THE HORIZON BOOK OF
GREAT CATHEDRALS

THE HORIZON
BOOK OF GREAT
CATHEDRALS

BY THE EDITORS OF HORIZON MAGAZINE

EDITOR IN CHARGE JAY JACOBS

INTRODUCTION BY ZOE OLDENBOURG

PUBLISHED BY American Heritage Publishing Co., Inc., New York

BOOK TRADE DISTRIBUTION BY Houghton Mifflin Company, Boston

PUBLISHED SIMULTANEOUSLY IN CANADA BY McClelland and Stewart Ltd., Toronto

HORIZON
BOOK DIVISION

EDITORIAL DIRECTOR
Richard M. Ketchum

GENERAL EDITOR
Alvin M. Josephy, Jr.

EDITOR, HORIZON BOOKS
Norman Kotker

Staff for this Book

EDITOR
Jay Jacobs

ART DIRECTOR
Arthur Korant

PICTURE EDITOR
Priscilla Flood

ASSISTANT EDITOR
Kristi N. Witker

COPY EDITOR
Priscilla Stone

TEXT RESEARCHER
Gail Fuhrer

EUROPEAN BUREAU
Gertrudis Feliu, *Chief*

AMERICAN HERITAGE
PUBLISHING CO., INC.

PRESIDENT
James Parton

EDITORIAL COMMITTEE
Joseph J. Thorndike, *Chairman*

Oliver Jensen

Richard M. Ketchum

SENIOR ART DIRECTOR
Irwin Glusker

PUBLISHER, HORIZON MAGAZINE
Paul Gottlieb

Sculptural representations of an Old Testament king and queen from the Royal Portal at Chartres Cathedral are shown in the photograph at right.

HALF-TITLE PAGE: *A twelfth-century knocker from the north portal of Durham Cathedral was supposed to provide sanctuary to fugitive criminals if they succeeded in grasping its ring before the law grasped them.*

TITLE PAGE: *The façade of Chartres' south transept with its three portals surmounted by a magnificent rose window is more imposing than the west, or main, front of many another major cathedral of the Middle Ages.*

Horizon Magazine is published quarterly by American Heritage Publishing Co., Inc., 551 Fifth Avenue, N.Y., N.Y. 10017. Printed in the United States of America. Library of Congress Catalog Card Number 68-29141

When the term "the Middle Ages" arises, our thoughts evoke cathedrals. We speak easily of the Europe of the Cathedrals or of the Civilization of the Cathedrals. The Europe of the impending millennium, the year One Thousand, had acquired a certain—although somewhat diversified—inward unity. This Europe had become an entity made up of differing countries holding in common a Christian religion and a Latin or Latinized culture. In both Norway and Spain, cultured men spoke the same language and were bound together by the same religious liturgy, and similar churches were being built in the two countries. This uniformity of worship was creating in the West the great International that called itself "Christendom," while the other Christendom, that of the Eastern church, was for all practical purposes excluded. The eleventh century saw consummation of the divorce between the two great Christian traditions.

The Church of Rome, for great stretches of time, was the only cultural power in the West and its sole ordering factor. Western civilization remained a religious one, by definition, while retaining and maintaining a strong Greco-Latin humanistic tradition. It was the search for a balance between these Christian and humanistic traditions that created medieval civilization, making way for the Renaissance as early as the twelfth century.

The eleventh century was the period of the stabilization of Europe; the twelfth, that of its expansion on the military and political planes, thanks to the impetus of the crusades; the thirteenth—its most brilliant epoch—the period of industrial and commercial expansion; the fourteenth, in part because of the Black Death, its moment of retrogression; and the fifteenth, the time of rebuilding. We read the history of medieval civilization in the cathedrals as if in a book—and, indeed, the cathedrals, collectively, *were* a book: the great stone record of a great culture.

What properly can be termed "Christian architecture" was first inspired variously by the Roman temple, which was round or octagonal, or by the typical Greek temple, which was rectangular and furnished with a double row of columns leading to a sanctuary. The first Christian innovation was the development of the cruciform plan, since the building was meant to symbolize Christ crucified. In the churches of the Eastern communion we find this cross broad and squarish, as it was also in the West in the Carolingian period. In Western Europe in the eleventh century, however, the cross becomes an elongated one with short transversal arms, and this basic plan was to remain unchanged in any significant way.

It was the eleventh century that introduced the great medieval church: a long nave with a powerful vault, sometimes flanked by two lower lateral naves separated from the main one by rows of pillars; an apse, semicircular and often built with radiating chapels surmounted by small cupolas in the Byzantine manner. The earlier central cupola

No single figure—not even Christ Himself—dominated the lives and thoughts of the cathedral builders as thoroughly as did the Virgin Mary. In city after city throughout medieval Europe cathedrals were dedicated to her and built in the hope of pleasing her. In the twelfth-century mosaic at left, William II, the Norman ruler of Sicily, offers the Virgin a model of his church (now the cathedral) at Monreale—one of the greatest buildings of the Romanesque era.

With Stone and Faith

ZOE OLDENBOURG

A medieval Bible illustration shows the construction of cathedral arches.

was replaced in this century by a square tower, while the windows of the nave became progressively larger. Then, toward the middle of the twelfth century, the broken or pointed arch (imported from the Moslem East, where its uses were for the most part purely decorative) was adopted by French architecture, stylistically and technically the most revolutionary of the times. The pointed arch vault provided greater solidity while requiring a lesser volume of stone than was needed for the half-round Romanesque vault. It was soon discovered that the pointed arch also permitted a more slender design and the construction of much taller vaults.

The perfect semicircular vault thus became sharpened, and the churches of the thirteenth century grew much higher than the so-called Romanesque cathedrals. They were also slimmer and more solid than those in the earlier style. To ensure that the enormous new naves would withstand the stresses they generated, the flying buttress appeared. In the process, walls became lighter, and truly immense stained-glass windows tended to replace mural decoration.

The upper part of the Gothic column of the thirteenth century retained, however, the massive nobility of the Romanesque pillar. But in the fourteenth century, although the plan of the structure remained unchanged, the vaults and columns became thinner and ribbed. These changes gradually led to an ever-increasing measure of sculptural ornamentation that made of the cathedral an immense lacework of stone. Although architectural style evolved rapidly in terms of time, it nevertheless remained consistent in each country, retaining a certain conservatism in Germany, being more influenced in Italy by the Roman and the Byzantine legacies, and clearly incorporating Moorish influences in Spain and in the south of France. Moreover, there was a single *type* of cathedral—found from Burgos to Reims, from Amiens to Naumburg, from Toledo to Canterbury—that demonstrated the existence of a truly international architecture, the visible sign of the unity of a civilization.

The evolution of architecture was paralleled by that of the plastic arts. Starting from the relative stability of Roman art, this evolution led to a variety of forms that made of the arts a perpetual negation of the past. The principle of such change is not inherent in the Christian religion: The Greek Church, in this very same period, remained steadfastly conservative, retaining a static outlook right up to the twentieth century. In the West, however, the art of the Middle Ages became an innovating, original art—starting with the second half of the eleventh century onward, when Europe became an area of intensive construction and, conscious of its power, affirmed independence of Constantinople, the "Second Rome." Before 1054, the date of the Great Schism between the Eastern and Western Churches, the West had been a somewhat "barbarian" emulator of Byzantium. The art of sculpture was still quite timid, since Western Christianity had long distrusted the carved image, which it likened to the idol of the past. In the tenth century, monks from the north of France looked with astonishment at the famous reliquary-statue of Saint Foy and asked themselves whether the southerners were not falling back into idolatry.

The fact is, though, that the peoples of western Europe were showing an increasing desire to incarnate their faith not only in the flat imagery of painting and mosaics but, more importantly, in "more real" images sculpted in stone, wood, or metal—a characteristic trait of Latin piety, which sought so much more to be fleshed-out and *incarnated* than did the Greek faith.

The twelfth century, from its very start, was a period of great sculpture. Although painters remained more-or-less disciples of the school of Byzantium, sculptors abruptly made theirs an altogether original art. Actually, they had no choice: Byzantine models did not exist, and the sculpture of Antiquity was despised as "pagan." The array of carvings adorning the Church of Moissac is the earliest of the great collective works of Western sculpture. Neither a copy of Antiquity nor a simple transposition in stone of the book illuminations from which, clearly, its inspiration was taken, the sculpture of Moissac was an altogether new art. Its most immediately striking feature is the skill of its compositions, in which decorative richness, precision of detail, and abundance of figures and ornamental motifs combine to produce an overall effect of perfect harmony. Even more striking, however, is the evidence of a decidedly positive attitude towards realism in the treatment of faces and in the choice of postures. At Moissac, the good rustic faces of the elders of the Apocalypse appear as if they had been carved from life models; the massive Christ with His heavy jowl makes one think more readily of some Carolingian king than of the Christs of Byzantine art.

Sculpture, at this time, was still only the ornamentation of sacred structures, a compromise between stylization and realism, between a self-sufficient art and mere architectural adornment, between the hieratic and the expressive—a compromise that is the characteristic of all the so-called archaic periods of the successive civilizations of man. There is an indisputable kinship in the smile of the kings of Chartres with those of the archaic Kores (or Persephones), Athenian prototypes entirely unknown to the sculptors of Chartres. Twelfth-century architecture, sculpture, and painting make up such a coherent whole that one feels that the least stone is an integral part of an immense organism imbued with life. It is this powerful sense of unity that charms us in the Romanesque basilicas. They may be ponderous, but they are imbued with the warmth of life directly expressed. Even in their exuberance they are homogeneous, because they are still rooted in centuries-old traditions while vivified by the influx of a new spirit working as the leavening of the graces of a robust youth, serene and still unaware of its power.

The statue-columns of Chartres or of Bourges are, quite frankly, *columns*. But they are more boldly conceived than the caryatids of Antiquity, since the shapes of the bodies are subordinate to the architectural line, while the faces, reflecting the intensity of life, share in the overall stylization by their inhumanly serene and somewhat fixed expressions. The great Gislebertus idealizes the figures of the Autun tympanum, not in the Byzantine manner but according to laws of his own invention, reminding us that the world of supraterrestrial realities differs in its nature from our own world. His Christ is one of the most beautiful of any in Christian art; He is transfigured and does not have a quite convincing human appearance; His is a grandeur that is not of this world. Such Christs would not have scandalized the religious feelings of the Greeks.

The respect—even awe—of his contemporaries for the medieval architect is evident in this fourteenth-century Bible illustration portraying God the Father as "Architect of the Universe."

When we consider the Christ of the Royal Tympanum of Chartres, which belongs to the end of the century, its difference from earlier Christ figures is striking. We see here a splendidly beautiful face, one that is noble, harmonious, shining with kindness; only the barely-hinted-at smile suggests a mystical thought. This face is superbly human, but at this early date, it must be stressed, it *is* human. Even more human is the Teaching Christ of the thirteenth century, the *Beau Dieu* of the south portal; although admirably expressing majesty and wisdom, He has come down from the heavens to stand on a base in front of the central pillar. The art of the thirteenth century had taken the decisive step; henceforth, sculpture was to be a humanistic, not hieratic, art.

On the north portal of Chartres the statue-columns display the strained transition between the earlier and later traditions. The heads, which are expressively mobile, are worthy of Michelangelo, but they seem unrelated—as if stuck on—to narrow, stiff bodies that lack the weightless grace of the statues of the Royal Portal. Beneath the porch of the Royal Portal, the effigies of Solomon, the queen of Sheba, and Saint Modesta no longer recall "columns" in any way; these are beautiful, slim human bodies whose carriage is graceful and free and whose faces have lost all traces of hieratic stylization. At Reims, the *Virgin* and the *Saint Elizabeth of the Visitation* (both of the thirteenth century) appear almost like Roman matrons. Only the lithe movement and the more-expressive faces reveal medieval characteristics. In actual fact, Rome never created a statue comparable to the *Saint Elizabeth* of Reims. That medieval sensitivity that was at once more refined and more anxious so transfigures this noble face of an aged woman that one forgets to admire the skillful play of drapery in concentrating only on this head.

After the classical age that was the thirteenth century, the medieval sculptors deformed and contorted their figures, not in the interests of idealization but of a realism that became equally exaggerated whether the aim was to depict gracefulness or violence. Thus, we have the "devout Christ" of Perpignan, in whom the tragic element, expressed in a veritable paroxysm of passion, almost equals the inhuman grandeur of the Romanesque Christs. And thus we have those charming Virgins with their swayed hips, remote heiresses of the *Smiling Virgin* of Amiens—overly slender, childish, almost coquettish, and far too human. From the fifteenth century onward the statue ceases to be an integral part of the building and lives a life apart and of its own. Fresco painting becomes the great sacred art as practiced by such men as Giotto, Fra Angelico, the Master of Moulins, the painter of the *Pietà* at Avignon, and the Spanish primitives. Painters covered the walls of churches with pictures that might just as well have been painted on canvas and framed. Although they started as part of the structure itself, the plastic arts conquered their dependence on architecture; the church became the mere pretext, instead of the sole purpose, of the work.

Stately witnesses to a past long renounced by us, the cathedrals remain fascinating. The tourist, arriving in a strange town, goes straight to the cathedral, the *duomo*, the *dom*. Cathedrals seemingly are without number; not necessarily beautiful, almost all are old. The

Some of the splendor of the first Gothic church can be seen in this painting of a Mass at St. Denis.

Middle Ages have remained quite alive in the cities and even in the humblest villages of Europe, thanks to their churches.

Rising above the invariably green lawns of Great Britain, one sees at Wells, at St. Andrews, the whitened and scattered skeletal remains of the ruined Norman cathedral. Of its beauty, which was great, nothing remains but a few lines and much to dream about. In contrast, most Gothic churches are still standing. Their creators might well be disappointed by their present looks, but they held their "doctorate in stonework" and their stone has stood up to the passage of time: The cathedral remains, even today, a "dream in stone." Look, for example, at the Cathedral of Beauvais. The city was the victim of heavy bombardment during World War II; entire sections leveled during that conflict have been rebuilt, leaving the cathedral to rise in the midst of vast low-cost housing projects. Beauvais Cathedral, in these new circumstances, seems sad, even vaguely grotesque, almost resembling an antediluvian monster—an enormous dragon of carved stone, black, dusty, gnawed by time, hollowed by the rains, but still more alive in its dignified old age than the flat white buildings that surround it. In 1945, in Caen, towering above apocalyptic heaps of collapsed and broken stones, of disemboweled bunkers, of mountains of rubble, the ancient cathedral—though mutilated, lacking roof and belfry—stood. At the end of World War I, Reims Cathedral still rose, blackened and half-stripped of its sculpted stone, in the midst of a flattened and fire-gutted neighborhood.

The Cathedral of Chartres was destroyed by fire in 1194, Canterbury in 1174, Rouen in 1200, Reims in 1210—and a much longer list could be drawn up. Indeed, it is to fires that we owe most of the Gothic cathedrals. Romanesque art has survived best in the great abbey churches, which were located away from towns and set in the midst of the large monasteries. These, because of their beauty and size, are worthy rivals of the cathedrals. The Romanesque cathedral has survived in a few instances: Notre Dame at Le Puy, whose walls, stripped of their frescoes, are of a dark red stone that confers on the church a shadowy warmth; the solemn and Roman starkness of the immense St. Sernin at Toulouse; the rich portal, so rich that it is almost barbaric, of Santiago de Compostela; the red marble of the Cathedral of Modena, used in Romanesque terms that are both heavy and sparsely adorned; and the great impoverished Cathedral of St. Albans with its colonnadeless nave. These survivors notwithstanding, most of the cathedrals that we recall easily date from the end of the twelfth century or belong to the thirteenth: Notre Dame of Paris; luminous Chartres, the shining rubies and sapphires of whose windows are set off by the cathedral's whitish walls and pillars; the broad and virtually naked cathedral with its immense windows at Poitiers; Amiens and the dizzying height of its main nave; the Spanish cathedrals with their main altars and choir stalls weighed down with wildly intricate gilded decoration; the Italian cathedrals, their interiors covered with white marble by the injudicious piety of the *Settecento*. Then, there is the vast and somber Cathedral of Toledo, a venerable Gothic structure in which, in the eighteenth century, a bishop had the idea of piercing above the choir a hideous little cupola adorned with paintings and Baroque sculptures, all blue and rose; the red Cathedral of Strasbourg, slim, seeming to limp with its single steepled tower,

A mason and a carpenter—probably hoping for promotion from apprentice to journeyman or journeyman to master—demonstrate their skills to a guild warden in the miniature above. In the drawing below, the thirteenth-century architect Villard de Honnecourt portrayed Offa, the eighth-century king of Mercia, as a building supervisor.

the highest in all Christendom; that enormous and proud Gothic pile, the Cathedral of Rouen—enriched by its external sculpture, blackened unevenly by time—that rises from a city of splendid ancient houses and old streets in which one senses the opulence of the city's Norman past. Finally, there is the *duomo* at Florence: austere, a bit cold, as if it were betrayed by its veneer of white, pink, and black marble—a veneer that makes it seem almost too new.

In Milan, on the vast Piazza del Duomo, ringed with tall buildings of the last century, rears up that shining, immense mass of stalagmites that is seemingly made of petrified frost crystals, gigantic candelabra, barbed spires and horns, that mass which we call the cathedral, and which has been defined as a "monstrous hedgehog" and a challenge to all spatial concepts. Decadent Gothic art could not reach beyond this. The thousand small shafts and pillars, the thorny lacework spires of this cathedral can only call, as their successors, for some evanescent structure made of spun glass and wind, some impossible crystal dream of a Gothic Piranesi. The great *duomo* has stood proudly for five centuries, but its only successor was the ponderous and massively pseudo-Roman St. Peter's in Rome.

All these unlikely dreams in stone share the nobility of bare stone, sometimes hard and gray, sometimes chalky, whitish, or of a warm, ochred yellow. On occasion they are red or purple or even black, like the Cathedral of Clermont-Ferrand. We know, of course, that originally the stone of these churches was not bare, as it is now, but most often painted or faced with marble like the Cathedral of Florence. The interior was always covered with frescoes, the exterior painted and partially gilded. Jean Fouquet, painting an imagined reconstruction of Solomon's Temple in the fifteenth century, saw it as a Flamboyant cathedral, gilded throughout.

Time has not tarnished the gold that lines the vaulting of the Byzantine-inspired churches because they were adorned with mosaics, as in Monreale, Cefalù, St. Mark's of Venice, or the Cathedral of Torcello. All these look to the most splendid of all cathedrals, that marvel of Christendom, St. Sophia of Constantinople, whose beauty was the adoring envy of the Venetians and of the Normans in Italy. But, in general, Western art of the Middle Ages, after the decadence of the Carolingian Empire, chose to ignore mosaics, contenting itself with frescoes, the "poor man's mosaics." The massive pillars of yellow stone were also painted, either in imitation of colored marble or striped with verticals and spirals. When visiting a cathedral, we should try to imagine these vast naves, these columns, walls, vaults, and chapels, despite their present bareness, as they originally were when covered with painting, often depicting scenes from the Bible, the Gospels, or the lives of the saints, adorned with suns and stars, with friezes of flowers, patternings of leaves, crosses and geometrical figures. And we may wonder how much differently we would be moved by the Royal Portal of Chartres were we to see it suddenly as it first was: resplendent with gilding and whites, blues, and purples; the eyes of the statues with shining painted pupils, the faces with pink lips and eyebrows and beards streaked with black or gold.

The Romanesque basilica took just as much account of color as it did of harmonious proportions. In the equally brilliant Gothic church, the stained-glass window replaced the fresco to a considerable extent, since the arts of glassmaking provide more dazzling color than any painted wall can. Churches were meant to be a feast for the eyes of our ancestors, whose taste stressed luster and rich, exuberant color, although sometimes they lacked balance and moderation in the pursuit of the beautiful. This fact should never be forgotten when visiting cathedrals, even though we are tempted, when confronted by so much bare stone, to imagine the Middle Ages as austere, even melancholy and fleshless. We must remind ourselves that these monumental structures, although they remain intensely alive, are merely the skeletons of the cathedrals of medieval times. Compared with what it was when first created, the cathedral, as we see it now, is like a venerable old lady whose noble carriage barely suggests the striking belle she must have been in her youth. We should not only recall the past splendor of the cathedral, much of whose external adornment is now lost, but also attempt to understand what the cathedral *was* during the progress of its own creation: the role it played at the heart of the city that saw its birth among the people whose stubborn or enthusiastic will alone caused its skyward thrust.

The Middle Ages undoubtedly had a greater passion for building than any other period. Western civilization was also producing estimable local literatures and encouraging worthy philosophers and theologians, but it seemed bent on finding its clearest expression in the most affirmative, the most positive, the most collective of all the arts—the art of building. In the twelfth century the countries of Europe were covered with castles and churches. It has been estimated that at that time there was a church for every two hundred inhabitants. Only the fires mentioned earlier explain why all the churches of France, Germany, Spain, and Italy are not today Romanesque. Most had to be replaced by Gothic equivalents, whose improved structural soundness accounts for their survival into our times.

In all ages there have been eminent men who, reasoning more or less in the style of "practical" men today, loudly condemned the cathedral as a monstrous waste of energy and money. In the twelfth century, Saint Bernard denounced energetically and indignantly what we think of as the very symbol of medieval faith, while Saint Francis, for his part, fled from all rich sanctuaries to preach poverty. A great current of rigoristic faith, as influential as it was heretical—exemplified by the Cathari of Albi or the tenets of the Waldenses—swept up some who looked upon the opulent official places of worship as the dwellings of Satan. In the thirteenth century the popular poet Rutebeuf jested somewhat bitterly of good king Saint Louis' mania for building and of his piety—piety that was costing his people almost more than they could bear.

The populace was poor. The money expended by the church for building could have been used to feed the famished—famines, even in the thirteenth century, were still frequent occurrences—or to maintain hospitals and schools. Thus, it could be said that the cathedrals cost hundreds of thousands of human lives. Immense riches were amassed; the church chose to deprive the poor and lavish those riches on building projects.

Once this fact has been noted, it should be acknowledged that every period of expansion has known similar immoderation, expressed through a seemingly unproductive display of wealth and al-

A manuscript illumination (above) illustrating the building of the Tower of Babel shows some medieval construction devices. The large wheel, worked like a treadmill, hoisted heavy loads. In the tapestry detail below, carpenters erect scaffolding at Notre Dame.

OVERLEAF: *The Gothic era began with the rebuilding of St. Denis, an abbey church, near Paris. In this fifteenth-century painting, King Dagobert oversees the construction of the west front.*

13

Although time has worn away most of the evidence, the majority of medieval sculptures were painted in vivid colors. In the detail above from a late thirteenth-century manuscript illustration, an artist seated on the steps of a church carefully applies polychrome to a newly carved statue of the Virgin and Child.

ways entailing a similar neglect of the poor. It must be remembered, however, that within this category of undertakings the construction of the cathedrals was at least the most democratic of projects and the one most justified by the public interests of its times.

The cathedral church was a public venture that no single element of society could underwrite. The decision to construct meant a more considerable effort than could be entailed in our time by the building of the Aswan Dam, the development of Brasilia, or even the boring of a tunnel under the English Channel. The medieval state had neither the legal authority nor the material power and means to undertake such tasks alone. As rich as it was, the church was also without these instrumentalities and could be only the initiator and the prime mover of the undertaking. In practice, it was the canons of a given bishopric who decided upon the construction of a new cathedral, after having tested public opinion, deliberated with their bishop, and consulted with the local nobility and the area's notables. It was the canonical chapter that collected the funds and directed the administrative aspects of the endeavor. To finance these gigantic undertakings the church could only levy occasional, invariably unpopular taxes and use the revenues from vacant vicarships and some part of the regular income of the chapter. Hence, for the most part, voluntary gifts had to be counted on.

Sometimes (but not always) the bishop would contribute substantially, and the king, the local duke or count, the secular lord of the town, would give as well. Noblemen, however, were always short of money, and monarchs like Saint Louis were rare; most of the money had to come from private individuals. If the cathedrals of the thirteenth century surpassed all others in their richness, it is quite simply because the bourgeoisie of the larger cities had become wealthy and chose to give more readily than in previous or later times. In France, the Rhineland, Flanders, and Italy, the cities where the bourgeois community had attained significant power were where the most sumptuous cathedrals were built. Money from trade—according to the thinking of the times, tainted money—went heavily into gifts to the church, mostly through legacies, which were not hampered by the clannish restrictions that had to be observed by the nobility in the disposition of its wealth. The guilds gave a great deal also, for reasons of local loyalty and of professional pride, ever attempting to outdo one another in generosity. No matter how much was given, though, the undertakings were always bottomless financial abysses, and the chapters would have to take up local public collections. When these, again, proved insufficient for the purpose, rounds were made in the outlying villages of the province, the countryside, and the castles, where holy relics were displayed by chapter representatives. To those who contributed, indulgences were granted to shorten by a number of days their future sufferings in purgatory.

Nevertheless, even these funds, though collected so laboriously, often proved still insufficient for the task. From the end of the thirteenth century on, in any event, it was rare for a cathedral to achieve uninterrupted completion, although completion might be accomplished one or two centuries later in the wake of some resurgence of local fervor. In most of the cathedrals the upper parts of the belfries and towers are of late (i.e., fourteenth- and fifteenth-century) construction—and often remain unbuilt. The Cathedral of Strasbourg has only one of its projected towers, and Reims lacks a second spire. It should be stressed that when work lasted for a century or more it was not because of any technical difficulties but simply for lack of money. When, in an exceptional case, a burst of popular enthusiasm spread beyond the confines of the province, the increased contributions speeded up the work. An instance of this acceleration is Chartres, destroyed by fire, except for the main portal and the south tower, in 1194. The veneration in which this sanctuary was held was such that sentiment caused gifts to pour in immediately, not only from all of France but also from foreign lands. Thus the reconstruction was completed in record time: Only twenty-six years were taken to finish the main body of the structure.

To finance the building of a cathedral was, it would seem, challenge enough, but further challenges, the technical problems the builders had to overcome, still amaze us today when we consider that the men of the Middle Ages had no other power source than that of man and his beasts of burden. The tasks taken on by these medieval builders would, however, have been terrifying to the Romans, although the latter were far better organized and had an immense labor force of slaves at their disposal.

The quarrying and the transportation of stone cost a fortune. At the four corners on the towers of the Cathedral of Laon we find statues of majestic oxen that, for once, are not symbols but rather the sculptors' homage to the good beasts whose efforts contributed so much to the building process. When Chartres Cathedral was being erected, peasants, bourgeois, and even nobles, under the impulse of pious enthusiasm, harnessed themselves by the dozen to enormous carts and dragged tons of stone over leagues of poor roads for days on end. But this was an unusual occurrence, and the transportation of building stone from the quarries to the church sites most often cost virtually as much as the stone itself.

The cathedral may have been an expensive undertaking, but at least it provided work for a very large number of workers. First among these were the quarrymen and stonecutters, since all stone was cut and shaped at the quarry according to drawings by the architect and only thereafter taken to the building site, frequently marked for its assigned place in the finished structure. Then there were the diggers, the laborers and all the skilled carpenters and masons, roofers, leadworkers, painters, and glassworkers.

The quarrymen, obviously, stayed on the job in one spot. All the others, by contrast, made up flying squads, traveling from one province to another. When money ran out on some cathedral construction site, thousands of masons and carpenters, certain of finding work elsewhere, would abandon the project on the spot. In the twelfth, thirteenth, and fourteenth centuries, the travel to and fro of such workers between France, England, Spain, and the Germanic countries was ceaseless. As constant travelers, the masons were the carriers of all new—and often subversive—ideas so that the discussions and brawls that took place in their "lodges" became notorious.

These workmen were poorly paid, but at least they were sure of their pay and never permitted quibbling about its established level. If in the building of the cathedrals the population was often exploited

ABOVE: *A fresco painter depicts the month of May.* BELOW: *A window from Chartres shows sculptors at work.*

17

by both the abusive collecting of money and the use of donations that could otherwise have relieved the poor, one cannot speak of exploitation of the workmen involved. Construction gave a livelihood to hundreds of thousands of men who left for more profitable locations the day their pay stopped. The cathedrals were not built by slave labor.

The basic building trade was that of the workers who specialized in the cutting and assembling of stone. Working closely with the masons were the men who compounded the mortar and positioned the stones. Construction also required great numbers of carpenters and timberworkers, many of whom were skilled engineers as well, since the whole project depended in large part on the perfection of scaffoldings and the design, placement, and practicality of hand winches, pulleys, and leverage systems. Such trades were passed from father to son, or even father to daughter, since we know of female masons and mortarmakers. Thus, we can think of entire families working side by side, but rarely do we find larger groupings, such as people from the same village. The mason, along with many others, was a nomad. Building workers, from the start, were recruited from among the rootless.

Let us imagine the immense vaults of Chartres, Beauvais, or Amiens in the course of their long and fevered elaboration: covered inside and out by an intricate network of timbers and scaffolds, with embankments and inclines of earth, noisily alive with the motion of pulleys and ropes skillfully used, where hundreds of men on dizzying scaffoldings handled stone blocks, often weighing as much as 2 tons, in an exercise in mathematical precision conceived by the mastermind of the architect. This latter was, obviously, both an engineer and the general foreman of the undertaking. William of Sens, who created the present Canterbury Cathedral, was the victim during its construction of a serious accident. Records show that work did not progress in his absence. Although he might attempt to give direction from his bed, it was up to him to oversee on the spot the placement of every single block.

The architects, many of whose names are a matter of historical record, were respected, eminent men, likened to the most learned. It was expected that they would be both mathematicians and artists—personalities of the first order, since on their expertise everything depended. But what of the sculptors? The names of several of them have come down to us, almost by accident, but some of the greatest still remain altogether unknown. In consequence of this, it has been concluded that theirs was a collective studio art executed by artisans. Hence arose the question whether the sculptor might not in his time have been considered a simple stonecutter somewhat more qualified than most. This question notwithstanding, once the plan for the cathedral's sculptures had been established by the architect and his design studio and approved by the church officials (without whose permission no work could be undertaken), the work was turned over to a team of sculptors, leaving them a broad area in which personal inspiration could be expressed. Through a certain uniformity imposed by style and subject, we perceive in the case of important sculptural masses a diversity of temperament. No one would confuse the sculpture of Autun with that of Vézelay, Chartres with Bourges, St. Tro-

Jean Fouquet painted King Solomon's Temple as though it were a Gothic cathedral. Note the gilded façade.

phime at Arles with Santiago de Compostela, or, later, the side portals of Chartres with Reims or Naumburg. And in each case, very great sculptors are involved.

Most of these sculptors are, as has been noted, anonymous. In the last century it was customary to admire the humility of these masters, whose devout piety and personal abnegation, it was thought, ensured their oblivion. Nevertheless, the sculptor of Autun, Gislebertus, carved his name in the very center of his tympanum, thus demonstrating that the artist was admired in the Middle Ages and that he was quite aware of his own merits. Those who did not imitate Gislebertus in this respect probably were confident of being famous enough not to have to sign their work. Jean de Chelles, one of the architects of Notre Dame in Paris, had his name carved in giant lettering on the wall of the structure; it originally must have shone strikingly, gold on a white ground. But since few now enter cathedrals to improve their knowledge from direct observation, depending rather on guidebooks, most people are better acquainted with the most-mediocre poets of the Middle Ages than with its greatest architects and artists.

The cathedral of a great town not only had to meet the tastes of its main underwriters, the notables, the guild leaders, the bishops, and the secular lords, but also had to be truly responsive to the wishes of the rest of the population. One need but point to the frigid Cathedral of Carcassonne or the cruel-looking Cathedral of Albi, both built by a hated power in humiliated lands, to understand that a cathedral unwarmed by popular approval could be only stillborn and lifeless.

Cathedrals were costly. Their size and sumptuousness revealed a number of quite profane motivations: the arrogant pride of the bishop or abbot under whose patronage the edifice was to be built (Abbot Suger, the builder of the Abbey Church of St. Denis, the first Gothic edifice, is a well-documented example of this arrogance), a similar pride felt by the canons, the aggressive local civic zeal of the upper bourgeoisie, and, finally, the competing spirit between neighboring cities. The impetus given by Suger in the middle of the twelfth century to an artistic renewal brought about the rivaling construction of Notre Dame in nearby Paris. Then, in the thirteenth century (and with the needs arising in the wake of destructive fires), cathedrals rose from the ground at an incredible pace, especially in northern France where there seems to have been a particularly intense spirit of competition. Chartres was started in 1194, Rouen in 1202, Reims in 1211, Amiens in 1220, Beauvais in 1225. In each of these structures can be seen a successive, constant, and probably quite conscious increase in the height of the nave, a fact that points to a deeply felt civic pride. It was deemed necessary that the local undertaking result in the "most beautiful of all"; hence, after the thirteenth century, the ever more-intense proliferation of external decoration that produced first the so-called Rayonnant and then the Flamboyant styles. Art was becoming virtuosity sustained by technical prowess, because visible signs of greater wealth were deemed necessary in any new or restored cathedral. In the last decadence of the Middle Ages, the prevailing collective sensitivity evolved in the direction of an anguished sentimentality that was both morbid and sensual, while genuine pious devotion deserted the cathedral to be better expressed in private chapels and family oratories. The cathedral was, therefore, to die from an excess of secular pride and vanity compounded by a competitive display of material wealth.

The luxury of the cathedrals was, first of all, an offering to God. Man needed this sacrifice by virtue of the instinct that impels him to believe in an unavoidable compensatory law: The extraordinary monument offered to God required of that same God the granting of extraordinary favors in return. In all ages man has offered sacrifices, going as far as self-mutilation or throwing his children into the fire. Dearly paid for, the cathedrals stand as eloquent witness to this belief in the virtues of the propitiating sacrifice, just as in their beauty they express an outpouring of deepest love.

This love was in no way an abstraction: The cathedral was the "Bible of the poor," its doctrine expounded by each capital of its pillars, each of its sculptured covers—teachings from which all, down to the most illiterate, were supposed to benefit directly. This teaching was both literal and symbolic, as in a great book of sacred numerals, of mystical types and forms, and of fleshed-forth meditations, all of whose meanings were familiar to everyone. From the primitive churchmen to the Quakers there have always been Christians who have been hostile to the "pagan" pomp that accompanies a church establishment. However, the men of the Middle Ages held a deep faith in the spiritual power of beauty.

In more-barbarous times, Queen Clotilda had ordered that churches be sumptuously decorated, hoping that by the sight of such beauty her pagan husband would be converted. In the tenth century the Viking prince of Russia, Waldemar, converted to Christianity because his envoys, dumbstruck by the beauty of St. Sophia in Constantinople, thought that they were among the angels and in the very presence of God—or so it was said. Beauty was, then, considered in itself as a means whereby the soul might be purified, and the beauties of the cathedrals testify as much to the credit of the worshipers as to the artists. The art of the cathedrals sought to be mediator between the flock and its God.

The house of God was, also, everyman's and, foremost, the house of the poorest. Its very size is evidence of this concern. Vaster and vaster churches were built because the urban population was increasing while the immense majority of worshipers were far from well-to-do. At Autun, in the second half of the twelfth century, the Cathedral of St. Lazarus was built *next* to the earlier Cathedral of St. Nazaire because there was no alternative to the requirement that any cathedral should be able to accommodate the entire population of its town. Eleanor of Aquitaine, queen of France, praying one day in the Basilica of St. Denis, exchanged the customary kiss of peace with the woman beside her, only to discover later, as an unpleasant surprise, that her neighbor was a prostitute. All were considered equal within the church, although the richer citizens usually found ways to reserve the best seats for themselves. The poor, however, believed to be closer to God, were more at home in the church than the rich could ever hope to be.

The Romans built circuses and theatres. The men of the Middle Ages, under the impetus of the church, constructed buildings destined to instruct and edify the crowds. Although cathedrals should

This cathedral scene by Peter Brueghel the Elder is part of a series on the Virtues. Although allegorical devices foreign to an actual service are included, Brueghel drew cathedral life much as it was lived, with its dense crowds of worshipers—crowds, incidentally, that must have derived an added benefit from their sardinelike proximity in cold weather.

not be compared with circuses, neither the spectacular nor the profit concerns of the older structures were neglected in these newer ones. By and in itself, the cathedral was spectacle. There was much to be seen in this museum of the sacred where all of the arts of the period were splendidly shown off. The religious ceremony, certainly, was a dazzling spectacle that brought on intense emotional reactions among the faithful. Besides, it was either in the cathedrals or before their portals that the great theatrical dramas of the Middle Ages, the mystery plays depicting the life of Jesus, Biblical scenes, and episodes from the lives of the saints, were enacted.

The cathedral was also a source of revenue. Rich and poor pilgrims, the tourists of the times, were drawn to it from all countries in larger numbers than today. Viewers came to see the new cathedral or to mark the progress of its building. Giving followed. With remarkable psychological insight, Saint Bernard wrote at an early date: "The sight of surprising and sumptuous vanities pushes man more to give than to pray." And elsewhere he wrote: "The more wealth is displayed, the more easily does one give." What was condemned by Saint Bernard became the very rule of the prelates of his century. Nevertheless, the cathedrals invariably cost more than they would ever take in.

A child born in Reims around 1210, when the cathedral was begun, could hardly hope to see it finished. Such a joy was reserved only for his great-grandchildren, since the lapse of time between the start and the completion was about that which separates us from the Civil War —something like a hundred years. The average building time for cathedrals varied from forty to eighty years, while the average life expectancy, low in the Middle Ages, was something like thirty years. Hence, during the twelfth and thirteenth centuries most of the inhabitants of medieval cities spent their lives in the shadow of unfinished cathedrals under active construction.

Most of the citizens of Chartres, Rouen, Toledo, Burgos, Cologne, or Pisa found themselves deafened by the unceasing noise of hammers, the creakings of winches, the rolling of stone blocks, and the strident cries of workmen. The life of the town was disturbed by an influx of nomadic workers who brought with them recurring civil disorders. Most of the residents in these times never saw much more of their cathedral than immense networks of scaffolding, supporting at all levels untold numbers of working men laboriously dragging skyward ponderous carved stones and pails of locally made mortar.

The cathedral was always consecrated well before its completion. Only the choir and the nave were necessary for this ceremony. The Cathedral of Chartres, although consecrated (and substantially finished) after only twenty-six years of intensive work, remained an active building site for decades thereafter and still lacks its north belfry. Construction work was often interrupted for years on end, only to be sporadically resumed. The faithful prayed in buildings without windows, with bare walls hidden under scaffoldings—buildings whose towers-to-be were then lowly structures masked by timbers and cumbrous hand-powered mechanical devices. Between religious services the workers took up their tasks. On hewn boards, perhaps a hundred feet up, masons sealed in the stones that made up the ribbing of the

A tenth-century cloisonné medallion from the cathedral treasury at Troyes bears a portrait of Saint Matthew.

vaults; painters plastered walls to be frescoed or, armed with buckets of color, worked on them or on colored sculptures. Outside, the stonecutters in a din of hammers chiseled the finishing touches of carved ornamentation while masons fastened statues or the panels of a tympanum onto the building. All this, while below, the recently carved statues were painted, and, on the higher scaffoldings above, enormous blocks of stone were slowly hoisted to the rising towers.

It was amid noise, incessant motion, the smell of paint, plaster, wood shavings, stone dust, sawdust, the runoff from lime, and the dung of horses and oxen that the population lived during the course of such an undertaking. They endured the disorders staged on the building site and those that took place in the lodges of the masons they lived with, along with the all-too-frequent kitchen fires, the din of the outdoor forges needed by the ironworkers and the sounds of the leadworkers' bellows, the stacks of rope, the piles of sand, and the mountains of baled straw used for the beds of the workers or for the protection of sculptures, windows, and flooring. The finished work was nowhere visible. Great events would be the installation of a new stained-glass window, the finishing of a new fresco, the placement of a new statue. The church in which the faithful prayed was constantly brought alive before their eyes by such occurrences. For long stretches of time dreams promised unknown beauty, and the faithful, sustained by their dreams, worshiped in the midst of ugly reality.

When seemingly completed at last, all new and dazzling, the cathedral was nevertheless not quite finished. The Middle Ages had a sort of genius for perpetual incompletion. Building went on for so long that it never could be halted. Complete at least in its essentials, although spires and towers might soar only in the dreams of the architects, the cathedral appeared to its elated possessors as the marvel of the century. To beautify it further, gifts poured in: rugs, tapestries, masterpieces of goldsmithing, precious stones for reliquaries. Lateral chapels were added, often in glaring conflict with the original plan. People had taken the habit of seeing their cathedral live and grow as if it were an animate thing. From time to time a fire would damage walls; lightning would bring down a belfry. Then architects, masons, and sculptors went back to work not only to repair but to invent new forms and expressions with a constructive passion that only the medieval West seems to have known to this degree.

In the past, even in the great towns, the countryside was close at hand. The city air smelled of hay, of smoke, of manure. The cities, with their streets always narrowed by houses as tightly confined within the municipal ramparts as the cells of a beehive, were filled with stables for horses and other beasts and with dovecots and chicken yards. The streets themselves were noxious quagmires. Fields and orchards were spread out at the very gates of the towns. Early in the thirteenth century, we are told, Philip Augustus of France, looking out from a window in the Louvre, was spattered by the mud thrown up by a passing cart and decided to pave certain streets of his capital. This is noteworthy only because Paris was at that time a great city, renowned for the beauty of its monumental structures and the vigor of its intellectual and commercial life. Notre Dame Cathedral was still a-building—towers and side portals were still lacking—but it was consecrated, painted (or whitewashed, at least), and adorned with stained-glass windows.

This cathedral dominated the Ile de la Cité, a stone ship set down upon another, the larger one floating in the Seine. It towered above its ancient town. Streets here were dark and crooked. Every square inch was employed to the limit; even the clear space before Notre Dame was hardly wider than an ordinary street. The crowded bridges were lined with two- and three-story houses, while behind this anthill island of la Cité was that other island, without houses and lush with greenery, on which the canons of Notre Dame set out their cows to graze. In most great river towns, the river itself, as lively as the streets, was covered with barges and small craft, ferries and floating timber. The banks of the stream were always muddy, furrowed by the carts, tamped down by the beasts that came to drink, trampled by the water carriers and the stevedores. The churches, often built side by side, took up the space of several houses each, even when they were of the smallest kind. They were always higher than the low-ceilinged dwellings. The city dweller lived more in the streets and in his churches than in his own abode.

When the bells of the cathedral rang out, all the town responded to their rhythm. The voices of the great bells not only announced religious services but also told of public joys and sorrows. Their resonant language was understood by all so that carillon, tolling, or tocsin was echoed in the houses and streets and felt by the citizens as some immense heartbeat of their town.

One went to the cathedral, morning and evening, to attend services. Half the day was spent there on Sundays and feast days. Baptisms, marriages, and funerals, prayers for the dead and prayers of thanksgiving, processions, prayers of intercession, exorcisms of evil spirits, priestly ordinations, excommunications and acts of public penance, victory festivals and lamentations over defeat, all such activity was focused in the cathedral. It was into the cathedral that preachers, coming from afar, attracted great crowds, much as in our times political figures organize great rallies. The cathedrals also served for the public meetings of princes and notables, for the communal councils held in the presence of the people. From the second half of the thirteenth century, the church, dominated by the Inquisition, would organize within the cathedral its spectacular heresy trials designed to strike terror into the faithful by each contrived auto-da-fé. It was also here that the convicted suffered flagellation. On Easter Eve the cathedral saw the lighting of the New Light, celebrating the Resurrection and the year's start, from whose flame a thousand tapers were lit and carried forth to light yet others throughout town and suburbs, spreading a joy renewed each year.

People agreed to meet in the cathedral to discuss private matters; beggars and pilgrims slept there on the straw-covered pavement. People ate there and joked there in the exuberant manner of the times. Even during divine services the quiet was relative. Abbot Suger, describing the crush one festival day in the Basilica of St. Denis, wrote of "howling men," of half-fainting women screaming "as if they were giving birth," while visitors, wishing to see the hallowed relics, were so belligerent that "the monks in charge of the reliquaries had no choice but to flee through the windows, taking the relics with them."

This intricately wrought reliquary shrine, the work of Nicolas de Verdun, an early thirteenth-century silversmith and enameler from the Champagne district, forms part of the treasury of Tournai's Cathedral of Notre Dame. The subject of the relief on the vessel's center is the Adoration of the Magi.

Such lusty devotion expressed the faith of a great civilization in the Middle Ages, although certain people of the times were already criticizing it as vain and superstitious.

As early as the twelfth century the church, by condemning Abelard, ruled against a critical mind that was, however, a deeply Christian one. Such a rift would broaden in the thirteenth century, creating the climate of suspicion between church and faithful that could lead only to the Renaissance and the Reformation. Perhaps the texture of the faith of the popular masses, for whom the cathedrals had been primarily intended, might seem to change but little as time went on, but this faith came to be sustained only by ever-poorer nourishment. After the Christ of Autun appears the one of Chartres, then comes the Christ of Perpignan and later the Christ of Grünwald, in a tragic evolution of a faith that became at once more humanized and more disincarnate. All this had to lead to the Christs of Raphael, such as in his *Transfiguration*, followed by those of Murillo and then of Ingres to wind up in the last century and much of this one with the commercial religious imagery whose insipidity, arrived at with less art, equals that of Raphael. Many Renaissance and Baroque churches, but few cathedrals, were built, since one does not demolish an ancient edifice to erect a new one in its stead. Sacred art more and more ceased to inspire secular art, finally attempting, clumsily and with bad conscience, to become indistinguishable from its classicizing counterpart. By then, religion was no longer symbolic of progress but rather of conservatism and finally of ignorance.

The cathedrals that had been despised for four centuries were returned to honor by the Romantics. The twentieth century rediscovered them, too, but sees them only as venerable historical curiosities, as masterpieces of times long gone, as some sort of Christian Parthenons. Even on Sunday they are almost empty now, the tourists more numerous than the flock. In many of their crypts the same relics are preserved in their ancient reliquaries, but they now attract the curious much more than the worshiper.

In the Middle Ages the possession of a chip of a bone belonging to Saint Lazarus ranked with any affair of state. The relic—or, sometimes, a miraculous image—became the living heart of the cathedral. The skull, the piece of tibia or jawbone, the remnant of rotted cloth, the splinter of bloodstained wood, the dried fingernail, the tooth, all of these sad, poor remains of a body or of some instrument of martyrdom were loved more fervently than the most beautiful work of sacred art. Seen as an incarnate bit of eternal life, considered more powerful than would be any radioactive material whose locked-up energy terrifies us today, the relic was the tangible sign of an unearthly reality. This reality was felt as primal, the remains by which it was denoted being considered mere perishable outward symbols. Thus, the sanctity of a cathedral was measured by the relics it enshrined.

Such was the power of the bones of Saint James—believed to be kept at Santiago, although the apostle had been executed at Jerusalem —that the constant influx of pilgrims created not only the Cathedral of Santiago de Compostela but convents, a prosperous town, a whole series of other towns as well, and churches and monasteries along the roads that led to Santiago. Even the Milky Way came to be called "the road of Saint James." Because the Virgin left no body to be

24

With its single spire pointing the way to heaven, Notre Dame keeps watch through a Paris night.

venerated and because odds and ends of clothing seemed too paltry, rediscovered statues of mother goddesses, perhaps pre-Christian in origin, were believed to be of supernatural beginnings and were worshiped at Chartres and at Le Puy, both major Romanesque cathedrals and the focal points of the greatest French pilgrimages. In the eyes of the men of the times, the beauty of churches was always less than that of their reliquaries, those little sarcophagi, small caskets, or hollow statues made of gold or silver or plated with gold, ornately carved and covered with enamels and precious stones. These latter were not valued as mere ornamentation but were thought of as imbued with sacred virtues and hallowed symbolism. Between the reliquary, whose value was often that of a year's pay for a royal army, and the fragment of broken bone that it contained, what worshiper could have hesitated for long?

St. Denis, the basilica of the French kings, was built for the relics of its patron saint; the Cathedral of Autun for the relics of Saint Lazarus; Chartres and Le Puy for their "black" Virgins. No church could be conceived without some seminal pretext of this sort. The relics won in the looting of Constantinople gave rise to many twelfth-century churches. Devotional piety permitted such thievery much as, in our own times, a good citizen may commendably steal another nation's secrets for the good of his own country. The faith of the Middle Ages drew its strength from this easy familiarity with the holy that made it see in every relic a living witness to the immediate presence of God.

Abbot Suger of St. Denis wrote in the early thirteenth century: "If the golden cups, amongst the Hebrews, served to receive the blood of goats and calves, how much more should we have to gather up the body and the blood of Jesus Christ, golden vessels and precious gems and all that is highly valued throughout Creation?" For the relic remained merely a secondary aspect of faith, whose main impetus lay in the sacrament. The first treasures of the churches were the chalices, the ciboria, and then the altars, the altar lamps, the crosses and lecterns, all of them studded with rubies, amethysts, sapphires, pearls, and rock crystal. The habits of the bishops were embroidered in gold and precious stones, and, in the instance, mere vanity was not in play. Everything here, from the golden chalice to the lowest step of the cathedral, stood as symbol of the sole supernal reality of the divine sacrament. Of such an attitude we may be sure that the people of the Middle Ages nourished an understanding that we can no longer comprehend nor imagine.

The cathedral, as the Bible of the poor, as a gigantic reliquary, as an image both of the cross and of the body of Christ, at once a Noah's Ark and a corner of God's Kingdom, was clearly in its own time the supreme expression of a great Christian civilization. Because the cathedral was too costly, too imbued with vain pride, so immoderate a folly that, even incomplete, it was to be enlarged over the centuries as if it were some new Tower of Babel, it also seemed to become irrelevant on the very day when man chose decisively to place himself first in the order of things. Luther and Erasmus, Michelangelo and Galileo, the Conquistadors and Machiavelli, Saint John of the Cross and Savonarola, found suddenly that, to affirm their faith, their thought, or their art, they no longer needed the cathedral.

25

A CATHEDRAL GLOSSARY

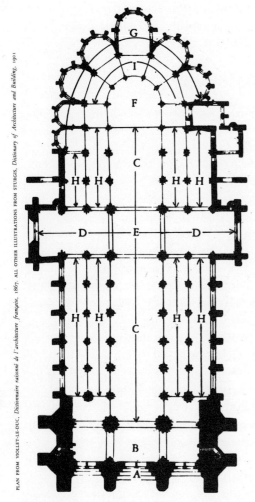

Romanesque arch

Lancet arch

Gothic arch

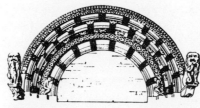

Archivolt

Bay

Floor plan, Troyes Cathedral

A. West front
B. Narthex
C. Nave
D. Transept
E. Crossing
F. Apse
G. Radiating chapels
H. Aisle
I. Ambulatory

ABBEY CHURCH. *A monastery church ruled by an abbot*

AISLE. *A longitudinal passage running parallel to the nave and usually separated from it by a succession of piers.*

ALTAR. *A table of wood or stone before which divine services are held and upon which the Eucharist is celebrated.*

ALTARPIECE. *A work of art, usually one or more painted panels, placed in the space above and behind an altar.*

AMBULATORY. *A sheltered place for walking, usually around an apse.*

APSE. *A projecting extension of a church, usually vaulted and semicircular, and almost invariably at the east end of the building.*

ARCADE. *A series of arches and their supporting columns or piers, usually roofed.*

ARCH. *Any of several types of curved, structural, self-supporting members used to span openings and to support a wall or other weight.*

ARCHIVOLT. *A molding, usually ornamented, around an arch.*

ATRIUM. *A central hall, usually of a Roman house; an open court leading to a church.*

BALDACHIN. *An ornamental canopy carried above a pope or other dignitary or standing over an altar; a ciborium.*

BALUSTRADE. *A row of balusters, or vase-shaped uprights, surmounted by a rail.*

BAPTISTERY. *A building, formerly separate but now frequently part of a church proper, used for baptismal ceremonies.*

BAROQUE. *Term for the style popular from the mid-sixteenth century to the end of the seventeenth; characterized by the use of elaborate scrolls, curves, and other symmetrical ornamentation.*

BARREL VAULT. *A continuous rounded vault unbroken by cross-vaults.*

BASILICA. *An oblong building ending in a rounded apse; an ancient Roman assembly hall or an early Christian church derived therefrom; a Roman Catholic church given high ceremonial privileges.*

BAY. *A recess or compartment, usually between buttresses, piers, etc., in a church wall.*

BISHOPRIC. *The seat, office, or territory of a bishop.*

BLIND DOOR. *A false door with no opening.*

BLIND TRIFORIUM. *A triforium having blind, or sealed, intervals between its columns.*

BOSS. *A raised or projecting ornament on a wall or ceiling.*

BRACCIO *(Italian; plural, braccia). Literally,* arm; *a unit of measure, roughly a yard.*

BRACKET. *A simple rigid structure used to support vertical loads, often in the shape of an L with the upright section attached to a vertical surface.*

BUTTRESS. *A projecting structure for support of a wall. See* FLYING BUTTRESS.

BYZANTINE. *Term for the style of architecture centered in Byzantium that reached its height during the reign of Justinian and was characterized by its use of the dome, pendentives, and mosaic decoration.*

CAMPANILE. *A bell tower, usually free-standing.*

CAPITAL. *The top of a column, pier, or pilaster, often ornamented.*

CAPOMAESTRO (Italian). *Literally, head-master; a chief architect.*

CARYATID. *A figure, usually female and draped, supporting an entablature.*

CATHEDRA. *A bishop's official throne.*

CHANCEL. *The portion of a church, usually to the east of the nave, that includes the choir and sanctuary.*

CHAPEL. *A chamber or recess for meditation, prayer, or subordinate services, usually with a separately dedicated altar.*

CHAPTER HOUSE. *A building in which a cathedral or monastery chapter convenes.*

CHEVET (French). *The semicircular or polygonal east end of a church; an apse.*

CHOIR. *The part of the chancel between the sanctuary and nave occupied by singers or clergy.*

CHOIR STALL. *A seat in the choir, usually elaborately decorated and enclosed at the back and sides, sometimes canopied.*

CHURRIGUERESQUE (style). *Term for the Baroque architecture of Spain and its Latin American colonies.*

CIBORIUM. *A free-standing canopy over a high altar. See* BALDACHIN.

CIMBORIO (Spanish). *A cupola placed over the crossing of a church.*

CISTERCIAN (style). *Term for the simple, sparsely ornamented architecture developed by Cistercian monks.*

CLASSICAL. *Term for the style based on the architecture of classical Greece and Rome developed during the Renaissance.*

Boss

Chevet

Clerestory

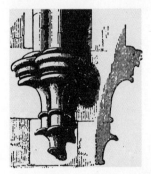

Corbel

Flamboyant tracery

CLERESTORY. *The upper level of the nave, transepts, and choir, pierced with windows.*

CLOISTER. *A covered passageway at the side of an open court, usually walled on the side farthest from the court and colonnaded on the other side.*

COLONNADE. *A series of columns, usually at regular intervals and usually supporting the base of a roof.*

COLONNETTE. *A small column, usually used in groups or clusters.*

CONSOLE. *An ornamental wall bracket, often used to embellish a keystone.*

CORBEL. *A supporting bracket projecting from the face of a wall.*

CORNICE. *The molded projecting crown of an architectural composition.*

CORONA. *The projecting portion of a classical cornice.*

CRENELLATED. *Furnished with battlements broken by spaces at regular intervals.*

CROSIER. *A bishop's or abbot's symbolic staff, modeled on a shepherd's crook.*

CROSSING. *The central opening, usually square, where a church's nave and transepts intersect.*

CROSS-RIBBED. *Supported (as vaulting) with intersecting ribs.*

CRUCIFORM PLAN. *A floor or ground plan laid out in the shape of a cross.*

CRYPT. *The vault, usually for burial, under the main body of a church; an underground chamber.*

CUPOLA. *A rounded roof; a dome, but usually on a smaller scale; a lantern.*

DECORATED (style). *English Gothic architecture characterized by geometric tracery.*

DOM (German). *A cathedral.*

DOME. *A hemisphere of masonry; a vaulted structure, curving upward and inward to a central point, that spans an open, circular, or polygonal area, usually at the crossing.*

DUOMO (Italian). *A cathedral.*

EARLY ENGLISH. *Term for the earliest Gothic style in England, introduced after 1190 and characterized by the use of lancet arches.*

FAÇADE. *The exterior (usually front) wall of a building; a west front.*

FENESTRATION. *The arrangement and design of windows.*

FLAMBOYANT. *Term for the Gothic style of the fourteenth, fifteenth, and early sixteenth centuries, characterized by flamelike window tracery.*

FLECHE. *A spire, especially one placed over a crossing.*

FLOOR PLAN. *The horizontal plan or layout of a building, as opposed to the elevation or vertical plan; ground plan.*

FLYING BUTTRESS. *An arched mass designed to transmit the thrust of a vault or an upper wall to an outer support.*

FOLIATE. *Leaf-shaped.*

FONT. *A receptacle for baptismal or holy water.*

FRESCO. *A wall painting executed in water-soluble pigments on freshly spread plaster.*

GABLE. *A wall at the end of a ridged roof, usually triangular and bounded by the roof slopes.*

GALILEE. *A porch, or occasionally a chapel, at the entrance to an English church.*

GLAZED TRIFORIUM. *A triforium having glass in the openings between its columns.*

GOTHIC. *Term given during the Renaissance to the architecture, popular in western Europe from the twelfth to the sixteenth century, characterized by the use of tall, slim masses, pointed arches, rib vaulting, and flying buttresses.*

GREEK CROSS. *An equilateral cross.*

GRILLE. *A decorative openwork screen, usually of wrought iron.*

GROIN. *The V formed by the supporting ribs of intersecting vaults.*

GROUND PLAN. *A floor plan.*

LANCET. *A tall, narrow window having an acute point at the top and no tracery.*

LANTERN. *A small tower or cupola; part of a cupola.*

LATERAL PORTAL. *A portal to either side of a central entrance.*

LATIN CROSS. *A cross having a longitudinal member and shorter transverse members; the type of cross used in the crucifixion of Christ.*

LECTERN. *A reading desk or stand.*

28

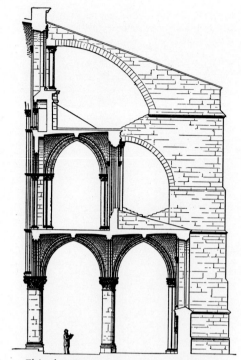

Flying buttress

Font

Perpendicular tracery

Pier (detail)

LINTEL. *The horizontal beam framing the top of a door or other opening.*

LOGGIA. *A roofed, open-sided gallery within a building, usually in an upper story and facing an open central court.*

MEDALLION. *A decorative tablet, set into a wall (where it usually bears an ornament in relief) or a window.*

MINSTER. *A monastery church; an important church or a cathedral.*

MOORISH (style). *Architectural style of Moorish workmen in the East, Spain, and Sicily, characterized by pointed, horseshoe, and double arches and elaborate openwork.*

MOSAIC. *A surface (usually wall) decoration made by inlaying small bits of colored glass or ceramic to form patterns or pictures.*

NAVE. *The main, longitudinal body of a church extending from the principal (usually west) entrance to the choir.*

NORMAN (style). *A variety of Romanesque architecture introduced into England at the Conquest and characterized by heavy masonry, round arches, and simple adornment.*

OCULUS (plural, OCULI). *A round (eyelike) window or other opening.*

OGIVAL. *Term for an architectural style characterized by the use of pointed arches; Gothic.*

OPENWORK. *Surfaces (usually carved) pierced to obtain a lacelike effect.*

PALLADIAN (style). *Of or like the sixteenth-century neoclassical architecture of Andrea Palladio.*

PERPENDICULAR. *Term given to the elaborate late stage of the English Gothic style, a product of the late fourteenth century.*

PIER. *A vertical support at either end of a lintel or arch; a mass of masonry, often of clustered verticals, used to reinforce a wall.*

PILASTER. *An upright, usually rectangular, projecting support for a wall.*

PILLAR. *An upright support; a free-standing column or shaft.*

PINNACLE. *A small turret or spire on a roof or buttress.*

POLYCHROME. *Multicolor decoration.*

PORCH. *A covered entranceway or waiting area at the front of a church, usually with a separate roof.*

PORTAL. *A door or entranceway, especially when ornate or imposing; the architectural setting for the doorways and porch of a church.*

PORTICO. *A porch or walkway with a roof supported by columns, often leading to the entrance to a building.*

QUATREFOIL. *A stylized floral motif having four leaves or lobes.*

RAYONNANT. *Term for the fourteenth-century French architectural style characterized by the use of radiating lines, particularly in window tracery.*

RELIQUARY. *A container for relics or other sacred objects.*

RENAISSANCE (style). *The style popular from the fourteenth to the sixteenth century, generally combining classical forms with new methods of construction.*

REREDOS (Spanish). *An ornamental screen behind an altar.*

RETABLE (or RETABLO). *A shelf or support above an altar for the altar cross, candles, floral displays, etc.*

RETROCHOIR. *The area behind the high altar or choir enclosure; in apsidal churches, the entire area east of the altar.*

RIB. *A salient stone arch that supports a vault and divides it into compartments.*

RIBBED VAULT. *A vault supported by a skeleton of arched ribs.*

ROCOCO. *An eighteenth-century style developed from the Baroque in France and characterized by extremely elaborate ornamentation.*

ROMANESQUE. *Term for the architectural style in use between Roman and Gothic times and characterized by the eleventh-century development of the round arch and vault, the substitution of piers for columns, and the extensive use of arcades.*

ROOD. *A crucifix, specifically at the entrance to a chancel.*

ROOD LOFT. *A gallery for the display of the rood and its screen.*

ROOD SCREEN. *An openwork partition that spans the end of the nave at the entrance to the chancel and supports the rood.*

ROSE WINDOW. *A circular window filled with symmetrical radiating tracery or similarly disposed stained-glass patterns.*

Reredos

Rood screen

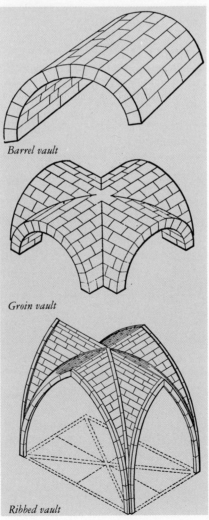

Barrel vault

Groin vault

Ribbed vault

SACRISTY. *A chamber where vestments and sacred utensils are stored; a vestry.*

SANCTUARY. *The part of a church where the altar is placed.*

SARACEN (style). *See* MOORISH.

SEE (episcopal). *The official seat and center of authority and jurisdiction of a bishop, the chief church of which is a cathedral.*

SILVERGILT. *Gilded silver.*

SPANDREL. *The space, usually decorated, between the exterior curve of an arch and the right angle that frames it.*

SPIRE. *A tapering pyramidal structure surmounting a tower; in more common usage, a steeple.*

STATUE-COLUMN. *A decorative, sometimes supporting, column in the form of a human figure.*

STEEPLE. *A church tower, usually surmounted by a spire.*

STRUTTING. *Wooden bracing, usually set diagonally, to strengthen a ceiling, spire, etc., from within.*

SUFFRAGAN. *Subordinate to an archiepiscopal see.*

TABERNACLE. *A receptacle for the consecrated Host and wine of the Eucharist.*

TRACERY. *Ornamental designs, often interlaced with branching lines.*

TRANSEPT. *Either of two lateral arms intersecting the nave of a cruciform church.*

TRANSITIONAL (style). *Term used to designate the first flowering of Gothic motifs in Romanesque architecture.*

TRASCORO (Spanish). *Retrochoir.*

TRIFORIUM. *A narrow second-story gallery or passage over either or both of the aisles that flank the nave.*

TRUMEAU (French). *A central pillar in a doorway; a support for the tympanum.*

TYMPANUM. *The space, usually decorated with sculpture or painting, enclosed within the frame of an arch, portal, or the triangle of a pediment.*

VAULT. *An arched masonry ceiling, usually of mutually supporting wedge-shaped stones or bricks.*

VAULTING. *Vaulted construction.*

Reims

THE CROWNING GLORY

The cathedral at Reims rises from the pavement like an immense sculpture, firm as a mountain yet delicate as Belgian lace. Auguste Rodin could sense its presence even in the darkness of night: "I cannot distinguish it, but I feel it. Its beauty persists. It triumphs over shadows and forces me to admire its powerful black harmony. It fills my window, it almost hides the sky. How explain why, even when enveloped in night, this cathedral loses nothing of its beauty? Does the power of that beauty transcend the senses, that the eye sees what it sees not?" Rodin was writing as a sculptor, concerned ostensibly with the physical and artistic, but there is in his words something of the mystical feeling with which the French have always regarded Notre Dame of Reims (seen at left as it was in the seventeenth century). For in the heart and history of the nation, Reims is to France what Canterbury is to England. Since 496, when Clovis, the first of the Merovingian kings, was baptized there, the city and its cathedral have been sacred to the French. To be crowned at Reims was to be undisputed king of France. Napoleon, who was not of royal birth, was crowned at Paris. So was the ten-year-old Henry VI of England, whose claim to the throne of France was never fully accepted by the French. King Henry IV, the only French monarch whose claim was in dispute, was crowned at Chartres. But it was to Reims that Joan of Arc brought Charles VII for his coronation in 1429, and her words confirmed both his and the cathedral's royalty: "Gentle King, from henceforth is fulfilled the pleasure of God who wished that you should come to Reims to receive your worthy anointing, by showing that you are truly king and him to whom the kingdom should belong."

Reims has had a Christian cathedral since 401 when Saint Nicasius dedicated a pagan temple to Mary. By the early thirteenth century several basilicas and churches had stood on the site. The last of these burned down in 1210, giving the energetic crusader and bishop of Reims, Albéric de Humbert, an excuse to build his own cathedral. He had been archdeacon at Notre Dame of Paris while that cathedral was being built, and in many respects—particularly in the cathedral's façade—the design of Reims was influenced by that of Paris. Five generations of builders and architects left their marks on the cathedral at Reims, but always on the basis of the original plan of Jean d'Orbais and always with a consistency of purpose that has left us with a structure of rare unity and beauty. The cathedral was all but complete by the end of the thirteenth century. The choir, transepts, nave, and towers were finished, and the great rose window was in place above the main portal. It remained only to perfect the details; for thirty years craftsmen lavished their attention on the carvings and statuary (like those on the spire at right) that cover the cathedral.

Because Reims, more than any other cathedral, has been sacred to the French, it has made an ideal target for the enemies of France. In striking it they struck at the soul of the nation. In 1914 and again in 1918 the enemy struck with a greater fury than ever before, pouring thousands of bombs into the cathedral, turning it into a furnace and mutilating its statues. But the structure stood, for it had been built on firm walls and foundations as well as on faith. Although the damage seemed irreparable, the cathedral was restored when the war was over, and today it stands as it stood before, a sacred symbol of France.

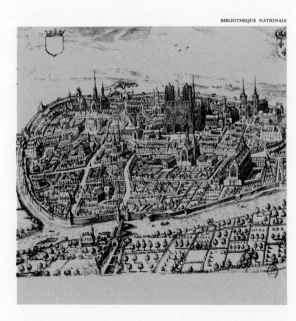

PORTAL. *A door or entranceway, especially when ornate or imposing; the architectural setting for the doorways and porch of a church.*

PORTICO. *A porch or walkway with a roof supported by columns, often leading to the entrance to a building.*

QUATREFOIL. *A stylized floral motif having four leaves or lobes.*

RAYONNANT. *Term for the fourteenth-century French architectural style characterized by the use of radiating lines, particularly in window tracery.*

RELIQUARY. *A container for relics or other sacred objects.*

RENAISSANCE (style). *The style popular from the fourteenth to the sixteenth century, generally combining classical forms with new methods of construction.*

REREDOS (Spanish). *An ornamental screen behind an altar.*

RETABLE (or RETABLO). *A shelf or support above an altar for the altar cross, candles, floral displays, etc.*

RETROCHOIR. *The area behind the high altar or choir enclosure; in apsidal churches, the entire area east of the altar.*

RIB. *A salient stone arch that supports a vault and divides it into compartments.*

RIBBED VAULT. *A vault supported by a skeleton of arched ribs.*

ROCOCO. *An eighteenth-century style developed from the Baroque in France and characterized by extremely elaborate ornamentation.*

ROMANESQUE. *Term for the architectural style in use between Roman and Gothic times and characterized by the eleventh-century development of the round arch and vault, the substitution of piers for columns, and the extensive use of arcades.*

ROOD. *A crucifix, specifically at the entrance to a chancel.*

ROOD LOFT. *A gallery for the display of the rood and its screen.*

ROOD SCREEN. *An openwork partition that spans the end of the nave at the entrance to the chancel and supports the rood.*

ROSE WINDOW. *A circular window filled with symmetrical radiating tracery or similarly disposed stained-glass patterns.*

Reredos

Rood screen

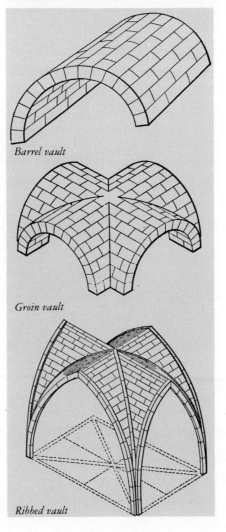

Barrel vault

Groin vault

Ribbed vault

SACRISTY. *A chamber where vestments and sacred utensils are stored; a vestry.*

SANCTUARY. *The part of a church where the altar is placed.*

SARACEN (style). *See MOORISH.*

SEE (episcopal). *The official seat and center of authority and jurisdiction of a bishop, the chief church of which is a cathedral.*

SILVERGILT. *Gilded silver.*

SPANDREL. *The space, usually decorated, between the exterior curve of an arch and the right angle that frames it.*

SPIRE. *A tapering pyramidal structure surmounting a tower; in more common usage, a steeple.*

STATUE-COLUMN. *A decorative, sometimes supporting, column in the form of a human figure.*

STEEPLE. *A church tower, usually surmounted by a spire.*

STRUTTING. *Wooden bracing, usually set diagonally, to strengthen a ceiling, spire, etc., from within.*

SUFFRAGAN. *Subordinate to an archiepiscopal see.*

TABERNACLE. *A receptacle for the consecrated Host and wine of the Eucharist.*

TRACERY. *Ornamental designs, often interlaced with branching lines.*

TRANSEPT. *Either of two lateral arms intersecting the nave of a cruciform church.*

TRANSITIONAL (style). *Term used to designate the first flowering of Gothic motifs in Romanesque architecture.*

TRASCORO (Spanish). *Retrochoir.*

TRIFORIUM. *A narrow second-story gallery or passage over either or both of the aisles that flank the nave.*

TRUMEAU (French). *A central pillar in a doorway; a support for the tympanum.*

TYMPANUM. *The space, usually decorated with sculpture or painting, enclosed within the frame of an arch, portal, or the triangle of a pediment.*

VAULT. *An arched masonry ceiling, usually of mutually supporting wedge-shaped stones or bricks.*

VAULTING. *Vaulted construction.*

AMIENS
BEAUVAIS • • LAON
ROUEN • • REIMS
COUTANCES • • PARIS • STRASBOURG
• CHARTRES
• LE MANS

• BOURGES
• AUTUN

ALBI •

FRANCE

Generations of historians have maintained that even had the history of the Middle Ages never been written, the medieval cathedral would still provide an almost complete record of the thought, beliefs, and aspirations of its time. In France, this stone history was written with particular fervor and eloquence. There, some six hundred major churches rose in a single century (1170–1270); and there, in a chain of mighty cathedrals that included such architectural masterpieces as Notre Dame, Beauvais, Chartres (below), Amiens, and Coutances, to mention just a few, was born and perfected the Gothic style—a style that gave renewed impetus to church building throughout western Europe and that made manifest the confidence of an age which, as the superb cathedrals illustrated on following pages show, believed that with faith, anything was possible.

Reims

THE CROWNING GLORY

The cathedral at Reims rises from the pavement like an immense sculpture, firm as a mountain yet delicate as Belgian lace. Auguste Rodin could sense its presence even in the darkness of night: "I cannot distinguish it, but I feel it. Its beauty persists. It triumphs over shadows and forces me to admire its powerful black harmony. It fills my window, it almost hides the sky. How explain why, even when enveloped in night, this cathedral loses nothing of its beauty? Does the power of that beauty transcend the senses, that the eye sees what it sees not?" Rodin was writing as a sculptor, concerned ostensibly with the physical and artistic, but there is in his words something of the mystical feeling with which the French have always regarded Notre Dame of Reims (seen at left as it was in the seventeenth century). For in the heart and history of the nation, Reims is to France what Canterbury is to England. Since 496, when Clovis, the first of the Merovingian kings, was baptized there, the city and its cathedral have been sacred to the French. To be crowned at Reims was to be undisputed king of France. Napoleon, who was not of royal birth, was crowned at Paris. So was the ten-year-old Henry VI of England, whose claim to the throne of France was never fully accepted by the French. King Henry IV, the only French monarch whose claim was in dispute, was crowned at Chartres. But it was to Reims that Joan of Arc brought Charles VII for his coronation in 1429, and her words confirmed both his and the cathedral's royalty: "Gentle King, from henceforth is fulfilled the pleasure of God who wished that you should come to Reims to receive your worthy anointing, by showing that you are truly king and him to whom the kingdom should belong."

Reims has had a Christian cathedral since 401 when Saint Nicasius dedicated a pagan temple to Mary. By the early thirteenth century several basilicas and churches had stood on the site. The last of these burned down in 1210, giving the energetic crusader and bishop of Reims, Albéric de Humbert, an excuse to build his own cathedral. He had been archdeacon at Notre Dame of Paris while that cathedral was being built, and in many respects—particularly in the cathedral's façade—the design of Reims was influenced by that of Paris. Five generations of builders and architects left their marks on the cathedral at Reims, but always on the basis of the original plan of Jean d'Orbais and always with a consistency of purpose that has left us with a structure of rare unity and beauty. The cathedral was all but complete by the end of the thirteenth century. The choir, transepts, nave, and towers were finished, and the great rose window was in place above the main portal. It remained only to perfect the details; for thirty years craftsmen lavished their attention on the carvings and statuary (like those on the spire at right) that cover the cathedral.

Because Reims, more than any other cathedral, has been sacred to the French, it has made an ideal target for the enemies of France. In striking it they struck at the soul of the nation. In 1914 and again in 1918 the enemy struck with a greater fury than ever before, pouring thousands of bombs into the cathedral, turning it into a furnace and mutilating its statues. But the structure stood, for it had been built on firm walls and foundations as well as on faith. Although the damage seemed irreparable, the cathedral was restored when the war was over, and today it stands as it stood before, a sacred symbol of France.

BOTH: BIBLIOTHÈQUE NATIONALE; MS. FR. 19093

The apse, from its five radiating
chapels to its ambulatory and choir (the interior of
which is shown above), rose in one
confident sweep between 1211 and 1241. During that time
the visiting architect Villard de Honnecourt stopped at the
building yard and made the sketches at right of the
exterior (top) and interior of the
chapels. The drawings differ slightly from the actual
design, suggesting that the cathedral's architect
made revisions in the course of construction.

*Like most French kings, Charles VII was crowned at Reims (left)
and took communion from the twelfth-century chalice of
Saint Remi (above) in 1422. But politics prevented Louis XVIII
from being crowned at Reims in 1814, and decorations (below)
planned for his coronation never were executed.*

Like most French kings, Charles VII was crowned at Reims (left)
and took communion from the twelfth-century chalice of
Saint Remi (above) in 1422. But politics prevented Louis XVIII
from being crowned at Reims in 1814, and decorations (below)
planned for his coronation never were executed.

Reims is a kingdom of stone
populated with five thousand statues of bishops,
kings, saints, devils, knights,
vassals, and craftsmen. Stone animals and birds
(like the one below) perch on its
pinnacles, and every type of leaf that grows
in northern France is said to be
reproduced on the cathedral's walls and towers.
Although the church was grievously
damaged by the shelling of World War I, it has
been restored to look much as it
did in the seventeenth-century engraving at right.

LEON D. HARMON—PHOTO RESEARCHERS

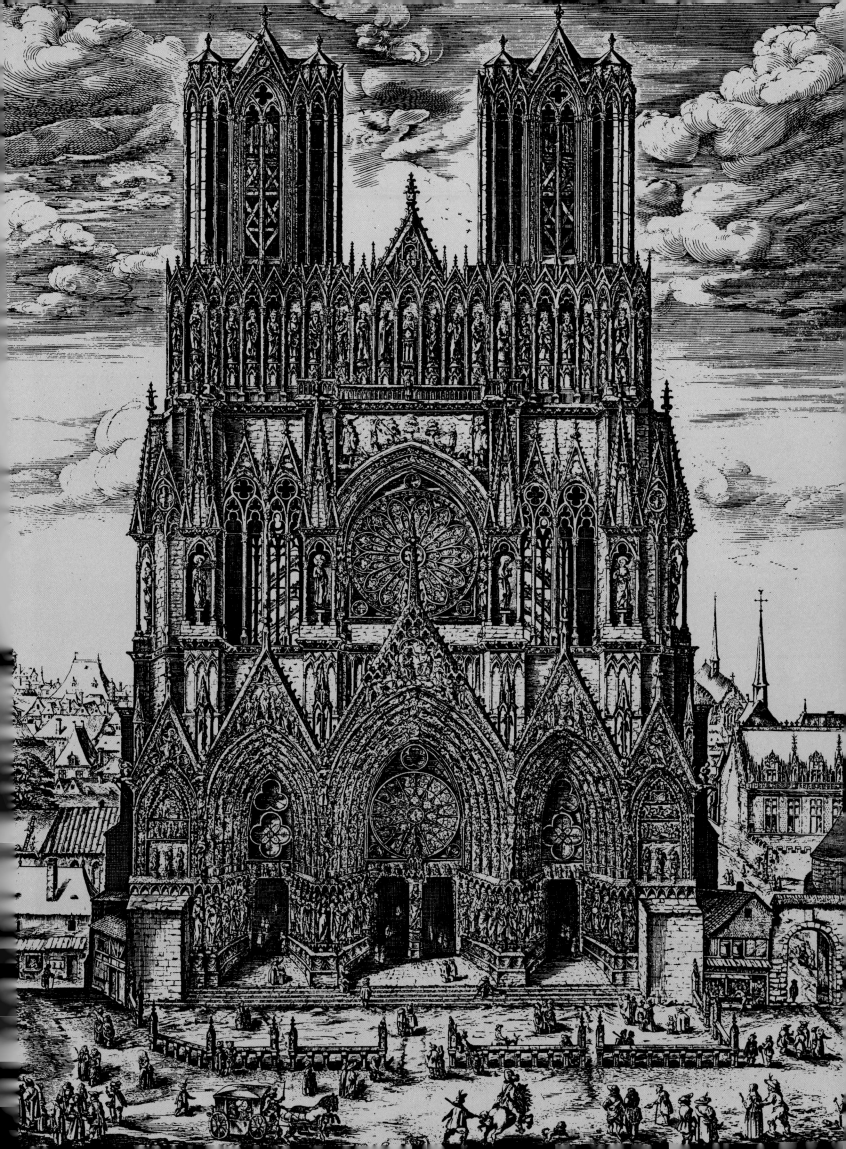

Amiens

A MODEL OF CONSISTENCY

An old saying has it that "the choir of Beauvais, the nave of Amiens, the portal of Reims, and the towers of Chartres, would together form the finest church in the world." Such a church existed perhaps in the imagination of Robert de Luzarches, for in his design of Amiens he came close to achieving it. Begun in 1220 over the charred ruins of a Romanesque cathedral, Amiens was in large part the product of the successes and failures of the other three cathedrals. The master builder of Chartres had just discovered that, by discarding the traditional gallery form of construction and relying instead on the support of buttresses and ribbed vaulting, he could make the aisles higher and open huge windows on the nave. It was too late for gloomy Notre Dame of Paris to benefit from this experiment, but for Amiens Robert built windows so high and wide that in the sixteenth century much of the glass fell out under the strain of its own weight and the battering of wind and hail. Although the windows were replaced and strengthened, most of the original stained glass was lost. Having noted that at Beauvais the highest choir in Europe had collapsed twice, Amiens' builders profited by the lesson and made their choir a few feet lower and more solid. Following the example of Reims, they also reduced to the extreme limit the thickness of Amiens' walls and pillars, thus allowing even more light to flood the great nave.

The simplicity and consistency of Amiens' design is a monument to the single-minded vision of its architects and builders. Unlike most other cathedrals, Notre Dame of Amiens bears no souvenirs of Roman or Byzantine predecessors. The choir of the Romanesque cathedral had been damaged little by the fire that destroyed its nave; yet when the new nave was finished in 1236, the Romanesque remains were completely demolished and a Gothic choir built from scratch. Amiens rose rapidly. The façade (right), inspired by that of Notre Dame of Paris, was finished by 1245, the choir by 1269. Pilgrimages to the cathedral's most famous relic, a part of the skull of John the Baptist recovered during the crusades, kept the building funds rolling in. Although chapels and the ill-suited towers were added much later, the cathedral was substantially completed before other builders with other ideas could destroy its unity and perfection—a fate which overcame many another cathedral. Amiens thus has the distinction of being in its entirety not only the largest cathedral in France but also one of the purest examples of Gothic architecture in the world.

40

*The problems of stress and
counterstress were resolved so deftly by the architect
of Amiens that the cathedral seems
to stand without effort. The main arches of the
apse and nave, seen in the
photograph at left, spring from remarkably slender
pillars to a height of 139 feet.
Windows occupy almost
half the total height. The graceful cross-ribbing
of the ceiling vaults (top right)
carries the weight of the roof downward to the pillars
and outward to the external
buttressing (bottom right). The
buttresses also take much of the weight of the walls.*

BOTH: JEAN ROUBIER

The façade of Amiens is a
complete theological, historical, moral, and natural
portrait of the thirteenth
century. "The Bible in stone," Ruskin called it.
Above, six apostles and prophets
stand in the central portal over a double row of
medallions portraying Virtues
and Vices. The rows of statues at right are from
the same door and represent,
from left, patriarchs of the Old Testament, the
tree of Jesse, old men of the
Apocalypse, saints, confessors, martyrs, and angels.

44

A CATHEDRAL BESTIARY

Although the demons and monsters so prevalent in cathedral sculpture may seem almost quaint to modern eyes, the men of the Middle Ages did not find them so. In a time when illiteracy was an almost universal condition and belief in a literal, waiting Inferno prevailed, the purpose of most cathedral sculpture was not decorative but didactic. It was intended, in short, to scare the hell out of its beholders, and there is every reason to believe it did a creditable job, presenting the horrors of damnation in living color (of which only faint traces remain today). The creatures depicted here and on the following two pages are typical of those that peopled the medieval French cathedral.

Gargoyle figures, originally simple disguises for waterspouts, evolved over the years into complex sculptures like the horned grotesque (bottom center) atop Notre Dame. Flanking it are two demons from the reliefs at Autun. The sky diver at right, also from Autun, represents Simon Magus, the sorcerer who gave his name to simony.

FAR LEFT AND FAR RIGHT: GIRAUDON; CENTER TWO: JEAN ROUBIER

BESTIARY

LEFT TO RIGHT: *Another Notre Dame gargoyle figure dines alfresco*
high above the streets of Paris; a devil
from Autun's west tympanum weighs the souls of the dead
to determine their ultimate disposition;
a colleague from Bourges carries off an unfortunate
who tipped the scales too heavily; a demon leers from
one of the Romanesque capitals at the Cathedral of Autun.

FAR LEFT: CULVER PICTURES, INC.; CENTER TWO: JEAN ROUBIER; FAR RIGHT: BELZEAUX—ZODIAQUE, FROM RAPHO GUILLUMETTE

The Gargoyle often makes his perch
On a cathedral or a church,
Where, mid ecclesiastic style,
He smiles an early-Gothic smile.
—Oliver Herford

Laon

A HEADSTART TOWARD HEAVEN

The year was 1112 and Gaudri, the bishop of Laon, was away in Rome, seeking the pope's pardon for a murder in which he was implicated. His Excellency was an erstwhile soldier of fortune who had grown rich under William the Conqueror and had gained his seat at Laon through simony. A tyrant who was far more interested in the care of his hawks and hounds than in the saving of souls—his own included—he was despised by a large portion of his flock, who took advantage of his absence to secure a communal charter for their town. On his return, Gaudri purchased revocation of the charter from Louis VI, whom he had invited to Laon to celebrate Easter. This maneuver enraged the townspeople, who retaliated by setting fire to the home of one of Gaudri's minions—a fire that, as chance would have it, first spread to the bishop's palace and then to his cathedral before devouring a sizable portion of the city. In the midst of the ensuing confusion, Gaudri and several of his supporters were put to death.

The Laonnais had rid themselves of their hated bishop, but in the process they had lost their cathedral, along with much of the town's wealth. Reconstruction funds were raised, however, by seven canons who traveled as far afield as the south of England, exhibiting sacred relics and begging aid. The resultant jerry-built cathedral apparently satisfied nobody; four decades later it was razed, and a new church was begun by Bishop Gautier de Montagne, who contributed his own funds toward the erection of a cathedral that, he hoped, would rival, if not surpass, those of Noyon and Sens, both of which were then under construction.

The site of the cathedral at Laon was tailor-made to the realization of the Gothic ideal. Located high on a ridge, the enormous edifice began at an altitude where its rivals left off, and it was the bishop's intention to double the height of the ridge, thereby making "as much for God as God had made for Laon." Only five of seven projected towers were completed, though, and only one of these was topped with a spire—which was pulled down during the French Revolution.

Laon's twin west towers (left) are unique for their subtle transition, as they rise, from the square to the octagonal, and for the herd of sixteen immense oxen that peer out from between the upper pillars. These great brutes commemorate the efforts of the beasts of burden that, according to legend, faithfully dragged huge blocks of stone up the hillside from the quarries below while the cathedral was under construction. The legend is further embellished by the story of one ox that turned up unbidden, relieved an exhausted fellow, completed the work at hand, and vanished as suddenly as it had appeared.

53

*I have been in many places as you
may see by this book: never anywhere have I
seen towers like those of Laon.*
—Villard de Honnecourt

*Airiness as well as height
contributes to the graceful proportions of Laon.
Open space was left wherever the
structure would sustain it, as can be seen
in Villard's sketch of the north
tower at left and in the photograph of the south tower
above. The nave walls (right) are also
riddled with windows and lofty galleries.*

Chartres

APOTHEOSIS OF THE GOTHIC

"Who has ever seen!—Who has ever heard tell, in times past, that powerful princes of the world, that men brought up in honor and in wealth, that nobles, men and women, have bent their proud and haughty necks to the harness of carts, and that, like beasts of burden, they have dragged to the abode of Christ these wagons . . . ?" The rhetorical question was put by a twelfth-century abbot in a letter to some colleagues; the occasion was his awe at the manifest piety of one of the greatest communal efforts of all time, the building of Notre Dame de Chartres.

Ordinarily, the construction of a cathedral was a matter of many decades or even centuries. Even the greatest churches tended to be stylistic hodgepodges as architects died and were supplanted by others, each in turn eager to shape the project to his own concepts, to leave his own mark to posterity. Chartres, however, has a remarkable stylistic unity that is attributable directly to the bending of those "proud and haughty" (and a multitude of humbler) necks. Because of the collective zeal of the people of Chartres, a project that might have dragged on for generations was completed in a scant quarter of a century. The result is both the purest example of the Ogival style ever constructed and a watershed in Gothic architecture. "For the first time," wrote Viollet-le-Duc, "one sees at Chartres . . . simplicity of construction, beauty in form, strong workmanship, structure true and solid, judicious choices of material, all the characteristics of good work. . . ." Henry Adams, taking a more subjective view, tells us that "Chartres expressed . . . an emotion, the deepest man ever felt."

Five previous churches, all of them highly flammable, stood on the site occupied by the present structure at Chartres. Fortunately, the fifth building did not burn entirely; along with the crypt, the mismated towers and the Royal Portal survived—and survive still as glories of French architecture. The south tower, Adams wrote, is generally recognized "as the most perfect piece of architecture in the world," while the Royal Portal moved him to declare that "you will see no other so complete or so instructive." Its tympanum (right) he found a sublime expression of the Church Triumphant. Indeed, almost everything about Chartres inspires the use of superlatives: the nave has been called the purest in France; the stained glass, with its renowned "Chartres blue," the finest anywhere. "Never in any period," rhapsodized the novelist J. K. Huysmans of the carving on the south bay, ". . . has a more expressive figure been thus wrought by the genius of man . . ."

French history consists in large part of the bending of proud and humble necks, but seldom in so noble an enterprise: "the struggle," in Adams' words, "of [man's] own littleness to grasp the infinite."

56

HENRY ADAMS ON CHARTRES

Henry Adams (1838–1918), a descendant of two American presidents, was one of the most enthusiastic and erudite of all cathedral buffs. Because he was first of all a historian, a visit to one of the great edifices of the Gothic period was not just the usual, dutiful tour of a pile of cold stone, but a trip backward in time that enabled him—and his readers—to experience with stunning intimacy the life and thought of the Middle Ages. Few writers have conveyed so vividly the spirit and aspirations of an epoch, along with its deep religiosity, as Adams did in this excerpt from his masterly study, Mont-Saint-Michel and Chartres.

If you want to know what churches were made for, come down here on some great festival of the Virgin, and give yourself up to it; but come alone! That kind of knowledge cannot be taught and can seldom be shared. We are not now seeking religion; indeed, true religion generally comes unsought. We are trying only to feel Gothic art. For us, the world is not a schoolroom or a pulpit, but a stage, and the stage is the highest yet seen on earth. In this church the old Romanesque leaps into the Gothic under our eyes; of a sudden, between the portal and the shrine, the infinite rises into a new expression, always a rare and excellent miracle in thought. The two expressions are nowhere far apart; not further than the Mother from the Son. The new artist drops unwillingly the hand of his father or his grandfather; he looks back, from every corner of his own work, to see whether it goes with the old. He will not part with the western portal or the lancet windows; he holds close to the round columns of the choir; he would have kept the round arch if he could, but the round arch was unable to do the work; it could not rise; so he broke it, lifted the vaulting, threw out flying buttresses, and satisfied the Virgin's wish. . . .

A single glance shows what trouble the architect had with the old façade and towers, and what temptation to pull them all down. One cannot quite say that he has spoiled his own church in trying to save what he could of the old, but if he did not quite spoil it, he saved it only by the exercise of an amount of intelligence that we shall never learn enough to feel our incapacity to understand. True ignorance approaches the infinite more nearly than any amount of knowledge can do, and, in our case, ignorance is fortified by a certain element of nineteenth-century indifference which refuses to be interested in what it cannot understand; a violent reaction from the thirteenth century which cared little to comprehend anything except the incomprehensible. The architect at Chartres was required by the Virgin to provide more space for her worshippers within the church, without destroying the old portal and flèche which she loved. That this order came directly from the Virgin, may be taken for granted. At Chartres, one sees everywhere the Virgin, and nowhere any rival authority; one sees her give orders, and architects obey them; but very rarely a hesitation as though the architect were deciding for himself. In his western front, the architect has obeyed orders so literally that he has not even taken the trouble to apologize for leaving unfinished the details which, if he had been responsible for them, would have been his anxious care. He has gone to the trouble of moving the heavy doorways forward, so that the chapels in the towers, which were meant to open on a porch, now open into the nave, and the nave itself has, in appearance, two more spans than in the old church; but the work shows blind obedience, as though he were doing his best to please the Virgin without trying to please himself. Probably he could in no case have done much to help the side aisles in their abrupt collision with the solid walls of the two towers, but he might at least have brought the vaulting of his two new bays, in the nave, down to the ground, and finished it. The vaulting is awkward in these two bays, and yet he has taken great trouble to effect what seems at first a small matter. Whether the great rose window was an afterthought or not can never be known, but any one can see with a glass, and better on the architectural plan, that the vaulting of the main church was not high enough to admit the great rose, and that the architect has had to slope his two tower-spans upward. So great is the height that you cannot see this difference of level very plainly even with a glass, but on the plans it seems to amount to several feet; perhaps a metre. The architect has managed to deceive our eyes, in order to enlarge the rose; but you can see as plainly as though he were here to tell you, that, like a great general, he has concentrated his whole energy on the rose, because the Virgin has told him that the rose symbolized herself, and that the light and splendour of her appearance in the west were to redeem all his awkwardnesses.

Of course this idea of the Virgin's interference sounds to you a mere bit of fancy, and that is an account which may be settled between the Virgin and you; but even twentieth-century eyes can see that the rose redeems everything, dominates everything, and gives character to the whole church. . . .

Looking farther, one sees that the rose-motive, which so dominates the west front, is carried round the church, and comes to another outburst of splendour in the transepts. This leads back to fenestration on a great scale, which is a terribly ambitious flight for tourists; all the more, because here the tourist gets little help from the architect, who, in modern times, has seldom the opportunity to study the subject at all, and accepts as solved the problems of early Gothic fenestration. One becomes pedantic and pretentious at the very sound of the word, which is an intolerable piece of pedantry in itself; but Chartres is all windows, and its windows were as triumphant as its Virgin, and were one of her miracles. One can no more overlook the windows of Chartres than the glass which is in them. We have already looked at the windows of Mantes; we have seen what happened to the windows at Paris. Paris had at one leap risen twenty-five feet higher than Noyon, and even at Noyon, the architect, about 1150, had been obliged to invent new fenestration. Paris and Mantes, twenty years later, made another effort, which proved a failure. Then the architect of Chartres, in 1195, added ten feet more to his vault, and undertook, once for all, to show how a great cathedral should be lighted. . . .

The rose window was not Gothic but Romanesque, and needed a great deal of coaxing to feel at home within the pointed arch. At first, the architects felt the awkwardness so strongly that they avoided it wherever they could. In the beautiful façade of Laon, one of the chief beauties is the setting of the rose under a deep round arch. The western roses of Mantes and Paris are treated in the same way, although a captious critic might complain that their treatment is not so effective or so logical. Rheims boldly imprisoned the roses within the pointed arch; but Amiens, toward 1240, took refuge in the same square exterior set-

ting that was preferred, in 1200, here at Chartres; and in the interior of Amiens the round arch of the rose is the last vault of the nave, seen through a vista of pointed vaults, as it is here. All these are supposed to be among the chief beauties of the Gothic façade, although the Gothic architect, if he had been a man of logic, would have clung to his lines, and put a pointed window in his front, as in fact he did at Coutances. He felt the value of the rose in art, and perhaps still more in religion, for the rose was Mary's emblem. One is fairly sure that the great Chartres rose of the west front was put there to please her, since it was to be always before her eyes, the most conspicuous object she would see from the high altar, and therefore the most carefully considered ornament in the whole church outside the choir. The mere size proves the importance she gave it. The exterior diameter is nearly forty-four feet. . . . The nave of Chartres is, next perhaps to the nave of Angers, the widest of all Gothic naves; about fifty-three feet . . . ;

An engraving by Benjamin Winkles shows Chartres in 1837.

and the rose takes every inch it can get of this enormous span. The value of the rose, among architects of the time, was great, since it was the only part of the church that Villard de Honnecourt sketched; and since his time, it has been drawn and redrawn, described and commented by generations of architects till it has become as classic as the Parthenon.

59

The details of Chartres are like jewels in a precious setting. At left, the rose window of the north transept. The sculpture over the right doorway of the west portal (above) depicts the Nativity and the Annunciation to the shepherds on the lower lintel and the presentation of Christ in the temple on the upper. At right are figures of Music and Pythagoras.

OVERLEAF: The figures on the south porch represent the Church in this world. At left are those from the central door: Saint James the major wearing a belt of shells, Saint James the minor holding a club, and Saint Bartholomew. At right, the gentle face of Saint Theodore from the statue in the Bay of Martyrs.

LEFT: JEAN ROUBIER; RIGHT: BELZEAUX—ZODIAQUE, FROM RAPHO GUILLUMETTE

THE EYE OF GOD

A Portfolio of Stained Glass

Henry Adams was not often at a loss for words, but even he hesitated to describe the stained glass of Chartres (whose north rose window is shown opposite): "One becomes, sometimes, a little incoherent in talking about it; one is ashamed to be as extravagant as one wants to be; one has no business to labour painfully to explain and prove to one's self what is as clear as the sun in the sky; one loses temper in reasoning about what can only be felt, and what ought to be felt instantly . . ."

Stained-glass windows were first used in the Byzantine churches of Constantinople, but as early as the fourth century the art had spread to southern France, as we know from a contemporary poet's description of the installation of a Byzantine window in a church at Lyons. In 550 Venetian and Near Eastern craftsmen installed a few of their glass windows in the first Notre Dame of Paris, but a hundred years later France had become so famous for its own stained glass that a British abbot was importing French artisans to glaze the windows of his abbey.

The original Byzantine windows were probably simple decorative designs set in plaster or stone to bring a touch of color to the gloomy interiors, but it was not long before these little jewels of light were being shaped into naïve portraits of saints and heroes and held together more delicately by ribbons of lead. As the art grew more sophisticated, the clergy became aware that these lovely windows which so enhanced the beauty of their churches could also have an educational value. Thus, in the last years of the tenth century, the storybook windows which illustrated in a series of panes the lives of the saints and biblical stories for the benefit of the largely illiterate church-goers of the Middle Ages began to make their appearance.

The art of making stained glass was a joint effort involving the designer, the glassmaker, and the painter, not to mention the builder who had to install the window without smashing it to bits. Properly stained glass, or "pot metal," was made by adding the color—manganese, copper shavings, red ochre, blue cobalt—to the molten glass. (The slipshod method was to paint on clear glass.) The glass was blown to the correct thinness and then put into an oven where it flattened into a plate. When the plate cooled, the glazier cut it to match the shape outlined on the designer's sketch; the designer scratched grooves on the glass to indicate details: a stalk representing a garden, an arch a palace, a few lines for a beard or the folds of a cloak. The painter filled in the scratches with enamel, perhaps adding a few strokes to suggest perspective, and then the glass was put into a kiln where the enamel was baked onto the surface. Finally the pieces were assembled into sections, soldered together with strips of lead, and handed over to the builders who assembled the whole in its proper place in the church.

With the evolution of the Gothic style in the twelfth and thirteenth centuries, the art of stained glass reached its height. The pointed arch, flying buttress, and weighted pinnacle allowed men to build higher and thinner walls than ever before and to open great windows on these towering walls. While stained glass had served only an ornamental function in the Byzantine and Roman churches, like a painting on the wall, it now became a major element, finding its perfect ethereal setting amid the soaring columns and graceful arches of the medieval cathedral.

64

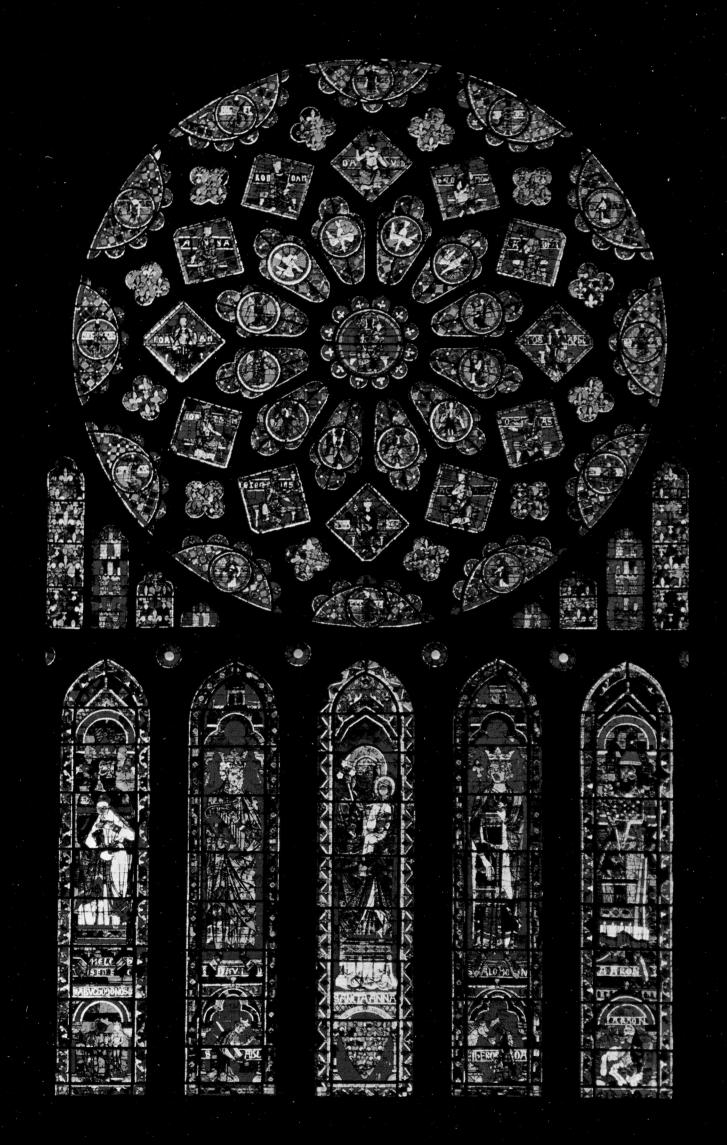

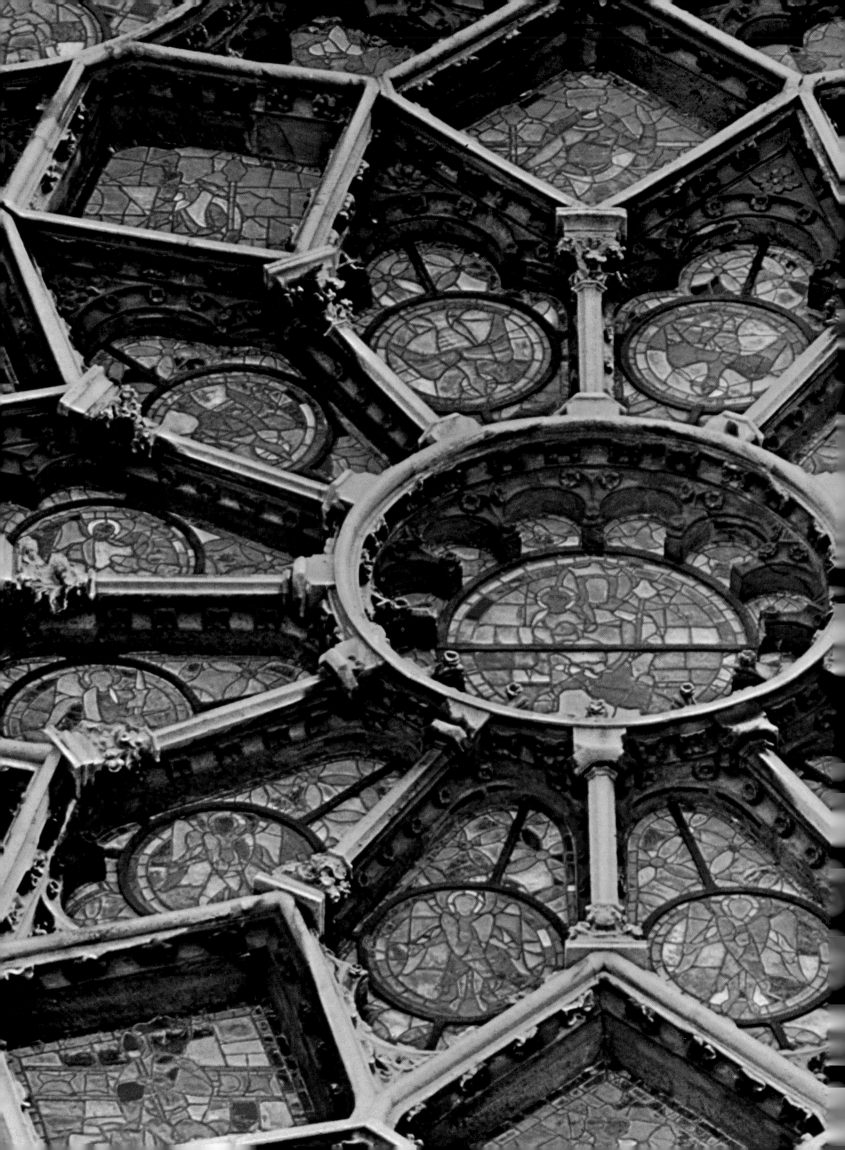

GJON MILI

"The western rose," wrote Henry Adams of the
great window in Chartres' west front,
"is one of the flowers of architecture which
reveals its beauties slowly without end."
Adams was as enthusiastic about the window's
exterior (left) as he was about the glass
itself: "Its chief beauty is in the feeling
which unites it with the portal, the lancets,
and the flèche." The Flamboyant window
tracery of Amiens' west front is shown below.

JEAN ROUBIER

OVERLEAF: A. *A detail from a nave window
of Chartres depicts an episode in the life
of Saint Lubin. B. Quatrefoil detail
from the Last Judgment window at Bourges.
C. A hunting scene illustrates the story of Saint Eustace
at Chartres. D. The minor Old Testament
prophet Zephaniah is portrayed in a choir
window at Bourges. E. Another Bourges portrait
represents Christ's ancestor, Nauhm.
F. A thirteenth-century border from Poitiers.*
A AND C: GIRAUDON; B, D, AND E: PETER ADELBERG; F: ARCHIVES PHOTOGRAPHIQUES

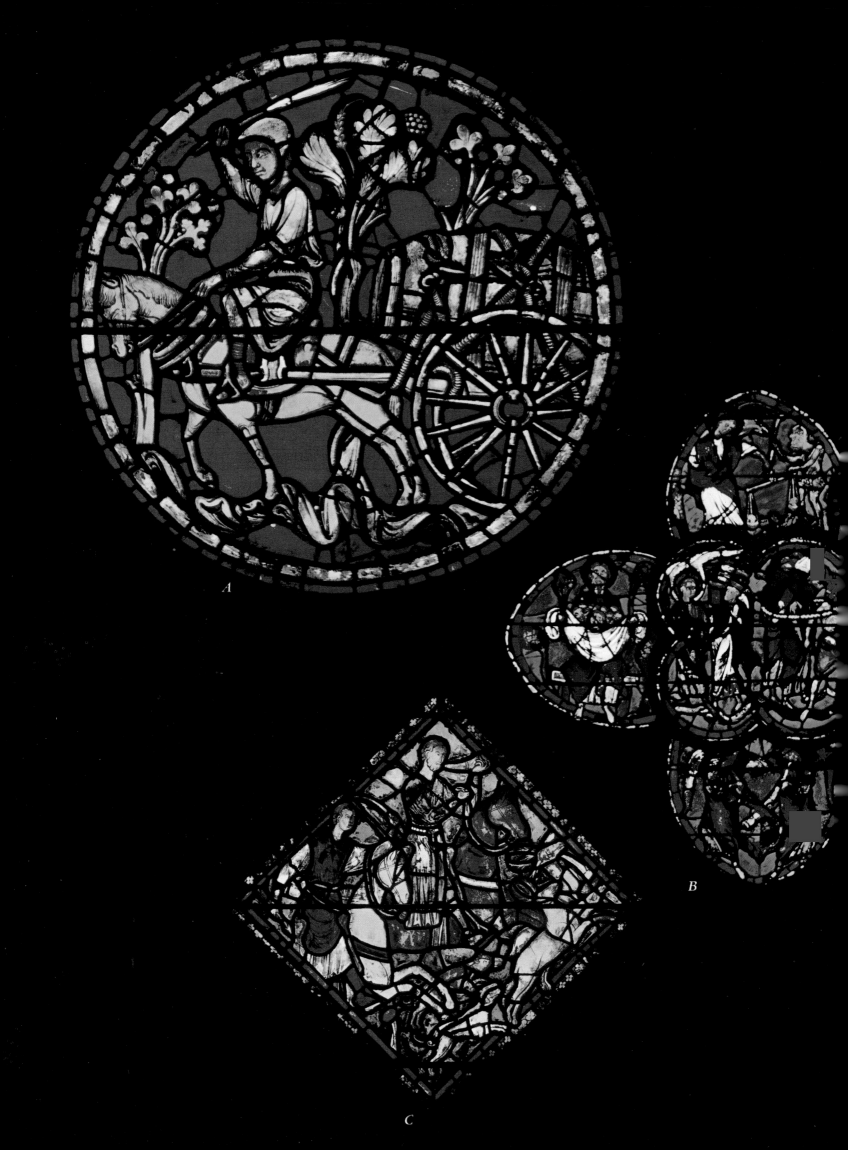

A

B

C

D   E

F

Even though it was altered from time to time and underwent extensive
restoration in 1861, the rose window (above) of Notre Dame's
south transept, which dates from around 1270, is still considered
one of the finest blossoms in the garland of glass flowers
produced in the Ile-de-France in the thirteenth century.
It depicts the triumph of Christ, with scenes from the New Testament.
RIGHT: A detail from an early thirteenth-century window at
Bourges Cathedral tells the story of Lazarus and the Evil Rich Man.

Bourges

FIVE GATEWAYS TO HEAVEN

In the third century the first of a succession of Christian churches was built in the hilltop city of Bourges (or, rather, just outside the city walls, since Christian converts were still considered pariahs by the community at large). A thousand years later, this succession was to culminate in one of the most magnificent of Gothic edifices.

Toward the end of the twelfth century, Henri de Sully became archbishop of Bourges and decided to replace the existing Romanesque basilica with a cathedral built in the style being developed in the Ile-de-France by, among others, Henri's brother Eudes, the bishop of Paris. Sully himself lived long enough to build only the crypt of the new cathedral—but what a crypt he built! The largest in France and the most splendidly designed, it was to serve not only as an ingenious substructure for the choir of the cathedral proper but also as a church within a church.

Sully was succeeded by Archbishop Guillaume, who continued the work, preached the Albigensian Crusade from an unfinished choir "open to the four winds," took a severe chill despite the heat of his exhortations, died of it, and won sainthood for his pains. In 1218 Guillaume's remains were transferred from the crypt to the by-then completed choir, where his poor old bones, kept warmer in death than in life, were enshrined in a golden reliquary behind the altar.

The cathedral was largely finished by 1324, and some years later John, duke of Berry, one of the great art patrons of the Middle Ages, commissioned designs from the architect Guy de Dammartin for the transformation of the west front. The façade—boasting five portals of varying size and shape, a great central gable, a pedestal of fifteen graceful steps, and Dammartin's enormous central window—is one of the unquestioned masterpieces of the Gothic era. So, for that matter, is the huge cathedral itself, a marvelous organization of space (the nave is unbroken by transepts) with stunning thirteenth-century stained glass, mighty flying buttresses (left) that soar upward in clean uninterrupted lines, and an extremely light, airy interior.

Ironically, this glory of French architecture was at the point of total destruction by Frenchmen when the Huguenots took the city in 1562. So eager were they to demolish the cathedral that some of them pulled the statuary of the west front down upon their own heads, while others attached mines to the pillars of the nave. Fortunately, a more practical member of their company persuaded them at the last moment to spare the edifice and convert it to a Huguenot temple. Thus was preserved one of Christendom's unique architectural monuments.

73

The exterior of Bourges' nave, looking like a huge oared ship with its array of angled supporting buttresses, is shown in the photograph at top left. The engraving by Jean Toubeau beneath it depicts the cathedral's west front as it looked in 1676. The tower on the left, the Tour de Beurre, *like several others in France, was financed by parishioners who paid for the privilege of eating butter during Lent.*

NOAH'S FLOOD
The story of the ark and the covenant is depicted in a series of thirteenth-century spandrel decorations on the cathedral's west front.

And God said . . . The end of all flesh is come before me . . . Make thee an ark of gopher wood

"And it came to pass after seven days, that the waters of the flood were upon the earth"

"And every living substance was destroyed which was upon the face of the ground"

"Also he sent forth a dove from him, to see if the waters were abated"

"And Noah began to be a husbandman, and he planted a vineyard"

"And he drank of the wine, and was drunken; and he was uncovered within his tent"

The choir (left), seen here through one of the arches of the ambulatory, contains some of the finest stained glass in all France. A detail (right) from the archivolt of the south portal, the most richly decorated portion of the cathedral, shows figures of prophets and patriarchs.

Albi

A MIGHTY FORTRESS

The Albigensian Crusade was over, after two decades of the bloodiest fighting France had ever seen ("I never saw so many heads fly as there," a Catholic general had written of the massacre at Toulouse; seven thousand heretics were roasted alive in the cathedral at Béziers). The forces of the church had at last vanquished the fanatical dissidents of the Languedoc, and the Inquisition had been instituted to root out any lingering traces of Manichaean apostasy. Peace prevailed, but it was an uneasy peace; the devastated cathedral-church of Albi served as an all-too-eloquent reminder of the folly of erecting a physically vulnerable house of worship in a potentially hostile region. Moreover, many nobles in the area still bitterly resented the loss of their traditional right to pillage episcopal property after a prelate's death.

In this parlous atmosphere, Bernard de Castanet, bishop of Albi, inquisitor of Languedoc, and vice-inquisitor of all France, chose not to avail himself of the dubious protection that setting his church within the town's castle walls might have offered. Instead, he determined to build an impregnable fortress, separated from the king's town by a moat; a fortress complete with drawbridge, portcullis, and keep, with ramparts, bastions, and even a guardroom for his soldiery. To this end Bernard established three monastic working orders and a system of taxation whereby a twentieth of all clerical income (and his own as well) was diverted to the project. Construction began in 1282 and continued for more than a century. The result was a mighty, thick-muscled, red brick structure (right) that stands foursquare above the river Tarn and its bridge like a manifest affirmation of faith.

Bishop Bernard's fortress was tested as early as 1422 (thirty years after its completion), when a band of marauding terrorists—a sort of free-lance army called the Routiers—besieged the cathedral after first razing the king's town across the moat. After some time and considerable wasted effort, the siege was lifted and the weary attackers moved on in search of easier prey. From inside the guardroom underneath the tower, the defenders doubtless peered through their loopholes at the smoldering ruins of the king's town and meditated profitably on the relative merits of religious and secular protection.

BOTH: JEAN ROUBIER

Two of Albi's most notable features date from the fifteenth century: the south porch (the cathedral's principal entrance), whose four arches are topped with delicate openwork carving, and the rood screen (above), which is generally conceded to be unsurpassed anywhere. The statuary of this masterpiece (one example of which is shown at left) is surmounted by a magnificent frieze of lacy canopies and pinnacles.

One could pass whole hours in contemplating this
lovely, ever-changing detail, in astonished wonder
that it was possible to find so many differing,
graceful forms, that it was possible to
carve from hard and brittle stone what today could
hardly be wrought in iron or in bronze.
　　　　　　　　　　　—Prosper Mérimée

*The bishops of Albi in the late fifteenth and
early sixteenth centuries were members
of the Amboise family and famous throughout
France as patrons of the arts. Several of them
employed artists imported from Italy
to decorate the cathedral's vaulting (above) and
walls. The small openings near the top of the
massive apse (right) allowed defenders
to pour boiling oil on would-be pillagers.*

The city and cathedral of Rouen have had a long, violent, and dramatic history—from the dark, declining years of the Merovingian dynasty (when the murderous Queen Fredegonde had the bishop Pretextatus slain at his prayers in the church), through the condemnation of Joan of Arc in the episcopal palace and her subsequent death at the hands of the English in 1431, to the destruction wrought by bombs during World War II. But the character of the city and its cathedral (which can be seen at left between the spires of the Church of St. Ouen) was determined primarily by Rouen's prominence in the history of the Norman era.

The invading Norseman Rollo was granted the district at the mouth of the Seine by a treaty made with Charles the Simple in 911. A year later Rollo had made Rouen his capital, and in 913, after his conversion to Catholicism, he began to construct a new cathedral. The history of this building is obscure, although it is known that it was continued by Rollo's successors. These rulers included Richard the Lion-Hearted, who was born at Rouen and who bequeathed his heart (now entombed in the present cathedral's choir) to the cathedral chapter after church treasures were sold to help ransom him from Austrians who had taken him captive during the Third Crusade. Rollo's building burned, along with most of the city, in 1200, a year after Richard's death. Nothing remains of it but the mid-twelfth-century Tower of St. Romain (named after the Celtic bishop who supposedly delivered the city from the monster "Gargouille") and the two lateral portals of the west front. Rebuilding apparently was begun within two years of the fire, and the main body of the cathedral was completed before the middle of the century.

Although Rouen was back in French hands by 1204 with the triumphal entry of Philip Augustus, the cathedral is Norman and English as well as French in character. The Norman style, the characteristics of which became more pronounced in the second third of the thirteenth century, features deeply cut profiles and a strong reliance on the effects of light and shadow, and the choir and chevet of Rouen Cathedral follow this style in the use of acute arches and multiple colonnettes. English forms, on the other hand, are evident in the later additions to the cathedral—the decoration of the façade with rows of statues in the manner of such English churches as Wells, Salisbury, and Lichfield. The panels and turrets over the lateral portals are Rayonnant. These additions, as well as the gables of the transept façades, were begun before the close of the fourteenth century. The English influence is even more obvious in the Flamboyant decorations of the west façade. The sixteenth-century central portal of this screenlike stone façade, which overwhelms the viewer with a dizzying collection of arches, spires, pinnacles, and carved foliage, was one of many gifts to the cathedral made by Cardinal d'Amboise, whose elaborate, primarily Renaissance tomb bears the Gothic statue of Temperance shown at right. Although this façade is regarded by some as symptomatic of a loss in vitality of the Gothic style—the separation of artist from architect and of form from function that reduces architecture to mere ornament—its richness and variety are still impressive indeed. In the words of the great art historian, Emile Mâle, "Rouen is like a rich book of Hours in which the center of the page is filled with figures of God, the Virgin, and the saints, while fancy runs riot in the margin."

Rouen

"LIKE A RICH BOOK OF HOURS"

85

The eighteenth-century engraving at left of Notre Dame of Rouen shows the Renaissance tower over the crossing, later replaced by a cast-iron spire—the tallest in France—after the tower was struck by lightning in 1822. In the right foreground are the almost military Tour St. Romain *and, beyond, the later* Tour de Beurre, *so called because it was built with money paid for dispensations to eat butter during Lent. Below and to the right are paintings of the cathedral at early morning, midday, and sunset (detail) by Claude Monet, showing the transfiguring effect of light on the lacy façade.*

OVERLEAF: *At the left is one of the lateral portals of the west front, which depicts the life of Saint John the Baptist; at the right, the* Portail des Librairies, *named for the bookshops that stood nearby.*

BOTH: JEAN ROUBIER

For eight centuries Notre Dame (left) has stood at the heart of Paris, grave and broad-shouldered, her buttresses rooted deep in the earth, her massive weight prevailing amid the storms that have swirled around her. The ground on which she stands, the eastern end of the Ile de la Cité, has been sacred to men since Celtic tribes first built wood and reed tabernacles to pagan gods on it. Over these tabernacles the conquering Romans built a temple to Jupiter in the reign of Tiberius. A Christian church stood here as early as the fourth century; in the sixth the walls of a basilica, thought to be the earliest shrine dedicated to the Virgin in Paris, rose beside the earlier church. On this spot in 1160 Bishop Maurice de Sully drew on the ground with his crosier the outlines of Notre Dame, the first of the truly Gothic cathedrals. A peasant boy who had risen to great wealth and power, Bishop Sully began planning the cathedral as soon as he had attained the episcopacy of Paris, devoting the rest of his life and fortune to the monumental project. He commissioned the unknown architect, raised funds (contributing from his own purse), and purchased a large number of houses which he ordered torn down. Through the rubble he had a new road built, over which materials could be transported through the crowded Cité (overleaf). He selected the artists, purchased materials, and chose the subjects for the sculpture and glass. Finally, his will paid the expense of having the roof covered with lead.

As work progressed, the heart of Paris was taken over by the construction crews. The roofless ruin of the fourth-century Church of St. Etienne, alongside the new excavation, became the major workshop where stone was carved for the new cathedral's first portal. Tents, worksheds, dormitories, dining halls, foundries, kilns, piles of timber, stone, sand, pulleys, and winches filled the streets, the square, and even the cloisters of the Merovingian basilica, soon to be torn down to make way for the nave, towers, and main façade of its successor. In 1163, with the foundations of the choir ready to receive the walls and shafts, the exiled Pope Alexander III, accompanied by Bishop Sully, King Louis VII, and all the notables of church and state, stepped through the dust and rubble to lay his hands and blessing on the first stone of the cathedral proper.

Notre Dame's 140 years of construction cover a major part of the Gothic period. The choir, completed in 1182, was begun when the Gothic style was escaping the last bonds of the Romanesque. In building the nave the architects were still exploring with caution the heights made possible by ribbed vaulting and flying buttresses, the latter device being employed for the first time at Notre Dame. They still retained the gallery form of construction for added support and thus were unable to build the large windows and slender pillars that make Amiens and Chartres so light and airy. Atop the towers of the western façade it was planned to build soaring steeples, but apparently the architects decided against this addition, for, although means and support were available, the spires were never begun. (The spire at the transept crossing was constructed in the nineteenth century.) But the graceful openwork, the height and perfect proportions of the towers, and the carving of the portals make the western façade a masterpiece of High Gothic. The engraving at right, from a drawing by Viollet-le-Duc, the cathedral's nineteenth-century restorer, shows the façade as it would have looked had the original builders completed the spires.

Notre Dame

AT THE HEART OF PARIS

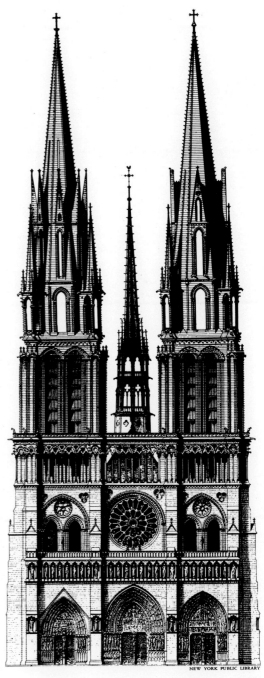

91

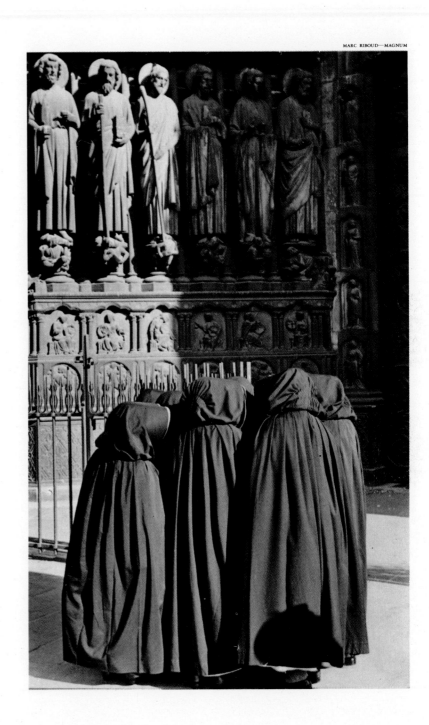

*Notre Dame's south portal, dedicated to Saint
Stephen, is decorated with eight
quatrefoil reliefs, of which four are shown
at left. The subjects of the carvings
are obscure, but may have
been meant to depict student life in the
thirteenth century. The nuns' habits in the
photograph at right strikingly
duplicate the draperies of the figures
that stand on the cathedral's central portal.*

WITNESS TO HISTORY

A Notre Dame Portfolio

For Frenchmen of the Middle Ages, wrote the art historian Emile Mâle, Our Lady was "all woman, regarding neither good nor evil but pardoning all for love." The history of Notre Dame has been the history of France: While she sheltered the humble in prayer her great gray walls were being marked by all the good and evil, all the desperate causes of that history. In the thirteenth century, while Notre Dame still echoed with the noise of masons and stonecutters, the crusaders came to the altar to swear fealty; when they returned from the Holy Land, they brought with them the Crown of Thorns, today still enshrined in the cathedral. Two centuries later during the Hundred Years' War, the streets around Notre Dame ran with blood when the Burgundians defeated the Armagnacs, slaughtering them to a man. With their factional wars tearing the French apart, the English Henry V was able to capture Paris in 1420 and, in a tradition already firmly established, probably came to Notre Dame to hear the hymn of victory and thanksgiving, the *Te Deum*. When Henry died shortly thereafter, his ten-year-old son was brought to the cathedral to be crowned king of the French and English. But those who cheered him in the cathedral square longed for freedom from the English yoke. Six years later they could cheer in earnest when Charles VII at last drove out the foreigners, triumphantly marched to Notre Dame, and heard the *Te Deum* himself.

Again and again violence reigned in the cathedral streets. In 1572 Catherine de Médicis repeated the Burgundian slaughter, this time in the name of religion. At her instigation, thousands of Parisian Protestants were cut to pieces by their Catholic neighbors on Saint Bartholomew's Day. The revolutionaries of the 1790's turned their fury on the cathedral itself, sweeping away its religion and destroying many of its statues. When further popular uprisings tore through Paris between 1830 and 1848, the cathedral was barricaded; but more than once the rioters broke through and ransacked the church. In 1871 the Communards even attempted to burn down the cathedral, but they were thwarted by a bucket brigade of interns from a nearby hospital. The Prussian bombing of Paris in 1870, depicted in the lithograph at left, did little damage to the cathedral, but during World War I the Germans did manage to drop a bomb through its roof. Peace came again, then war again: Nazi convoys were sabotaged by the Resistance near the cathedral square; open rebellion broke out in 1944 as Allied troops approached the city and then rushed up the tower stairs to ring the bells of victory. Snipers were still firing from the roof tops on August twenty-sixth when General de Gaulle, like so many before him, heard the *Te Deum* at Notre Dame.

The events that swept round the cathedral were not all somber. The mystery and miracle plays of the Middle Ages brought gaiety to the cathedral square. There, visiting merchants from the Orient displayed the wonders of the East. In the seventeenth century Louis XIV, the Sun King, held festivities constantly, and most of them included a *Te Deum* at the cathedral. Always a great showman, he once insisted on a lavish cathedral ceremony simply to renew a Franco-Swiss alliance. And when the tragedies of war were only memories and the blood long since had been washed away by the rain, there were *Te Deums*, royal marriages, and church holidays when world-weary hearts could be eased by the hope of heaven and cheered by the glittering splendor of festive pageantry.

97

A RABELAISIAN VISIT

Notre Dame was already a venerable edifice in 1535, when François Rabelais (c. 1494-1553) published Gargantua. *In this excerpt (illustrated at left), Rabelais emphasizes Gargantua's great size by contrasting the giant with the cathedral.*

After a few days' rest, Gargantua went sightseeing. He attracted the attention of all the townsmen because Parisians are such fools, dolts and gulls that a mountebank, a hawker of relics and indulgences, a mule with a bell on its neck or a fiddler on a street corner, collects a greater mob than the most distinguished . . . preacher.

They thronged so thick about that he said in a loud clear voice:

"Upon my word, I think these boobies want me to pay my welcome here and give the Bishop an offertory. Quite right, too! I'll treat them! They'll get their drink! I recognize my obligations and liquidate I shall!—but only *par ris*, for sport!"

Then, smiling, he unfastened his noble codpiece and lugging out his great pleasure-rod, he so fiercely bepissed them that he drowned two hundred and sixty thousand four hundred and eighteen, exclusive of women and children.

By sheer fleetness of foot, a certain number escaped this mighty pissflood, and reaching the top of the Montagne St. Geneviève, beyond the University, sweating, coughing, hawking and out of breath, they began to swear and curse, some in anger, others in jest. . . .

But, whatever protector each invoked, . . . all cried:

"*Nous sommes baignés par ris*, we are drenched *par ris*, for sport."

Accordingly, the city which Strabo . . . calls Leucetia—the name, signifying "whiteness" in Greek, pays a pretty tribute to the thighs of the local ladies—was, ever after Gargantua's exploit, named *par ris* or Paris.

And, since at this new christening every single townsman present swore by all the saints in his parish, the Parisians, who are made up of all nations and all varieties of man, will quite naturally swear at, to or by anything. Indeed they are not a little presumptuous and conceited, whence Joaninus de Barranco in his *Liber de Copiositate Reverentiarum* or *Of the Abundance of Venerable Things* opines that the word *Parisian* comes from the Greek *Parrhesieus*, a bold talker.

His account liquidated, Gargantua considered the great bells in the Towers of Notre Dame and made them ring out most harmoniously. The music suggested to him that they might sound very sweet tinkling on his mare's neck when he sent her back to his father laden with Brie cheese and fresh herring. So he promptly picked up the bells of the Cathedral and carried them home.

BOTH: BIBLIOTHEQUE NATIONALE

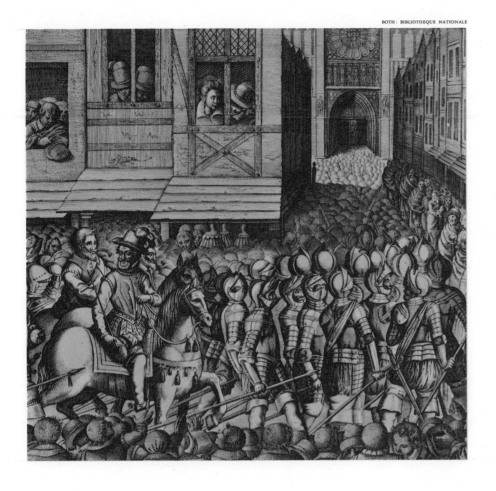

AN EXPEDIENT MASS

The popular and productive reign of Henry IV began, as
did so many others, with a triumphal march to Notre
Dame for a singing of the *Te Deum*. Although his marriage
in 1572 had precipitated the Saint Bartholomew's Day
massacre of the Huguenots, Henry had little difficulty
with the fine points of religious dogma. He bounced back
and forth like a shuttlecock between Protestantism and
Catholicism, thus more than once saving his life and
eventually winning for himself the throne of France. A
lengthy siege of Catholic Paris had no effect, but as soon
as Henry converted for the second time to Catholicism
("Paris is worth a Mass," he is supposed to have said),
the war-weary citizens threw open the city's gates. In
March, 1594, Henry, astride a white horse, entered Paris
and made his way to the cathedral amid the cheers of
the jubilant populace. Those who still mistrusted the
king's religious scruples were tossed into the river Seine.

ABOVE: *Henry IV makes his way through the Paris crowds to the
cathedral, whose main portal can be seen in the background of
this sixteenth-century engraving.* RIGHT: *A somewhat later
engraving shows troops entering the cathedral to celebrate a
victory over Spanish forces at the battle of Avein in 1635.*

TRIUMPHS AND TRAVESTIES

As befits the solemn grandeur of Notre Dame, the celebrations and ceremonies held within her walls have usually been lavish in the extreme. When the Feast of the Assumption was celebrated in the thirteenth century, the cathedral was hung with tapestries and the pavement covered with sweetly scented flowers and herbs. Two centuries later, when times were harder, grass from the fields of Gentilly had to suffice. At Pentecost flowers, torches, and pigeons were tossed from the windows to represent the descent of the Holy Ghost. Coronations, marriages, royal baptisms, and church holidays naturally brought forth the richest decorations, but even a funeral could be splendid. In 1735, for example, the bier of the queen of Sardinia rested beneath an ermine-trimmed canopy. Even the revolutionaries of 1793 required pageantry, bizarre though their brand may have been. In place of the Mass, they held a feast for the Goddess of Reason, who was, as André Maurois was later to write, "all too present in the flesh."

The funeral of the queen of Sardinia is shown in the eighteenth-century engraving at right. In the slightly inaccurate depiction of Notre Dame's interior (below), a German artist portrayed a popular dancer from the opera enthroned as Reason in 1793.

*For Napoleon's coronation as emperor in 1804 both he and his
court dressed in Roman style. Napoleon invited the pope to attend
the ceremonies and then asserted his independence of Rome by
placing the crown on his own head. The final canvas made from
this sketch by Jacques Louis David portrays a Napoleon less rude,
though still imperious, and a Pope Pius VII slightly less sullen.*

VICTOR HUGO AND NOTRE DAME

By 1831, Notre Dame was in a sad state of disrepair, but the publication that year of Victor Hugo's Notre-Dame de Paris *launched a propaganda campaign that culminated in its restoration. Two excerpts from the novel follow. In the first, Hugo (caricatured above) angrily describes the cathedral's decline.*

On the face of this aged queen of our cathedrals we always find a scar beside a wrinkle. *Tempus edax, homo edacior*—which I should translate thus: "Time is blind, man stupid."

If we had leisure to examine with the reader, one by one, the different traces of destruction left upon the ancient church we should find that Time had had much less hand in them than men, and especially professional men. . . .

Time, by a slow and irresistible progress raising the level of the city, occasioned the removal of the steps; but if this rising tide of the pavement of Paris has swallowed up, one after another, those eleven steps which added to the majestic height of the edifice, Time has given to the church more perhaps than it has taken away; for it is Time that has imparted to the façade that somber hue of antiquity which makes the old age of buildings the period of their greatest beauty.

But who has thrown down the two ranges of statues? —who has left the niches empty?—who has inserted that new and bastard pointed arch in the middle of the beautiful central porch?—who has dared to set up that tasteless and heavy door of wood, carved in the style of Louis XV, beside the arabesques of Biscornette? The men, the architects, the artists, of our own days.

QUASIMODO IN THE BELL TOWER

He hurried, out of breath, into the aerial chamber of the great bell, looked at her attentively and lovingly for a moment; then began to talk kindly to her, and patted her with his hand, as you would do a good horse which you are going to put on his mettle. He would pity her for the labor she was about to undergo. After these first caresses he shouted to his assistants in a lower story of the tower to begin. They seized the ropes, the windlass creaked, and slowly and heavily the enormous cone of metal was set in motion. Quasimodo, with heaving bosom, watched the movement. The first shock of the clapper against the wall of brass shook the woodwork upon which it was hung. Quasimodo vibrated with the bell. "Vah!" he would cry, with a burst of idiot laughter. Meanwhile the motion of the bell was accelerated, and as the angle which it described became more and more obtuse the eye of Quasimodo glistened and shone out with a more phosphoric light. At length the grand peal began: the whole tower trembled; rafters, leads, stones, all groaned together, from the piles of the foundation to the trefoils of the parapet. Quasimodo then boiled over with delight; he foamed at the mouth; he ran backward and forward; he trembled with the tower from head to foot. The great bell, let loose, and, as it were, furious with rage, turned its enormous throat first to one side and then to the other side of the tower, and thence issued a roar that might be heard four leagues round. Quasimodo placed himself before this open mouth; he crouched down and rose up, as the bell swung to and fro, inhaled its boisterous breath, and looked by turns at the abyss two hundred feet below him, and at the enormous tongue of brass which came ever and anon to bellow in his ear. This was the only speech that he could hear, the only sound that broke the universal silence to which he was doomed. He would spread himself out in it like a bird in the sun. All at once the frenzy of the bell would seize him; his look became wild; he would watch the rocking engine, as a spider watches a fly, and suddenly leap upon it. Then, suspended over the abyss, carried to and fro in the formidable oscillation of the bell, he seized the brazen monster by the earlets, strained it with his knees, spurred it with his heels, and with the whole weight and force of his body increased the fury of the peal. While the tower began to quake he would shout and grind his teeth, his red hair bristled up, his breast heaved and puffed like the bellows of a forge, his eye flashed fire, and the monstrous bell neighed breathless under him. It was then no longer the bell of Notre-Dame and Quasimodo: it was a dream, a whirlwind, a tempest, vertigo astride of uproar; a spirit clinging to a winged monster; a strange centaur, half man, half bell; a species of horrible Astolpho, carried off by a prodigious hippogriff of living brass.

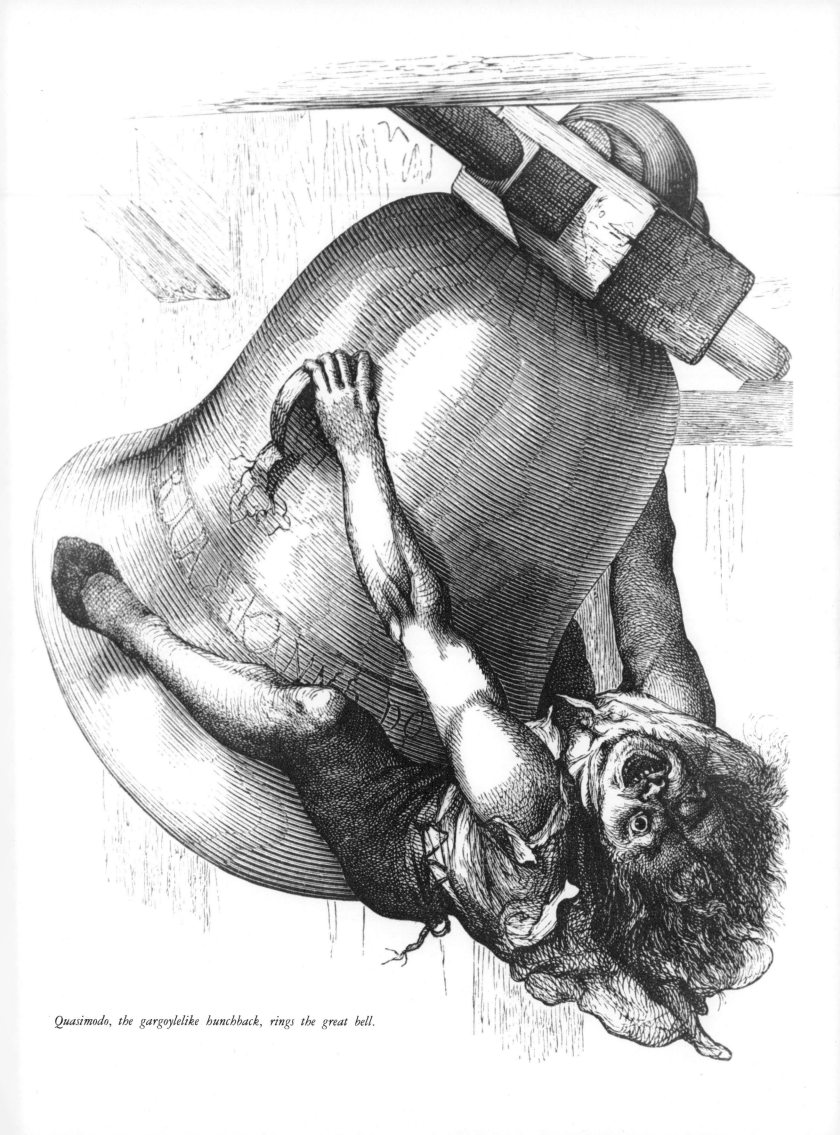

Quasimodo, the gargoylelike hunchback, rings the great bell.

Strasbourg

THE MOST
GOTHIC OF SPIRES

"This is German architecture, our architecture! Something of which the Italians cannot boast, far less the Frenchmen." So said the poet Goethe in a youthful essay praising the thirteenth-century architect Erwin von Steinbach, whose "wildness" of inspiration, according to Goethe, transformed the stones and mortar of Strasbourg's Cathedral of Notre Dame into the truest possible expression of *Deutschheit emergierend*—emerging German nationalism.

What young Goethe did not know, or had forgotten, was that French Gothic had been the most widespread and eagerly copied style of architecture Germans—including Erwin—had ever known and, indeed, that many of the details of Strasbourg bear strong resemblances to the French abbey church of St. Denis, the first Gothic building; to the cathedrals of Troyes and Laon (which Erwin knew); and to Notre Dame in Paris. Moreover, the famous statuary adorning Strasbourg's portals, piers, and arcades is derived from the Reims school of sculpture, and its representations of the Last Judgment and of the prophets are regarded to this day as French sculpture, comparable to similar works at Sainte-Chapelle in Paris.

Steinbach was not the only inspired architect to contribute to the building of the cathedral. The Parler family, in collaboration with others, worked out the designs for the west front (opposite). Sometime around 1385, Michael Parler, whose brother Peter was renowned for his earlier work at Prague Cathedral, executed the drawing at left for the arcade, with its row of statues representing the twelve apostles of the New Testament.

Strasbourg has been used to the blending of French and Germanic elements, and questions of national identity have long played a part in the history of the city and its cathedral. After all, both belonged to Germany and France by turns, and even when it was technically French, the cathedral—rising from amidst the quaint houses that surround it—seems always to have inspired the kind of German nationalism that Goethe trumpeted. This was true as far back as 1262, when the building was still Romanesque and consisted of nothing but a nave and apse; at the time, burghers of Strasbourg, asserting their independence from the Rome-directed bishop who ruled their lives, first claimed the cathedral as their own, and then, in a bloody battle at Oberhausbergen, thoroughly trounced the bishop and his forces. Thereafter, as a demonstration of their freedom, the townsmen gratefully assumed financial responsibility for the reconstruction of their cathedral. They hired the leading architects of the day, Erwin among them, and saw to it that the entire structure was rebuilt in the latest Gothic style. For years the builders worked steadily on the nave and façades, until stylistic innovations and financial shortages caused changes in the original plans. These temporary setbacks notwithstanding, the burghers passed down their desires, from generation to generation, and finally the last major component, the jagged single spire, which has been called "the most Gothic of all spires," was completed in 1439.

Whether Strasbourg's cathedral is really German, French, both, or neither, it has continued to generate extravagant praise. Georg Dehio, the twentieth-century art historian, like Goethe, could not contain his admiration for Erwin's work. It was, he said, "the most beautiful thing that was ever devised in the Gothic style anywhere in the world."

The "most Gothic of all spires" rises high over the
city of Strasbourg in a nineteenth-century
facsimile (opposite) of an anonymous engraving of
1590. Some artistic exaggeration
becomes apparent when the print is compared with the
photograph of the cathedral below; in the
latter the spire, lofty as it is, takes a somewhat
more squat form. Strasbourg's sculpture
is remarkably well preserved because of the durability
of its red sandstone from the Vosges region;
this can be seen from the condition of the
thirteenth-century figure (at right) from the
cathedral's world-famous "Pillar of the Angels."

BOTH: JEAN ROUBIER

They were giants who built this cathedral!
—Auguste Rodin

The sculptures of the cathedral's
south portal (much restored after being mutilated
during the French Revolution)
illustrate the parable of the Wise and Foolish
Virgins. The gay blade at the
far left represents Folly. Seen frontally, he is
garbed in the robes of a noble;
his naked back, however, swarms with reptiles.

JEAN ROUBIER

Beauvais

PRIDE BEFORE A FALL

Beauvais Cathedral, wrote the novelist J. K. Huysmans, is "a melancholy fragment, having no more than a head and arms flung out in despair, like an appeal forever ignored by heaven." In height and airiness the cathedral represents the apogee of the Gothic style; its choir at 158 feet is the tallest in the world; its transepts are exquisite. But Beauvais is only half a cathedral, for it is entirely without a nave.

Plans for the cathedral were begun with high hopes in 1225. Amiens, thirty-odd miles to the north, was only five years under way, but already its grandeur was apparent to the bishop of Beauvais, Milon de Nanteuil. *His* cathedral, he decided, must surpass all others in height and beauty. Construction of the choir began in 1225 under the direction of Nanteuil's equally ambitious successor, Guillaume de Gretz. But it and the cathedral's apse (right) were hardly finished when, because of weak buttressing or inadequate foundations, the vaulting crumbled and the roof fell in in 1284. The cathedral was rebuilt somewhat more solidly. This time repairs took about forty years, draining away funds that might otherwise have been spent on the nave. Epidemics, civil disorders, and the Hundred Years' War ended further construction until 1500, when the first stone was laid for the transepts. Those who donated funds were allowed by the bishop to eat butter and cheese during Lent. The canons contributed a part of their salaries, King Francis I made a generous donation, and the pope accorded indulgence to any who prayed at the cathedral's seven altars *and* left alms. With the transepts completed, construction funds were again in short supply. The dome of St. Peter's was rising in Rome, however, and promised to outsoar any edifice in Europe; his competitive spirit aroused, the bishop of Beauvais borrowed money, sold a large part of the cathedral treasure, and accepted an architect's plan for a spire to rise 492 feet above the cathedral pavement—40 feet higher than the dome of St. Peter's. In the autumn of 1569 it was finished: a graceful, elegant shaft of stone with a flèche of oak, topped by an iron cross. But the bishop's triumph was an anxious one, and, in the interests of safety, plans were advanced for reducing the weight of the cross, for taking it down altogether, or for building a nave to lend the tower added support. All in vain. On Ascension Day, 1573, just after the congregation had left the church, the supporting columns crumbled under the strain and the proud spire came crashing down, a heap of rubble. The resultant damage to the choir was repaired, but the Gothic era was ending. The nave was never begun; so Beauvais stands, truncated, unfulfilled, a sad monument to the temerity of its builders.

110

JEAN ROUBIER

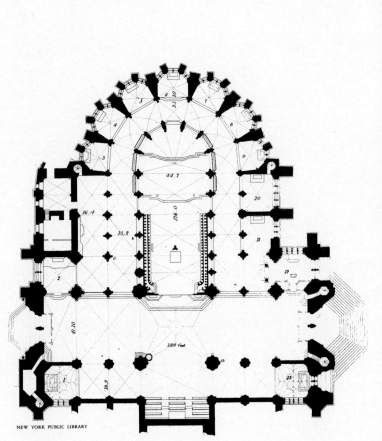

NEW YORK PUBLIC LIBRARY

Beauvais' curiously truncated form is best seen
in its floor plan. The cathedral's
Flamboyant south facade (above), built by Martin
Chambiges in the first half of
the sixteenth century, is partly Renaissance in
style, as can be seen in its
wooden doors (opposite), which date from 1535 and
depict the lives of Saints Peter and Paul.

Autun

A BIBLE IN STONE

Gislebertus hoc fecit. With this inscription—displayed with unprecedented prominence—the greatest sculptor of the Romanesque era proclaimed his satisfaction with the supreme effort of his life: the relief decorations for the Cathedral of St. Lazarus at Autun. Almost nothing is known of Gislebertus himself, except that he came to Autun around 1125 after serving for some time as a master sculptor at the abbey church of Cluny and that he spent the next ten years carving some sixty capitals for various parts of the cathedral, along with several more ambitious pieces. From the sculptures' remarkable uniformity of style, it is obvious that Gislebertus was a mature artist at the height of his powers when he began his work at Autun; and from the assurance, grace, and ease with which his works were executed, it is just as obvious that, unlike his contemporaries, he was, in André Malraux' words, "not a primitive—but a Romanesque Cézanne."

The sculpture of Gislebertus was not always so highly regarded. In the eighteenth century his work was thought to be primitive indeed, if not downright barbaric, and in 1766 the canons of Autun covered the reliefs of the tympanum and apse with plaster and marble. The carvings soon were forgotten, remaining so for seven decades. Then a priest of Autun who dabbled in archeology chipped away at the plaster obscuring the tympanum and uncovered a portion of a superbly designed *Last Judgment*.

Bit by bit the sculptures of Gislebertus came to light: In 1866 a broken slab of stone was discovered in the wall of a nearby house, where some long-forgotten scrounger with a taste for whimsy had used Gislebertus' *Eve*, possibly the most sensuous female figure in all Romanesque art, as a building block (it has since been moved to the Musée Rolin in Autun); in 1939 a quantity of marble was removed from the apse, where it had obscured a magnificent group of capitals; and in 1948 a carved head of Christ was recovered and returned to the tympanum, thereby completing the restoration undertaken almost ninety years earlier by Viollet-le-Duc.

The sculpture of Gislebertus is most striking for its sure grasp of form and rhythm. The artist, though, was not one to skimp on detail. In *The Dream of the Magi* (shown on the capital at left), for example, the underside of the bed is rendered with meticulous care, even though it is almost invisible from all angles. Despite his lavish use of detail, however, it is believed that Gislebertus seldom spent as much as a full week on the carving of a capital. He worked far more slowly and carefully than was his habit on the superb *Last Judgment*, however, and it was there, directly beneath his majestic central figure of Christ, that he proudly inscribed the three words, "Gislebertus made this."

*Originally, Gislebertus' reclining
Eve was flanked by figures of Adam and Satan
(whose clawed hand, pressing the
fruit-laden limb of the Tree of Knowledge toward
Eve, is visible near the upper
right-hand corner of the carving below). No
description survives of the figure of Adam, but
his head must have been quite close to that of
the seductively whispering Eve.*

OVERLEAF: *A number of capitals for the
choir of St. Lazarus depict various episodes in
the story of the Magi. In the carving
shown here, one of the three kings offers his gift
to the infant Jesus, while another
tips his crown in a regal gesture of reverence.*
JEAN ROUBIER

BELZEAUX—ZODIAQUE, FROM RAPHO GUILLUMETTE

*The west tympanum of St. Lazarus (above) is the most ambitious
of the individual works created by Gislebertus
during the decade he spent at Autun and the one he chose to
sign with the inscription that appears below.
Although the cathedral (right) was named for the brother of
Martha and Mary, lepers of the twelfth century
mistakenly believed it was named for another Lazarus, their own
patron saint; to accommodate the enormous
number of these unfortunates who came to Autun, a well-ventilated
shelter was attached to the cathedral.*

GIRAUDON

The military engineer Sebastien le Prestre, Marquis of Vauban and marshal of France under Louis XIV, was renowned chiefly as an expert in the architecture and deployment of trenches. At Coutances in Normandy, however, he lifted his gaze heavenward from the mud and exclaimed: "Who was the sublime madman who dared launch such a monument into the air?" The monument in question was "Le plomb," the octagonal Norman lantern tower of the Cathedral of Notre Dame at Coutances. The sublime madman, according to scholarly consensus, was Geoffroy de Montbray, the energetic eleventh-century bishop of Coutances, who is said to have died happily contemplating from his bedroom window the proud golden rooster which, in the Norman fashion, surmounted the central tower with which he had crowned his church.

Geoffroy, who like his notorious confrere, Bishop Gaudri of Laon (see page 53), was to serve under William the Conqueror as a warrior-priest in England, had inherited a moribund Romanesque cathedral in 1048 from his immediate predecessor. As it happened, the church itself was just about *all* that Geoffroy fell heir to; nothing, it seems, remained in the episcopal coffers after the Norman sack of Coutances earlier in the century, and the new bishop sent emissaries as far afield as Calabria in southern Italy in search of funds with which to rebuild his church. These were provided by the expatriate Normans who then ruled the region.

Besides putting up the great central lantern tower (beneath the interior of which Vauban is supposed to have spread a blanket as an aid to prolonged contemplation), Geoffroy began the choir (shown in the photograph at left, looking toward the nave) and completed the façade and the two towers of the west front—towers, incidentally, that are characteristic of Norman architecture. As Henry Adams put it: "What the Normans began they completed. Not one of the great French cathedrals [i.e., cathedrals in major cities outside Normandy] has two stone spires complete of the same age, while each of the little towns of Coutances, Bayeux, and Caen contains its twin towers and flèches of stone as solid and perfect now as they were seven hundred years ago."

Of the central tower, which rises 190 feet above the floor of the nave, Adams (as impressed in his own way as Vauban was in *his*) had this to say: "Neither at Chartres, nor at Paris, nor at Laon, nor at Amiens, nor at Reims, nor at Bourges, will you see a central tower to compare with the enormous pile at Coutances." Of course, Villard de Honnecourt, as noted earlier, considered those of Laon the greatest of all towers, central or otherwise. If there is a special region of heaven reserved for cathedral lovers, the thirteenth-century French architect and the twentieth-century American historian probably are even now arguing the merits of their respective favorites.

Aside from its great Romanesque lantern (which is illuminated by two stories of windows) and twin west towers, Coutances is not an overpowering edifice. Relatively devoid of the embellishments that distinguish the great Gothic cathedrals of France (its own Gothic elements date from after a fire that swept the church in 1218) and modest in its dimensions, it has been praised for a simplicity and integrity of line and proportion too austere for some, but which have led many to call it the most nearly perfect of all Norman cathedrals.

Coutances

FAITH AND NORMAN BLOOD

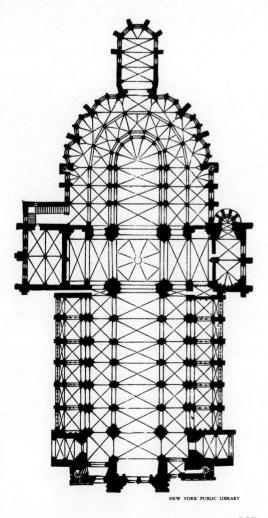

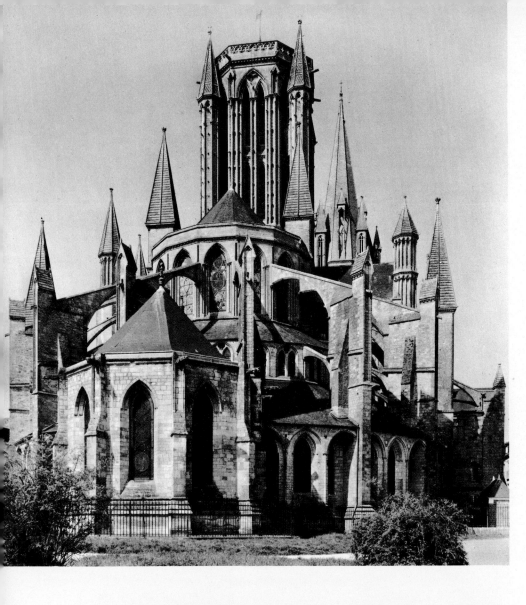

ALL: JEAN ROUBIER

Bishop Montbray's enormous eleventh-century
lantern tower (top left) rises
high above Coutances' chevet, which was patterned
on that of Le Mans. The photograph
at bottom left shows the tower's interior as
seen from the pavement of the
crossing, where the eighteenth-century
enthusiast Vauban lay supine in
contemplation of its grandeur.
OPPOSITE: As tall as the lantern is, only its
surmounting balustrade is visible above the
façade when the cathedral is
approached from this angle, and the twin Norman
towers seem Coutances' dominant feature.

DURHAM

ELY

LONDON
WELLS · CANTERBURY
SALISBURY · WINCHESTER

ENGLAND

"Then on Midwinter's day, archbishop Ealdred hallowed him king at Westminster; and he pledged him on Christ's book." Thus did a contemporary chronicler describe the coronation of William the Conqueror, and thus began England's great age of cathedral building. Sir Winston Churchill was later to write: "Once the secular conquest had been made secure [William] turned to the religious sphere. . . . and by 1087 the masons were at work on seven new cathedrals. . . ." Norman elements are still apparent in such cathedrals as Durham (below), but the evolution of English church architecture continued—as the following pages show—through a magnificent Gothic period to the rebuilding of St. Paul's, London's great Renaissance cathedral, in the seventeenth century under the direction of Inigo Jones and, later, Sir Christopher Wren.

HERSCHEL LEVIT

Winchester

WHERE "ENGLAND" WAS BORN

In 634 Bishop Birinus, leading a mission from Rome, came to Britain to undertake the conversion of the West Saxons. His first convert, King Kynegils, was probably baptized at Dorchester, but the episcopal see was soon transferred to Winchester. There, in the Saxon church in 828, Egbert was crowned king and issued an edict naming his realm England—the country of the Angles. There also King Alfred was crowned in 871 and buried at the century's end. Had Alfred's kingdom been perpetuated by his successors, Winchester, not London, most certainly would have become the center of British government, and the cathedral that eventually arose there would have become the English coronation church.

The history of Winchester's cathedral began in 1079, following the Norman invasion, when William the Conqueror's cousin, Bishop Walkelyn, erected a church in Norman style. In 1107, shortly after William Rufus was buried within the church, its central tower fell onto his tomb, an occurrence taken by many to be a sign of heavenly wrath over the interment within the church of the wicked Red King.

Walkelyn's structure underwent further, if less abrupt, changes in the early thirteenth century when one of his successors, Godfrey de Lucy, tore down its east end and rebuilt it in the then-popular style, later called Early English. The nave (opposite) was converted from the Norman to the Perpendicular style in the fourteenth century, but the most important architectural change came between 1487 and 1493, when Bishop Peter Courtenay added a bay to the east end (at foreground in the photograph below), thereby making Winchester the longest church in England.

Although Winchester Cathedral's importance waned as that of Westminster Abbey gained, it served throughout the Middle Ages as a scene for many regal ceremonials, including the weddings of Henry I to Matilda and Henry IV to Joan of Navarre. In the seventeenth century Winchester was damaged badly during the Great Rebellion when Parliamentary troops stabled their horses in the nave, and a mob of rebellious peasants, finding only bones where they had expected treasure, vented their wrath by hurling the relics at the stained-glass windows of the choir. By 1653, the cathedral had deteriorated so badly that it was condemned to be razed. At the last moment, however, it was spared and underwent no further indignities until 1967, when it became the subject of a very popular vaudeville-parody song.

A. F. KERSTING

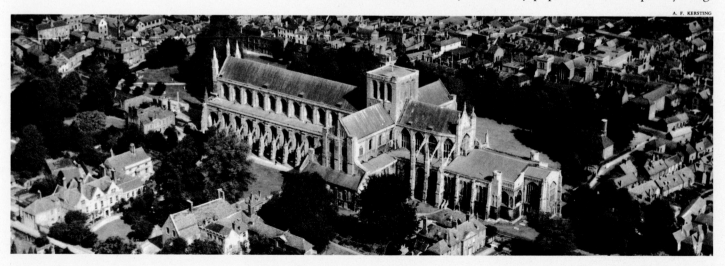

The cathedral's baptismal font, the work of
craftsmen imported from Belgium late in
the twelfth century, is made of dark Tournai
marble and decorated with relief scenes
from the life of St. Nicholas of Myra. The font
is supported by five pillars. In the scene
below (a detail from which is shown opposite),
the saint (with crosier) bestows a
dowry on the daughters of an impoverished noble,
thereby saving the three young ladies
from spinsterhood and dishonor. The fine
textural detail of the reliefs can
be seen in the decorative medallion at left.

134

The choir of the Cathedral of Wells in England is depicted in the cutaway picture above, engraved early in the nineteenth century.

BUILDING THE CATHEDRALS

A Construction Portfolio

"The horizontal," wrote Victor Hugo, "is the line of reason, the vertical the line of prayer." Appropriately, then, the International Gothic, the monumental building style of medieval Christianity, is a vertical architecture of emphasized heights and de-emphasized widths, of tall, linear proportions that bypass perpendiculars as they soar heavenward in chorus, arch inward and upward, then—still rising—meet. It is a colossal, man-dwarfing architecture, and yet, unlike classical architecture—traditionally the architecture of reason—it is conceived from the inside out, embracing as it dwarfs. To be detached from the Gothic is difficult, for its effectiveness comes not so much from its massiveness as from the vast, enveloping spaces shaped by its vaults and colored by ever-changing light beams rushing downward through stained-glass windows.

But the architecture of prayer is also an architecture of reasonable structure. It has a skeleton and a shell and a logical arrangement of elements that balance, support, and strengthen the uprising, arching, and intersecting members. It was said that the cathedrals were erected by the will of God; but it also took elaborate human organization, the application of geometry, and the technological inventiveness of reasoning men.

Although the aim of Gothic structural principles—the achievement of design unity and the interior duplication of "universal," or heavenly, illumination—was common to all countries that participated in the cathedral crusade, the application of principles varied from place to place. Thus, unlike the international architecture of our own time, the Gothic was international more in spirit than in detail. Each nation brought its own traditions, attitudes, experiences to the building procedure and reworked the principles in its own image. In Spain, for example, the remains of early Iberian art—a tradition of linear, geometric, intricately patterned art—affected the decoration of portals and tympanums. Through the lingering influence of the Moors, the forms characteristic of Islamic art—the horseshoe arch, the slender minaret, the bright mosaic decoration—also worked their way into the Spanish Christian cathedrals. The result was a Gothic richer in decoration, more elaborate in construction, and less simply conceived than the architecture of the North.

Topography, too, played a significant part. In France, where most cathedrals were built within towns or villages, the structures rose higher and narrower than they did in England, where they were erected in the country, surrounded by parks. As significant a difference between French and English churches sprang from the boatbuilding experience of the English, who put this skill to use. Timber roofs and woodworking, rather than stone vaults and stone sculpture, characterize English interiors.

And, of course, there was the influence of national character. The cathedrals of the Germanic North were similar to those of France, though more symmetrical, generally better constructed; and, understandably, more predictable. In their later churches, the Germans, who were fonder of rules than the French, achieved a greater uniformity of design; but their chronic rule making also made building procedures increasingly complicated. So difficult did it become to learn and follow all the rules that when the Renaissance introduced simpler methods, the masons were glad to shift, and the Gothic slowly waned.

137

FROM ROBERT BRANNER, *La Cathédrale de Bourges*, EDITIONS TARDY, 1962

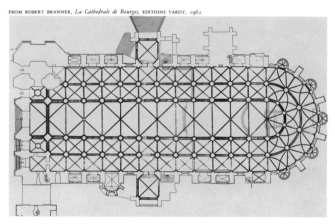

The floor plan of Bourges Cathedral follows the basilican form.

The basilican plan was the basic layout of Gothic cathedrals. Although its shape resembles a Latin cross, and despite occasional medieval assertions that the shape had theological significance, the plan did not have a religious origin and was in fact based on the ancient Roman basilica. Consisting of a nave and a rounded, vaulted apse, the basilica was used for most early Christian churches. As the Middle Ages and church building progressed, it remained the standard form. Protruding transepts and the subdivision of nave and apse evolved during the Romanesque era.

While there is no typical basilican plan, the diagram above illustrates the standard elements incorporated in the plan of most Gothic cathedrals. The nave was composed of a wide center section flanked by aisles. The crossing—the area, often domed, where nave and transepts intersected—was sometimes floored with a labyrinth or mosaic. The apse contained at its center the choir, surrounded by a circular corridor called the ambulatory, off which small, frequently circular chapels were built. Portals were located at the front of the nave and at each end of the transepts. As a rule—indeed, with only a handful of exceptions—the apse faced the East.

Within the nave, two rows of columns or piers—clusters of slender pillars—were erected parallel to one another. The squares or rectangles formed by each set of four piers are called bays. In the early Romanesque period, arches were constructed across the nave from one column to the one opposite. The series of round arches created the half-cylinder shape known as the barrel or tunnel vault. Later, when the achievement of height became a desirable factor, the masons erected much larger round arches across each bay from the top of one pier to the one *diagonally* across from it. Because the diameter of a square is half again as long as the sides, the crisscrossing, diagonal arches over the bay were much higher than the side-to-side arches. And to reach the same height on the sides as on the intersection of the diagonals, the masons made the side arches pointed. This was called the groin vault.

Scaffolding in a Gothic cathedral under construction underwent several stages. Before the first vertical elements were raised, large poles were secured in big buckets of sand and joined together with small platforms from which the piers were raised. The piers themselves then became scaffolding supports, as did the framework of the arches on top of the piers. Because most bishops wanted to begin using the cathedrals as soon as possible, scaffolding in later stages of the construction process was suspended from structural elements, leaving the floor clear and available for services. Many other bishops, however, frowned on this procedure and preferred to use the basement or the chapels until the structure had been finished.

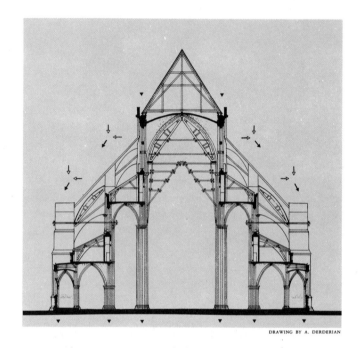

DRAWING BY A. DERDERIAN

Arrows show transmission of thrust through flying buttresses.

Before the Gothic era, arches were supported and centered by improvisational and sometimes less-than-ingenious ways. There are, for instance, records of churches being built on top of and around huge mounds of shaped earth, which later had to be removed. In the Romanesque era, it was not unusual for the masons to raise a mound of earth in an arch shape on a platform, build the stone arch around it, then lower the mound and hope that the arch would remain in place. Gothic centering was done, as above, with a wood falsework of struts and braces over which an inner skeleton of wood framework (which remained in place) was erected. Wedge-shaped stones were placed over the inner framework, and the falsework was removed. Whether or not the vault stayed in place remained to be seen: There are records of numerous disasters when the support was removed. If it remained, workmen plastered the vault, and then a painter arrived and added his embellishments to the area that the plasterers had just covered.

The elevation of the vault (illustrated above) was generally divided in three parts. The first level, rising to about half the total height of the piers, was the arcade, which usually corresponded to the height of the exterior walls. Level two was the triforium. Wood was placed from the arcade tops to the exterior walls and from those walls to the top of the triforium, making a triangular shaped passageway at the triforium level. The top level, which was itself an exterior wall, was fittingly called the clerestory (clear story). As this level rose higher in the Gothic years, the conventional buttresses used to support round arches proved inadequate. To counter the downward-outward thrust of the new ribbed vaults, the masons used flying buttresses—arched supports that extended outward.

The extraordinary legions of medieval humanity that built the great edifices of Christian Europe were as inconsistent in mood as they were in make-up. A great proportion of the workers did not want to be there at all: They were there because they had been conscripted or because they could find no other way to stay alive. Pay, although regular, was meager; the wardens in charge of the various workcrews were frequently brutal; even the wandering monks who arrived periodically at the site to pray for the workers, and the entertainers with their dancing bears who came to entertain them, often stole the camp blind during the day. Some of the men might have wanted to learn something, but few of them were rewarded; for the masons were a secretive group, huddling together in the lodge that was built on most cathedral sites, keeping all the methodology of their skills behind closed doors.

The common laborer, the hardest-working member of the construction team, was never entrusted with any responsibility that might require judgment. If he were assigned to the forest, he would be instructed specifically which trees to chop down; and at the stone quarry he would be told which stone to cut; even then, he was permitted to cut only the largest blocks from the sloping quarry wall. The smaller blocks were chiseled by roughmasons, the professional stonecutters responsible for the stone blocks which formed the basic outer structure.

If the forest and quarry were connected to the building site by waterway, the laborers built barges on which to float the timber and large blocks of stone. If all the transportation were overland, the matériel had to be hauled to the site occasionally by oxen, steers, and horses, more frequently by the men themselves serving as beasts of burden. Smaller pieces of stone were transported by barrowmen. The one-wheeled barrow requiring only one man to push it was a luxury; more common was the wheelless barrow carried by two men. At sundown, the barrowmen were responsible for the collection and hauling of the rubble left in the quarry, for this waste was often used to fill in the space between the double-thickness walls.

However hard the work and whatever their attitude about being there, the laborers were seldom victims of unchanging routine. The master mason seemed to be everywhere at once, often accompanied by the bishop. When these two were together, an argument was almost inevitable, and the men were perfectly willing to suspend work and witness the exchange. Similarly, the master might find it necessary to reprimand one of his assistants, and his lecture was another welcome diversion. Equally entertaining were the fistfights that erupted regularly among the men. Although less welcome, illness, injury, or death were also common reasons for work stoppage.

Because the clergy constantly frightened the peasantry with grim portraits of the Last Judgment and pointed to floods, famines, plagues, and other disasters as examples of man's sinfulness and God's wrath, the workers lived in perpetual fear. Every misfortune on the building site was regarded as an indication of the presence of demons, and so every misfortune signaled a pause in the work so that the evil spirit could be dealt with. Proper dealing required prayers to the appropriate saint.

Every major construction job employed a number of masons: The master mason was in charge, functioning much as a modern architect does. His agents on the site were one clerk and several wardens. The clerk, or keeper-of-the-works, handled most of the business details: He had to keep financial records and make estimates of the personnel and matériel needed, the time required for each building phase, and so forth. The wardens were the construction foremen, and very often they were held responsible for any errors made by the common laborers, the attitude being that laborers should be assigned nothing beyond their capabilities. Roughmasons cut and laid the stone. Freemasons shaped the softstone used for doors and windows and around joints. Hardstone cutters were masons who worked in marble and alabaster, carving the statuary and decoration—in other words, the sculptors. Most of the time the stonecutters worked in the lodge, but occasionally, to save time and money, they did all but the most detailed cutting at the quarry.

Masons were usually paid by the piece. Each stone that they cut was marked twice: once with their initials and once with a symbol corresponding to the place where the stone would be placed on the structure. Before the stone could be taken to the building site, the master mason or a warden had to inspect the stone and mark it with his initial. If the stone was later found to be faulty, both the mason and the inspector were fined up to two days' pay. On payday the paymaster would inspect all the work done since the previous payday, record each mason's tally, add a bonus or subtract a small penalty according to quality, and compute the mason's wages.

Beneath the masons but above the common laborers were the workers known as famuluses. The famulus was usually a young boy who had attracted the attention of a mason and who served as a mason's helper—dressing stone, mixing mortar, keeping the tools sharpened and in good repair. If the mason decided that the boy was capable of becoming a mason, the famulus served a seven-year apprenticeship during which he was permitted to do some simple stone carving. Since the lodge and not the employer paid the famuluses, the masons were very particular. After his apprenticeship the youth was awarded the degree of bachelor, or companion. At this level he was assigned a work-thesis to complete. If the wardens of the lodge judged that he had satisfactorily demonstrated his ability, the young mason was awarded the rank of master, which meant that he was a full-fledged mason. He celebrated his accomplishment by presenting each of the wardens with a gift of a pair of gloves and by paying for a feast for the whole lodge.

Although more and more young men were allowed to become masons as the demand increased during the Gothic age, the shortage of masons was never eliminated. The steady accumulation of stone dust in the lungs of masons made their life expectancy very short, and the well-paid masons began to realize the dangers and often worked only long enough to save money to buy an inn, brewery, or farm. They would occasionally come out of retirement at the request—or insistence—of the bishop, but their fees were higher than ever, and they began delegating responsibility to lesser laborers to avoid risking their own health. In consequence, the skill and pay of the common laborer began to increase.

The only way for the stonecutter to buck the system and express his individuality or disenchantment with the church was through his work. All art was regimented according to the medieval concept of order. Each carved saint or sacred figure, each painted religious scene had a definite form or way of being portrayed, and it was supposed to be invariable; for each was based on certain theological formulas. To change them was equal to heresy.

The Virgin Mary, for example, always had to be shown wearing shoes, although God, Jesus, the apostles, and the angels were always shown barefoot. Such signs as the halo, the nimbus, details of appearance and costume were used to identify subjects instead of the facial expressions or gestures that might have been appropriate. But in the thirteenth century, the artisans began to take more liberties, and their figures began to take on a certain identifying expressiveness. The earlier conventions were only gradually eliminated, however; were an artist to eliminate them completely and rely entirely on his own sensitivities when giving figures separate identities, he would certainly have been chastised.

The masons traveled vast distances looking for work. (In the thirteenth century, several French masons were working as far away as Turkey.) They rode in rude and undoubtedly uncomfortable carts, but at least these were covered so that they made an adequately sheltered dwelling place while en route. Highways and roads were barely traversable. Packs of wolves lived in the forests and preyed upon travelers, as did bands of robbers who took not only money but everything of value that was portable. Travelers usually went in caravans for safety, and the masons were often accompanied by painters, woodcarvers, glaziers, and mosaicists who might be carrying valuable goods such as colors or wood that they used in their work. The mason's rich clothing also helped to attract thieves. At night, guards were posted around the caravans to keep watch against the human or carnivorous predators.

The fifteenth-century illustration above shows a medieval construction team at work. Conferring at left are the patron and bearded mason.

A typical Gothic cathedral, superimposed on its floor plan (A), is shown here in various imaginary stages of completion—stages that do not necessarily reflect the progression of actual cathedral construction. The vaulting of the north aisle (B) and clerestory (C) and the framework of the nave roof (D) can be seen to the east of the transepts in the cutaway section of the drawing.

142

Salisbury

"A BLONDE BEAUTY"

"I have traveled all over Europe in search of architecture, but I have seen nothing like this," was the reaction of Augustus Pugin, the nineteenth-century architectural critic, on first seeing Salisbury Cathedral. The historian John Motley was not so easily captivated, sizing up his impression as simply "too neat"; but to the novelist Henry James, who put a little sex into his appraisal, Salisbury was "a blonde beauty among churches."

In early Norman times Bishop Herman fixed his episcopal see at Old Sarum, and a cathedral was built there in the late eleventh century by Bishop Osmund, who also compiled *The Use of Sarum*, the model for all service books in southern England. The Old Sarum site, however, was far from ideal. There was no water, and the cathedral's perch on a high, barren hill exposed it to winds that were both dangerous and annoying: "When the wind did blow they could not hear the priest say Mass." Added to this disadvantage were constant quarrels between the clergy and the king's soldiers, and finally, in the early thirteenth century, the bishop Richard Poore decided to move. Having tried the usual methods of finding a new location (arrows shot at random, dream interpretation, etc.), the bishop spoke to the abbess of Wilton, who told him what he probably did not want to hear—to take some of his own land 2 miles away. He did, and the present cathedral was begun in 1220. The building (the south view of which, as seen from the cloisters, appears in J. M. W. Turner's nineteenth-century water-color drawing at left) has the distinction of being the only Gothic cathedral begun on a site totally unencumbered by previous architecture, and to this circumstance it owes its particularly symmetrical layout and design. Finished very quickly—in only thirty-eight years—it was consecrated in 1258 by Archbishop Boniface of Canterbury in the presence of King Henry III and became the first example of pure, unmixed Gothic style in England.

The cloisters, seen at right from the outside, were begun in geometrical Decorated style between 1263 and 1270 by Bishop de la Wyle and are the oldest and largest in any English cathedral. (The library above them, incidentally, houses one of four original copies of the Magna Carta.) In the fourteenth century the presiding bishop, Wyvil, requested permission of King Edward III to strengthen the cathedral close with stones from the church at Old Sarum. The king approved, and Norman stones and carvings from the old edifice now form part of the wall of the close. At about the same time the upper stories of the tower and the spire were added, generating fears that the increased weight would prove too great for the piers and light arches of the crossing. To forestall this possibility, flying buttresses and girders were added in the fifteenth century.

Although Ludlow's soldiers were quartered in the cathedral during the Civil War, they behaved with exceptional mildness, and little damage resulted. The cathedral did not fare as well, however, during an eighteenth-century "restoration" by James Wyatt, of whose efforts the historian Harry Batsford writes, "In no other cathedral did the hand of this stucco-Gothic mandarin fall more heavily."

Salisbury's spire (404 feet), the highest in England, is a well-known landmark of the Wiltshire countryside and can be seen for miles. The cathedral exerted a peculiar fascination over John Constable, who made it the subject of many of his finest paintings.

The cathedral's thirteenth-century nave, with its ten
bays divided by Purbeck marble columns, is shown
—looking west from the choir—in the photograph at
left. The austerity of the design is derived in
part from the Cistercian architecture of the period.
The vaulting at right was photographed from
the floor of the nave. The tomb effigies below
represent Sir Thomas George and his Swedish wife,
both of whom were members of the court
of Elizabeth I. The graceful double arch shown at
bottom right was built at the transept
entrance late in the twelfth century as a precautionary
measure when the downward thrust of the
central tower threatened to buckle the walls below.

JAMES BOWEN

A. F. KERSTING

HERSCHEL LEVIT

OVERLEAF: *Salisbury was a favorite subject of John
Constable (1776–1837), England's greatest landscapist
after Turner (pages 144 and 283). This view of
the cathedral and its setting was painted around 1829.*
THE TATE GALLERY, LONDON; SKIRA

A. F. KERSTING

A. W. KERR

*A particularly beautiful example of fan vaulting
(above) rises from a single central pillar
to support the ceiling of the cathedral's octagonal
chapter house. Medieval English carpentry was
famed for its complexity and ingenuity. The
internal strutting (left) of Salisbury's spire,
which has not measurably deviated in position for
over a century, is in every sense of the
term a tour de force.*
OPPOSITE: *The terrific pressure exerted
by the weight of the spire and central
tower is evident in the bending of the supporting
piers as they approach the vaulting.*

Ely

ANTICIPATING THE SPACE AGE

In the year 673, Queen Etheldreda of Northumbria established a Benedictine abbey in the East Anglian town of Ely. Three centuries later the abbey was rebuilt and reconsecrated by Ethelwold, the bishop of Winchester; during the last years of the Saxon era, it became one of England's greatest religious centers. After the Conquest, Simeon, a kinsman of William the Conqueror and former prior of Winchester, was appointed abbot. He set about enlarging the existing church, and work began in 1083; the transepts and east end were finished by 1106, thirteen years after Simeon's death and three years before the elevation of the church to cathedral rank. The Norman nave, an immense structure of surprising buoyancy, was probably finished around 1189, a decade or so before the addition of the Galilee, or west porch, at the direction of Bishop Eustace.

In the second quarter of the thirteenth century, Bishop Hugh of Northwold added considerably to the length of the choir by installing six magnificent new bays, but much of his work was undone in 1322 when the cathedral's central tower toppled into the choir. This apparent disaster contributed to the greater glory of the church, however, by providing a brilliant team of artisans with an opportunity to exercise their talents on behalf of the ruined crossing. The architect Alan of Walsingham and his extraordinarily gifted carpenter, William Hurle, constructed a church-wide central octagon that has since been called "perhaps the most beautiful and original design to be found in the whole range of Gothic architecture" and capped it with "the only Gothic dome in existence": a wooden lantern, itself octagonal, but so set that its angles are juxtaposed with the faces of the immense octagon that supports it. (The exterior of the structure can be seen at the center of the photograph below, and the interior of the dome is shown opposite.) What Walsingham and Hurle accomplished has been likened by one modern critic to the structures of the Space Age.

Twelve imposing Late Norman bays line Ely's nave
(seen at left from the crossing). Alan of Walsingham's
great octagon is visible in the right side of the
photograph. The Prior's Door (opposite), which opened
onto the cloisters (which since have been destroyed),
was built in 1140 for Bishop
Goodrich. The relief on its tympanum, which depicts
Christ in Majesty, may have been the basis
for a twelfth-century manuscript illumination (above)
for the sermons of Saint John Chrysostom, now
in the collection of the cathedral library at Hereford.

Although the present cathedral (opposite) was begun in 1074 and finished in 1503, little construction took place between 1184 and 1379. "Bell Harry Tower" (right side of photograph) was begun just after the Conquest and finished around the beginning of the sixteenth century. It has been called the "noblest Gothic tower in existence" and mightily impressed the Dutch scholar Erasmus, who found that it "struck religious awe into the heart of the beholder." Edward IV, The Black Prince, who died in 1376, lies buried beneath the effigy shown above. The door (right) through which Thomas Becket went to his death in 1170 has been known since that time as "The Door of the Martyrdom."

"What idle and coward knaves have I nourished as vassals, that faithless to their oaths, they suffer their lord to be mocked by a lowborn priest!" The time was early December, 1170, and the Plantagenet king of England, a monarch given to ungovernable rages, had just learned that the man he hated above all others had eluded seizure at Dover, re-entered England safely after a six-year exile in France, and was making his way like a conqueror to his episcopal throne. The king's rhetoric was perhaps more effective than it was meant to be; four armed knights quietly slipped from the royal presence and set out for the city of Canterbury and its cathedral. Thus began the last act of one of the most dramatic struggles in English history: a fight for supremacy between church and state conducted by once-inseparable companions; a fight that was to culminate in bloody murder on the cathedral floor, in defeat and anguish for the survivor, and in triumph and eternal glory for the victim.

Henry II and his lowborn priest were well matched. Both were proud, learned, articulate, witty, and popular. Both had served with distinction in the field. Except perhaps for his hot temper, Henry was the very model of kingliness. He controlled not only England, but half of France and, through his marriage to Eleanor of Aquitaine, the largest fortune in Europe.

Thomas Becket, the young archdeacon of Canterbury and an expert in canon law, had begun his rise to power soon after Henry's accession, when the king chose him as his counselor and favorite. Becket, who despite his humble origins cut a more resplendent figure than the king himself, was, like Henry, a man of implacable will.

Just how unbending Thomas could be did not become evident until the king succeeded in having his crony (who as archdeacon was only a minor cleric) elected archbishop of Canterbury. Henry thereby expected to provide himself with a rubber stamp who would see to it that the church in no way impeded affairs of state. How wrong he was! The elegant Becket (who had once boasted a personal retinue of seven hundred knights) immediately exchanged his finery for a hairshirt and monk's robes, gave up his hawks and hounds, and proceeded to champion the papacy with all the energy and ardor he had once expended on jousting matches.

The two men soon clashed—on the issue of church revenues, on the right to punish criminous clerks, on Becket's refusal to obtain a papal dispensation that would have enabled Henry's bastard brother to marry advantageously. Becket (who is shown disputing with the king in the fourteenth-century miniature at right) remained obdurate on every point, even when the pope himself interceded on Henry's behalf. But if Becket was stubborn,

Henry was both stubborn and crafty, and by a series of carefully calculated maneuvers he at last forced the archbishop to flee for France in 1164.

Six years later, with their quarrel ostensibly resolved, Becket returned to England and again defied Henry. At this juncture the king flew into one of his famous rages, and the four knights departed for Canterbury, where a waiting Becket—having refused to bolt the doors because it was "not meet to make a fortress of a house of prayer" —announced that he was "ready to die for my Lord." He was hacked to pieces in the transept of the cathedral.

POST MORTEM

The murder of Becket (which is shown opposite in a thirteenth-century miniature) achieved for the egotistical archbishop what he most deeply desired: martyrdom, glory, and sainthood. For Henry, however, this grisly demonstration of knightly fealty was the occasion for an agony of lamentation and remorse—and for the murderers themselves, it led to flight, exile, and a near-lynching. Politically, the murder brought the king nothing but a slight diminution of his power within the realm and a considerable loss of prestige among the horrified nations of Europe.

At Canterbury Cathedral, rumors of miracles began to spread within hours of the murder. Invisible hands were said to have lighted the candles beside Becket's body; his voice was heard among the voices of the choristers during the singing of the *Introit;* the blind and the halt were restored to health by praying to the martyr or making contact with his relics. The cathedral soon became England's great pilgrimage shrine, to which, in Geoffrey Chaucer's words, "From every shire's end/Of Engleland to Canterbury they wend/The holy blissful martyr for to seek."

Wells

ENGLISH ART TYPIFIED

Wells Cathedral's Saxon predecessor was founded in the year 704 by King Ina near a spring, "The Wells," from which the town derives its name. When the episcopal see established there in 909 by Edward the Elder was transferred by Bishop John de Villula to Bath in 1090, much of Wells fell into ruins and a bitter rivalry which was to last several hundred years developed between the two towns.

In 1135, Robert of Lewes became bishop and revitalized Wells. He rebuilt most of the cathedral in the Norman style and ordered the town's market, previously held in the church, to be moved elsewhere so that services could be carried on in a more appropriate atmosphere. His efforts were short-lived; the building was torn down when Bishop Reginald Fitzjocelin began construction of the present Gothic cathedral (calling it "an honour due to God") around 1176. Then, about a decade and a half later, Bishop Savaric arrived on the scene, calling himself "bishop of Bath and Glastonbury." The resident monks objected vociferously to this self-imposed title, whereupon an enraged Savaric stormed their abbey and had them beaten and imprisoned. This deed apparently was one of Savaric's few positive actions, and his successor, Jocelin de Welles, inherited a church that had been allowed to fall into an advanced state of decay. Jocelin set about completing Reginald's work, added the glorious west front (right) with its wide screen of some 350 statues, and relinquished all claims to Glastonbury. In 1218 the Bath-Wells rivalry was eased somewhat. This was followed by the merger of their names in the title by which the bishopric is still known: "Bath and Wells."

During the Protestant Reformation in the seventeenth century the church was plundered, the Lady Chapel destroyed, and much of the see's land seized by the infamous duke of Somerset. To make bullets, Somerset's men stripped the lead from the cathedral's stained-glass windows ("I would that they had found it scalding," lamented an old chaplain of Wells). In 1685 Monmouth's men "caroused about the altar," and, had not one officer restrained them with his drawn sword, they might have wrought considerably more destruction.

"Though one of the smallest, it is perhaps, taken altogether, the most beautiful of English cathedrals," writes the architectural historian Sir James Fergusson of Wells. "Externally, its three well-proportioned towers group so gracefully with the chapter house, the remains of the vicar's close, the ruins of the bishop's palace, and the tall trees with which it is surrounded, that there is no instance so characteristic of English art." The cathedral's most unusual feature, however, is its large fourteenth-century inverted double arch, dedicated to Saint Andrew, which supports the weight of the central tower.

The tomb of Bishop Drokensford (opposite), who
presided at Wells from 1309 to 1329, is
located in the Chapel of St. Katherine and is
distinguished by the softness and color of
its design. The capitals of the south transept
date from the thirteenth century and
illustrate the parable of the thieves in the
orchard. One of the series, depicting a farm hand
beating one of the thieves, is shown at top
left. The fifteenth-century alabaster panel at
left represents the Trinity, although the
Holy Ghost, logically enough, is not visible.
A capital from the nave (above) is known to be of
the thirteenth century, but its subject is uncertain.

The elaborate fan vaulting of
Wells' chapter house (top left) contrasts
sharply with the simplicity of that
of Salisbury (page 150); and, in
contrast with the slender elegance of
Salisbury's inverted arches (page
147), those at Wells (one of which is
shown at bottom left), which also
bear some of the thrust of the central
tower, are strikingly muscular.
The so-called Heavenly Stair, whose
soft, timeworn beauty is shown in
the photograph at right, leads to Wells'
chapter house (through doorway on
right) and to the gallery over the
choir (at the head of the staircase).

Durham

A MONKISH MISOGYNIST

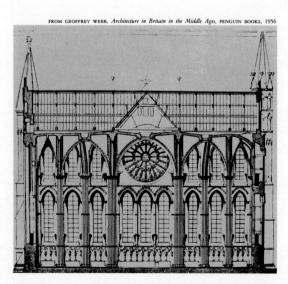

In 652, seventeen years after an episcopal see was founded at Lindisfarne on the north English coast, one Cuthbert became a monk there. In 687, at the end of a lifetime in the church, he announced his determination to be buried in the cathedral and to have his remains stay with it, even in the event that the cathedral later be moved. Loyalty to the saint was not tested until the Danish invasion in 875, when a contingent of monks, complete with remains, fled Lindisfarne for more salubrious climes. After a century's stay in Chester-le-Street, they moved on, after Cuthbert, according to legend, appeared in a vision and suggested a move to Dun-holm, a place familiar to none of them. As the monks were searching, however, they overheard two women speaking of a lost cow "down in Dun-holm" (the hill meadow), and it was there, the modern Durham, that in 995 they began a cathedral to receive Cuthbert's bones. Two sieges by the Scots destroyed this structure, but its replacement, a large Norman building begun in 1093 by Bishop William of St. Carileph, survives as the present cathedral.

His bones safely in place, Cuthbert remained an active influence on Durham's design. From the handle of the north door hangs a ring that in earlier times granted the "peace" of Saint Cuthbert to fleeing fugitives; in a niche of the north wall stands a copy of an original sculpture of the famous Dun Cow; and the Galilee Chapel results from Cuthbert's paranoid view of women. Forbidden by the good saint to approach his shrine, ladies were given a separate chapel in which to worship (the term "Galilee" is thought to refer to Galilee of the Gentiles, implying that this part of the church was less sacred than the rest), and a cross imbedded in the pavement at the far end of the nave still marks the spot beyond which they could not pass.

Because it was built after the first wave of Norman construction (when engineering techniques had advanced perceptibly), Durham Cathedral is structurally sounder than such earlier churches as Canterbury and Winchester. Unlike most cathedrals, it grew not by replacement but by accretion. Durham, according to the critic Sir Alfred Clapham, is "the most complete and least altered of all the early Anglo-Norman churches, and may be considered the finest, and organically the most perfect achievement of the Anglo-Norman school." It is also the earliest surviving example in England of a completely rib-vaulted church, and its transverse arches, finished in 1133, are probably the earliest high-vault pointed arches anywhere.

The Norman choir, originally ending in an apse, underwent alterations in the late thirteenth century and now terminates in the Chapel of the Nine Altars, a detail of which (showing a rose window added in the eighteenth century) appears at left. The cathedral's solemn interior, whose full length can be seen in one unbroken view (right), gives a particularly individualistic effect, largely because of its plan of alternating square and circular piers, incised and decorated by remarkable patterned carving and zigzag moldings.

Samuel Johnson described the interior of Durham Cathedral as producing an impression of "rocky solidity and indeterminate duration," a description that could also be applied to its exterior. The cathedral's setting—it is placed in the center of a peninsula, surrounded almost entirely by loops of the river Wear—is, like the church itself, one of the grandest and most beautiful in England.

*Yet well I love thy mixed and massive
piles, half church of God,
Half castle 'gainst the Scot.*
                    —Sir Walter Scott

The nave of the cathedral is supported by
alternating circular columns and
clustered piers (left), which were marked
at the quarry for easy assembly at
Durham. The massiveness of the cylindrical
columns, dating from the eleventh
and twelfth centuries, is in no way
diminished by the geometrical incisions
on their surfaces. The fresco (above) of the
cathedral's patron Saint Cuthbert is
generally considered to be one of the finest
wall paintings of the Transitional period.
OPPOSITE: *The cathedral viewed
from the southwest with the river Wear in
the foreground of the photograph.*

St. Paul's

"MAY I RISE AGAIN"

The first major restoration of St. Paul's in London, begun in 1634, had the curious distinction of having been financed, at least in part, with the wages of sin. The church had been in a sorry state of disrepair since the reign of Elizabeth I, when it was badly damaged by fire—and even in its earlier, undamaged state it had been no architectural triumph. In 1620, under James I, Inigo Jones, the first great English architect of the Renaissance, was appointed Surveyor of Works. A program for the restoration of the cathedral was drawn up, and quantities of Portland stone were transported to the site. At this point, however, funds ran out, and the work stopped before it had really got started. It was not until the rise of William Laud under Charles I that the project again got under way. Laud became bishop of London in 1628 and, five years later, archbishop of Canterbury. From Canterbury he ceaselessly harangued the British clergy, using all the suasion at his command, in his efforts to raise funds for the restoration. Coal taxes were levied expressly for the cathedral's use, and fines for such transgressions as adultery, incest, and swearing were used to pay for the work.

Financial problems were not the only ones Laud had to cope with. A clutter of private houses abutting the site was razed, thereby incurring the wrath of the dispossessed citizenry; Portland stone earmarked for St. Paul's was stolen before it left the quarries; press gangs so effectively combed the Fiddler's Green for seamen that it became difficult to secure crews for the transport of whatever stone had not already been abstracted; and a continuing series of quarrels between labor and management led to to frequent defection by masons, carpenters, and other workmen.

All these troubles notwithstanding, the work proceeded, and by 1642 Jones had more or less completely transformed the cathedral's exterior in what one architectural historian has called "a gallant attempt to make a Classical silk purse out of a Gothic sow's ear." What Jones did was to rework the west front in the Palladian style and make it a sort of backdrop for an immense Corinthian portico. This solution, while hardly ideal, was a tour de force of improvisation and England's outstanding example of Classical architecture. Unfortunately, Londoners had only twenty-four years in which to appreciate it. The façade—along with a good deal of the church proper—was destroyed in the great fire of 1666.

The next reconstruction of St. Paul's was accomplished by the greatest of all English architects, Sir Christopher Wren, who in 1675, after submitting several preliminary designs, devised a system of screen walls and hidden flying buttresses that gave the cathedral's exterior (a decorative detail from which is shown at left) an extraordinary cohesiveness. Then, by synthesizing the ideas of Bramante and Michelangelo, Wren created an inner and an outer dome, constructed like two layers of onionskin, and so achieved maximum grandeur internally and the distinctive external silhouette (right) that ever since has been a London landmark.

Curiously, as Wren was laying out the shape of his great dome on the cathedral floor, he asked a laborer to bring him a flat stone to be used as a marker. The workman picked up the first bit of rubble that came to hand: a fragment of a gravestone that bore on its surface the single Latin word *Resurgam*, "May I rise again." The cathedral did.

The choir's Baroque vaulting is shown at left,
and its imposing high altar can be seen
in the photograph below.
OPPOSITE: The library staircase in the cathedral's
southwest tower rises in a magnificent spiral
above the ornate ironwork of Jean Tijou,
an artisan imported from France, who was
also responsible for most of the screens
and grilles found in the cathedral's choir.

In this anonymous seventeenth-century painting, James I (in balcony at center) hears a sermon at St. Paul's.

THE LAND'S EPITOME

A St. Paul's Portfolio

St. Paul's Cathedral, one authority has commented, stands in relation to the cathedral at Canterbury as the people of England do to the king. It has never been England's chief religious center. Yet, struck by lightning, burned and bombed, cluttered at times with bookstalls and food stands, thronged almost daily with worshipers and whisperers, St. Paul's has been heart and symbol of London, and thus of English life, for centuries. There in the spring of 1169 a messenger from the exiled archbishop Thomas Becket announced to the congregation the excommunication of the bishop of London—and then had to be smuggled out under another man's cloak to avoid injury. There John Wycliffe was called to trial for heresy in 1377. There in 1514 Henry VIII, wearing a "gown of purple satin and gold in chequers, and a jewelled collar worth a well of gold," put on the cap and sword sent by the pope as symbols of his rank. At St. Paul's Cross outside the cathedral the contest between Henry and the pope over the king's divorce and over control of the English church was angrily debated. There preached John Colet, friend to Erasmus, in the sixteenth century, and the poet John Donne in the seventeenth. There both those great deans of St. Paul's were buried, as were the poet Philip Sidney, the architect Christopher Wren, Lord Nelson, and the duke of Wellington. There Queen Elizabeth I heard herself called "an untamed heifer" by a Puritan named Dering. The doughty Elizabeth, who tried to pacify through compromise the fierce battle between Catholic and Protestant interests, once took the Spanish ambassador to hear Dean Alexander Nowell preach at St. Paul's Cross, and when the dean began attacking the use of images in worship (obviously offensive to the Spaniard, though not to Elizabeth personally), she abashed Nowell into strangled

silence by shouting, "To your text, Mr. Dean, to your text! We have heard enough of that! To your subject!" There, some years later, were displayed on the walls a number of Spanish ensigns captured in the defeat of the Invincible Armada. Shakespeare often walked past the cathedral on his way to and from the theater. Four members of Guy Fawkes' plot to blow up Parliament were executed, drawn, and quartered outside the cathedral in 1605. During the Commonwealth, soldiers and horses were housed inside. The composer Handel played the organ at St. Paul's with the regular organist, Maurice Greene, working the bellows. "Handel, after 3 o'clock prayers," recorded the contemporary music historian Charles Burney, "used frequently to get himself and young Greene locked up in the church together; and in summer often stript unto his shirt, and played away until 8 or 9 o'clock at night." There George III gave formal thanks for his temporary return to sanity in 1789. There in 1913 suffragettes planted a homemade time bomb (which failed to explode) under the bishop's throne. There, with the British and American flags hung side by side over the choir entrance, the decision of the United States to enter World War I was celebrated. St. Paul's was in the way of only British shells—stray duds—in that war, but in the next it was not so lucky: One bomb hit the choir; an incendiary set the dome afire; another bomb came through the roof of the north transept and exploded. But the cathedral's schedule of services was interrupted only once, and that briefly. And when, during the traditional watchnight service held in the crypt beneath the cathedral on the eve of the turn of 1945, a V-2 rocket landed nearby and shattered one of the few crypt windows still intact, the congregation caught its breath—and then laughed.

177

*The Saxon version of St. Paul's—built in the seventh century—
burned in 1087. Rebuilding was begun by William the Conqueror's bishop of London but was not finished until 1240. Its
tall spire (above) was a landmark and St. Paul's a medieval
center for the debate of religious and political questions. The
heresy trial of Wycliffe (below) was an example. Having been
cited for his attacks on the worldly character of church and
churchmen, the Oxford theology professor came surrounded by
protectors, including John of Gaunt, duke of Lancaster, and Sir
Harry Percy, and the nobles' behavior almost brought on a riot.*

A TRIAL—AND TRIBULATION

*On February 23, 1377, as Wycliffe arrived at St. Paul's, Lon-
don talked angrily of a rumored proposal to eliminate the post
of Lord Mayor and to give the marshall of England the same
rights of arrest in the city as he had elsewhere. The marshall
was Harry Percy, and the proposal, it was said, had been made
that very morning by the duke of Lancaster. Wycliffe's arrival
at the church was described thus by a contemporary chronicler:*

Thys sonne, therefor, of perdition, John Wiclyffe, was to
appear before the bishopps . . . to be converted for mar-
vellous wordes that he had spoken, Sathan, the adversarye
of the whoole churche, as ye beleaved, teachynge hym:
. . . in the waye he was animated by his companions not to
feare the . . . bishopps, whoe in respect of hym were un-
learned, nether yet the concourse of the people, seynge
that he was walled in on every syde with so many knyghtes.
His body was now broughte into St. Paul's church . . .,
where such a multitude of people was gathered togeather
to heare hym, that yt was harde for the noble men and
knyghtes (the people lettynge them) to pass through, and
even by & by with this occasion they were persuaded
craftely to pull back with there handes there scholer, that
he might escape deathe entended him by manye bishopps.
The devill found a way, that fyrste a dissension beynge
mayde betwene the noble men & bishopp, hys answer
might be differed. Truly when the people . . . stayed to
geave place unto the noble men, Syr Henry Percye
abusynge hys authoryte miserably pricked forwardes the
people in the churche, whiche the Bishopp of London
seying, prohibited him to exercyse such authoritye in the
church, saynge that yf he had knowne he wolde have used
hym selffe so there, he sholde not have come into the
churche yf he coulde have letted him, whiche the duke
hearynge was offended, and protested that he wolde
exercyse suche authorytye whether he wolde or not. When
they were come into our Ladyes chappell, . . . the foresayed
John also was sent in by Syr Henrye Percye to sytt downe,
for because, sayed he, he haythe much to answeare he
haith neade of a better seate. On the other syde the
byshopp of London denyed the same, affyrmynge ye to be
agaynst reason that he sholde sytt . . . Hereupon very
contumelyous wordes did ryse betwene Sir Henrye Percye
and the bishopp, & the whoole multitude began to be
troubled. And then the duke began to reprehende the
bishopp and the bishopp to turne then on the duke
agayne. [The exchange of insults continued.] Then the
duke whysperynge in his eare, sayed he had rather draw
hym furth of the churche by the heare then suffer such
thynges. The Londoners hearynge these words, angerlye
with a lowd voice cried out, swearynge they wolde not
suffer ther Bishopp to be injured . . .

ALL THINGS TO ALL MEN

Paul's Walk, the center aisle of the great cathedral, "is the Land's Epitome, or you may call it the lesser Ile of Great Brittain," wrote a churchman sarcastically in 1628, the year William Laud became bishop of London and inaugurated an era of reform for St. Paul's. "The noyse in it is like that of Bees, in strange hummings or buzze, mixt of walking, tongues and feet . . ." For much of its life St. Paul's was market place, employment agency, factory, playground, and flophouse for the city, and many were the complaints about this desecration. The grounds and the cathedral were so open that using them as a shortcut between streets became a common practice. A lay vicar, John Ramsey, noted in 1598 that worship was disturbed by the constant passage of "Porters, Butchers, Water-bearers, and who not?" And since the area was a thorough-fare, businesses sprang up in and around the cathedral: "The south alley [aisle] for usurye and poperye; the north for simony and the horse-fair; in the midst for all kinds of bargains, meetings, brawlings, murthers, conspiracies . . ." Varlets seeking employment and prospective masters met at St. Paul's. Lawyers staked out pillars as offices. Books, tobacco, and tailoring were hawked there. Trunks were hammered together; glass, lumber, wine, and other goods were stored on the premises. Plays were given. Beggars and drunks slept in the church. Rubbish and dung collected there in heaps, and huts leaned against the walls outside. The antics of children were a constant distraction. As early as 1385 a bishop of London spoke of boys shooting birds, playing ball, and breaking windows in the cathedral. And Ramsey was explicit in a report to his bishop two centuries later about "boys (saving your reverence) pissing upon stones in the Church . . . to slide as upon ice, and so . . . hurt themselves quickly."

Architect Inigo Jones (portrayed above) was chosen to renovate St. Paul's in 1620, as Laud spurred the razing of the sheds and shops that contributed to its disrepair. Jones' work included the construction of the Roman-style west portico (below). In the detail from a Jacobean painting above at left, a gentleman and a prospective employee, typical of those who met at St. Paul's, confer.

A GREAT POET PREACHES

John Donne (above) wrote erotic poetry in his youth, but the eloquent sermons that he preached during his tenure as dean of St. Paul's from 1621 to 1631 are considered to be among the best in English. The following is from a 1625 sermon on Psalms 63:7: "Because thou hast been my help, therefore in the shadow of thy wings will I rejoice." London was then in the grip of the plague.

. . . It is a blessed Metaphore, that the Holy Ghost hath put into the mouth of the Apostle, *Pondus Gloriae*, That our *afflictions* are but *light*, because there is an *exceeding*, and an *eternall waight of glory* attending them. If it were not for that exceeding waight of glory, no other waight in this world could turne the scale, or waigh downe those infinite waights of afflictions that oppresse us here. . . .

All our life is a continuall burden, yet we must not groan; a continuall squeasing, yet we must not pant; and as in the tendernesse of our childhood, we suffer, and yet are whipt if we cry, so we are complained of, if we complaine, and made delinquents if we call the times ill. And that which addes waight to waight, and multiplies the sadnesse of this consideration is this, That still the best men have had most laid upon them. As soone as I heare God say, that he hath found *an upright man, that feares God, and eschews evill*, in the next lines I finde a Commission to Satan, to bring in Sabeans and Chaldeans upon his cattell, and servants, and fire and tempest upon his chil-

dren, and loathsome diseases upon himselfe. As soone as I heare God say, That he hath found *a man according to his own heart*, I see his sonnes ravish his daughters, and then murder one another, and then rebell against the Father, and put him into straites for his life. As soone as I heare God testifie of Christ at his Baptisme, *This is my beloved Sonne in whom I am well pleased*, I find that Sonne of his *led up by the Spirit, to be tempted of the Devill*. And after I heare God ratifie the same testimony againe, at his Transfiguration, (*This is my beloved Sonne in whom I am well pleased*) I finde that beloved Sonne of his, deserted, abandoned, and given over to Scribes, and Pharisees, and Publicans, and Herodians, and Priests, and Souldiers, and people, and Judges, and witnesses, and executioners, and he that was called the beloved Sonne of God, and made partaker of the glory of heaven, in this world, in his Transfiguration, is made now the Sewer of all the corruption, of all the sinnes of this world, as no Sonne of God, but a meere man, as no man, but a contemptible worme. As though the greatest weaknesse in this world, were man, and the greatest fault in man were to be good, man is more miserable then other creatures, and good men more miserable then any other men.

. . . Our Saviour Christ . . . sayes, *That hee would have gathered Ierusalem, as a henne gathers her chickens under her wings*. And though the other Prophets doe (as ye have heard) mingle the signification of Power, and actuall deliverance, in this Metaphor of Wings, yet our Prophet, whom wee have now in especiall consideration, *David*, never doth so; but . . . rests and determines in that sense, which is his meaning here; that though God doe not actually deliver us, nor actually destroy our enemies, yet if he refresh us in the shadow of his Wings, if he maintain our subsistence (which is a religious Constancy) in him, this should not onely establish our patience, (for that is but halfe the worke) but it should also produce a joy, and rise to an exultation, which is our last circumstance, *Therefore in the shadow of thy wings, I will rejoice*.

I would always raise your hearts, and dilate your hearts, to a holy Joy, to a joy in the Holy Ghost. There may be a just feare, that men doe not grieve enough for their sinnes; but there may bee a just jealousie, and suspition, too, that they may fall into inordinate griefe, and diffidence of Gods mercy; and God hath reserved us to such times, as being the later times, give us even the dregs and lees of misery to drinke. For . . . God hath accompanied, and complicated almost all our bodily diseases of these times, with an extraordinary sadnesse, a predominant melancholy, a faintnesse of heart, a chearlesnesse, a joylesnesse of spirit, and therefore I returne often to this endeavor of raising your hearts, dilating your hearts with a holy Joy, Joy in the holy Ghost, for *Vnder the shadow of his wings*, you may, you should, *rejoyce*. . . .

Etiam periere Ruinæ

The Wren Society Publications, VOL. XIV, 1937

THE CATHEDRAL AFIRE

Fire was a constant menace. The steeple had been hit by lightning in 1561, and the damage done by the resulting fire had not been completely repaired by 1666, despite Jones' work. The steeple was still not rebuilt; scaffolding was still in place around the tower. In the wee hours of September second in the dry summer of that year, flames burst out in a bakehouse in Pudding Lane; the Great Fire of London had begun. That night embers landed on the scaffolding at St. Paul's, and the church burned fiercely. To exacerbate matters further, great heaps of flammable goods had been stored in the church's precincts in the illusory hope of divine protection. Stones, according to one eyewitness, exploded and flew through the air "like grenadoes," and the lead of the cathedral's roof first buckled under the intense heat, then poured, molten, into the streets below. "One sees only a huge heap of stones," remarked another shocked witness after the fire, "cemented together by the lead with which the church was covered."

In the seventeenth-century engraving above, the cathedral is engulfed by flames at the height of the Great Fire of London in 1666. By the time the conflagration had been got under control, only a charred and shattered corner of the choir still stood, as can be seen in Thomas Wyck's contemporary drawing at right.

ALL: *The Wren Society Publications*, VOL. I, 1924

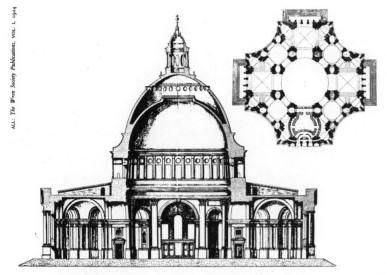

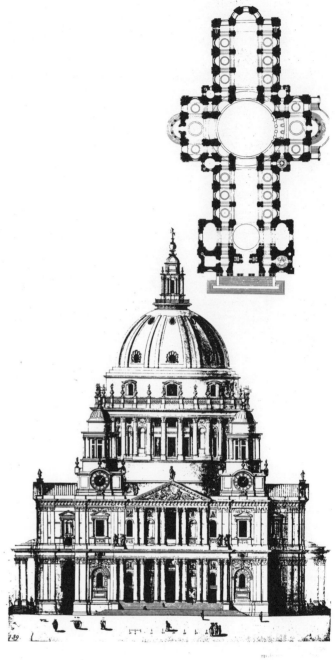

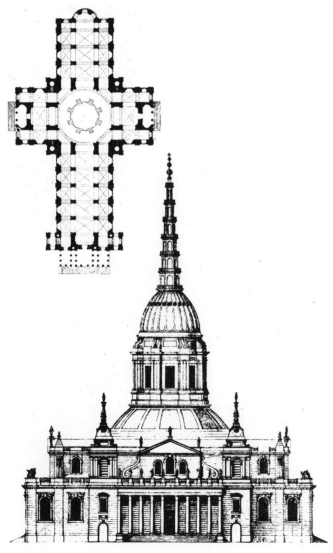

Plans for the reconstruction of St. Paul's Cathedral, which had been extensively damaged during the Great Fire of 1666, occupied Christopher Wren for almost fifty years through four major designs and numerous revisions. The first plan, for rebuilding the deteriorating—and now fire-scarred—old cathedral, was submitted in 1670; the last, a design for the dome of the nearly completed structure, was probably not settled upon until 1697. In the years between, Wren produced three major designs: the domed Great Model (above left) in 1673, which was rejected because it lacked the traditional long axis from nave to choir; the more conventional Warrant Design of 1675 (left); and the final plan (above), which incorporated elements of the two earlier ideas.

OUT OF THE ASHES

He was, wrote John Evelyn, a "miracle of youth." By the time he was thirty-four, in the year of the Great London Fire, Christopher Wren had already established himself as one of England's leading scientists. He had been professor of astronomy at Gresham College in London and now held the Savilian chair of astronomy at Oxford, but his interests also included mathematics, physics, weather, inventing, and architecture. He had helped found the Royal Society of London for the Advancement of Science. Before the fire he had been working on a plan to rejuvenate old St. Paul's, which the Commonwealth had left in worse condition even than Laud and Inigo Jones had found it. He had gone to France to study architecture in 1665 and, back in England, discussed his ideas for St. Paul's at a meeting in the cathedral six days before the fire. Now, with London in ruins, he was commissioned to lay out a plan for the rebuilding of an entire city. His bold blueprint for London—delivered in less than a week—was not accepted, but he designed many of the new buildings, including, among others, the Custom House, the Temple Bar, a theatre, more than fifty churches, and the new St. Paul's. Because of the enormous costs of reconstructing London, it was thought at first that St. Paul's would have to make do with a limited repair job. Wren believed this a poor idea and was not surprised when, during the restoration, a column caved in and convinced the authorities that the cathedral should be rebuilt from scratch. "Reverend Sir," he wrote the dean of St. Paul's, "I . . . must comfort you as I would a friend for the loss of his Grandfather by saying in course of nature you could not longer enjoy him, so many and so evident were to me the signs of its ruin, when last I viewed the building." And so, what remained of the old structure was torn down—a difficult task because the molten lead had fused the stones together much more effectively than cement. Wren offered two striking designs, which were rejected, and then a third, which was accepted in 1675. He was given permission by the king to amend this "Warrant" design as he went along—which he began to do immediately. The cornerstone was laid in 1675. By then Wren had been appointed surveyor-general to the crown and had been knighted. Despite his work for the king and his other building projects in the city, he managed to visit the cathedral regularly and toward the end was hauled up to the top of the structure in a basket, the better to oversee the work.

Wren, who died in 1723 at the age of ninety, is shown holding one of his designs for St. Paul's in the engraving above at right. The architect had a passion for detail and personally designed many of the smaller embellishments for his buildings, including the one shown in his meticulous pen-and-ink drawing at right.

FOR GOD AND QUEEN

During the reign of Queen Anne (1702–14), a yearly ceremony of general Thanksgiving was held in St. Paul's in honor of the successful prosecution of the War of the Spanish Succession, a conflict that arose from the attempts of Louis XIV to extend French power by placing his son on the disputed throne of Spain. Anne was an aging, gouty woman, and her visits to the cathedral—she usually tottered there on the arm of her favorite, Sarah Churchill—were more painful than joyous. It was during one of these visits, the Thanksgiving of 1708, that the infamous "Screw Plot" came to light. This was a Tory fiction according to which a group of dissident Whigs removed the screws and bolts from St. Paul's roof in the expectation that it would then fall in upon the heads of Anne and her ministers.

The general Thanksgiving ceremony of 1706, held at St. Paul's in commemoration of the duke of Marlborough's defeat of the French at the battle of Ramillies, is depicted in the engraving above by Robert Trevitt. Two years before the death of Queen Anne in 1714, a statue of the last Stuart monarch and first ruler of the United Kingdom was erected outside St. Paul's west front. In the late Victorian view at left, the monument (which since has been replaced by a copy) can be seen in the midst of London traffic, with figures representing England, France, Ireland, and America at the queen's feet.
OPPOSITE: *During the restoration of St. Paul's in the 1920's, a team of English artists made this detailed isometric drawing.*

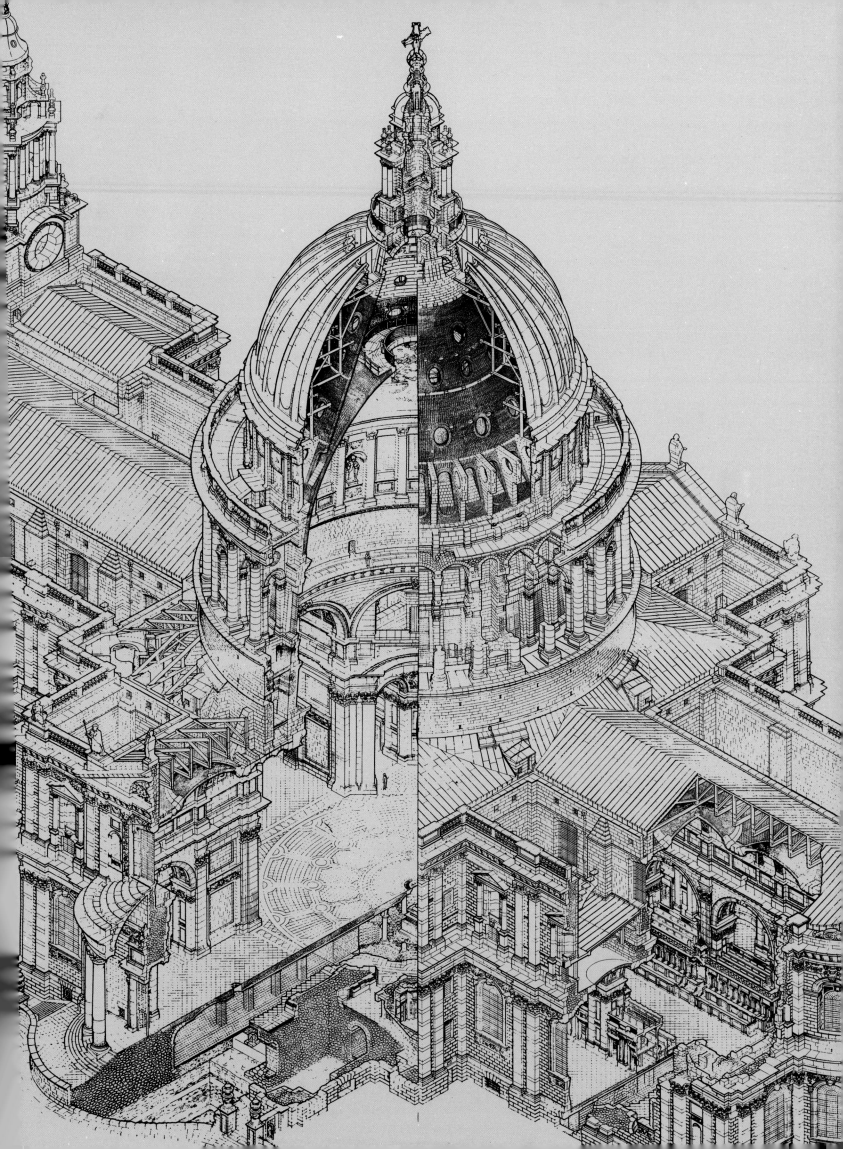

COLOGNE
AACHEN   FREIBURG
MAINZ
WORMS
SPEYER

GERMANY

Charlemagne, according to a ninth-century chronicler, "began . . . many works for the advantage and beautifying of his kingdom. . . . Chief among them . . . the Basilica of the Holy Mother of God, built at Aachen, a marvel of workmanship." Although he himself was an illiterate, Charlemagne became the first great patron of the arts and architecture in the Germanic lands and a prime mover in the Germans' conversion from barbarism. And although the so-called Carolingian Renaissance was more a renaissance of intent than of accomplishment, it did usher in an age of cathedral building that was to pass through a magnificent Romanesque period and to culminate in a series of soaring German cathedrals, such as the double-spired edifice at Regensburg (shown in the photograph below)—cathedrals that rank with the greatest Gothic structures ever built.

Speyer

WITNESS TO GREATNESS

Eight German rulers were buried in the vast Romanesque Cathedral of Speyer, and two of France's most illustrious leaders, Louis XIV and Napoleon Bonaparte, so admired the massive, highly original sandstone structure that they gave express orders to their conquering troops to protect the edifice if they could (those of Louis XIV could not, and the building was gutted in 1689).

The cathedral was begun about 1030 by Conrad II, the first of the Salian emperors, who wished to erect a family tomb "in a place beloved by him." About nine years later, his wish was fulfilled, and he was laid to rest in the new building. His body reposed there, with those of seven of his successors, until the seventeenth-century War of the Grand Alliance, when fires set in the city of Speyer by the soldiers of Louis XIV raged through the cathedral's interior. The destruction uncovered the imperial tombs, and the French troops scattered the emperors' remains. Today only stone monuments indicate where the rulers' bodies once lay.

Emperor Henry IV, a grandson of Conrad II, played a large role in the construction of the cathedral and also, in 1076, left from it on his celebrated walk of repentance to Canossa. Under his direction the vaulted ceiling of the crypt was installed as a bolster to the floor of the chancel, which had been weakened by floods. A succession of fires and wars in the following centuries necessitated building and rebuilding, much of it following faithfully the original Romanesque designs of the eleventh century. The exceptional additions of Corinthian capitals and mosaic inlays were the work of Italian craftsmen employed by Henry and his successors to embellish the austere interior. Around 1700, a number of Baroque elements were introduced when a new western section was added to the already immensely long (432 feet) nave.

Thus rebuilt and extended—it was now the largest Romanesque church in Germany—Speyer's cathedral stood proudly before the oncoming armies of Napoleon, which, in 1805, were headed for Vienna across the Rhine. When generals Soult and Davout entered Speyer in September, Napoleon gave them strict orders to leave the cathedral untouched, and this time the French troops obeyed.

The building they spared (the eastern towers are shown at left) is a monument to the greatness of German Romanesque architecture and a striking reminder of the power of the medieval Holy Roman Empire.

LALA AUFSBERG

*Speyer's crypt (left) was constructed in the
eleventh century and restored in 1857;
Conrad II, Henry IV, and other German emperors were
buried here. The city, its cathedral, and the
Rhine River are shown in the seventeenth-century
engraving below by Matthew Merian.*
OPPOSITE: *In the miniature, Henry III,
the son of Conrad II, dedicates the cathedral
to the Virgin with the help of the empress Agnes.
The cathedral's nave and choir are shown at right.*

RHENUS

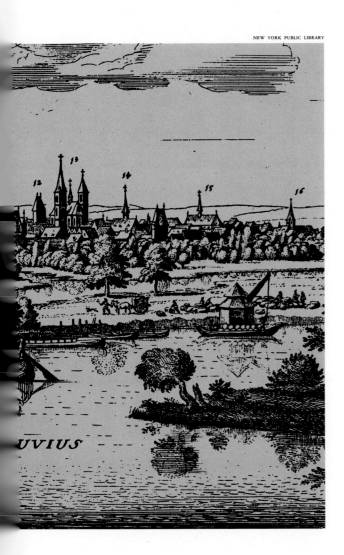

Mainz

INSULT AND INJURY

It was the first month of the year One of the new French Republic—or, according to more conventional reckoning, September, 1792. The army of the French people, under General Adam de Custine, was marching toward Austria, stronghold of the *émigrés* and homeland of the hated Marie Antoinette. One of Custine's chief objectives was Mainz, ancient fortress of the Rhine and site of the eleventh-century Cathedral of St. Martin, a glorious Romanesque structure built in praise of God and the Holy Roman Empire. General Custine apparently had little regard for either: Upon occupation of the city, he turned the cathedral into an abattoir, a storehouse for salt and corn, and a stable for his cavalry. For ten months St. Martin's was subjected to these indignities; then the Prussians recaptured the city after a siege during which the cathedral's walls were partially damaged. In 1795 the French reoccupied Mainz, and two years later Napoleon exchanged the city for Venice in the Treaty of Campo Formio.

The stately old cathedral had certainly seen better days. Dedicated in 1009, it was the coronation site for the Holy Roman emperor Conrad II, the builder of Speyer Cathedral. In 1114, Henry V married the eleven-year-old daughter of Henry I of England in Mainz Cathedral. There, too, in the fifteenth century, Mainz-born Johann Gutenberg, then in the process of setting off a communications explosion, probably worshiped between stints at his newly invented printing press.

For nine hundred years—until the twentieth century—the red sandstone cathedral had its ups and downs, literally and figuratively; major construction occurred in almost every century, but all this tinkering with the foundations and the relentless ravages of fire and war finally took their toll. During World War I, it was discovered that the pillars supporting the walls were dangerously rotted and that extensive underpinning was required immediately to save the cathedral from caving in. For ten years—during the war and well into the 1920's—builders worked intermittently to save the edifice. Then, when everything seemed once more to be in order, World War II visited *its* destruction on the whole city, and the old cathedral again suffered extreme damage. Since the war, however, extensive restoration has taken place; once again the cathedral stands as the historian Henri Daniel-Rops described it, "sturdy, and yet charged with poetry." In the photograph at left, its towers may be seen overlooking the clustered buildings of Mainz, the Rhine, and the land beyond the river.

193

*The massive eight-ribbed vault of the cathedral's choir
is shown in the photograph opposite. The choir
itself was begun late in the twelfth century.
The illustration above, a detail from a view of the city
by the Swiss engraver Matthew Merian, shows the
cathedral as it looked in the first half of the seventeenth
century. The elaborate tracery (top right) by
Master Gerthener from the cathedral's Memorial Chapel
(formerly the chapter house) dates from around 1420.
The east choir of the cathedral, which was given a coat
of red paint in the eighteenth century, is shown at right.*

Mainz' choir screen, two details from which are shown here, was completed around 1329 by the anonymous sculptor now called the Naumburg Master, an artist who some years before had worked in France. The almost insufferably smug expression on the moon-faced individual above was intended to signify the joys of a heavenly reward for piety on earth. Members of the anguished group opposite, however, are paying for their misdeeds in life.

Cologne

ACROSS SIX CENTURIES

When the Prussian emperor Frederick I stormed Milan in 1162, his major accomplishment—for residents of Cologne at least—was the "liberation" of the relics of the Three Magi from the bell tower of a Milan church. These precious relics that, according to legend, had been in Milan for eight centuries (having been sent there from Constantinople by Constantine the Great) were carried off to the German city of Cologne by a splendid procession, depicted in Augustin Braun's seventeenth-century drawing at left.

A century later, when the powerful archbishop Conrad decided that an imposing shrine was required to house the relics, the dilapidated structure that had served as Cologne's cathedral since the fourth century providentially caught fire and was allowed to burn itself out. Master Gerard, an architect who had recently returned to Cologne after assisting the designers of Amiens, was put in charge of the new project and drew up plans for a chancel in a distinctly French Gothic style. Gerard did not live to see the realization of his designs, but his successors followed them faithfully and in 1322 the chancel was consecrated. Its lofty vault, whose ribs spread like rays (Rayonnant) to a height of 150 feet, is clearly reminiscent of the chancel at Amiens and was characterized by the nineteenth-century Swiss historian Jacob Burckhardt as "the peerless manifestation of a great and heavenly genius."

However ambitious the cathedral's plans may have been, and despite such embellishments as some splendid sixteenth-century stained-glass windows, only the structure's south tower came near to completion, rising high enough, anyway, to accommodate a bell hung in 1437. Once they had a bell and a chancel for communion and prayer, the residents of Cologne, it appears, found financial support of further construction unnecessary. Work slowed appreciably, then came to a halt, and was entirely abandoned in 1560. Its resumption, however, was only 282 years away.

In 1842, King Frederick William IV announced that the unfinished cathedral would be completed "in the spirit of the brotherhood of all Germans and of all faiths." Because of certain long-lost documents that had just turned up in the city of Darmstadt, this fraternal and ecumenical spirit was enabled to extend backward over a period of six centuries. The Darmstadt papers included medieval elevations and ground lines for the cathedral's unbuilt main towers, transepts, nave, and west spires. Frederick William's grandiose scheme called for nothing less than the completion of the cathedral exactly as it had been conceived originally—and as though the prolonged delay had never occurred. Work on the building began in 1842 and progressed rapidly until 1880, when with the completion of the four-storied towers and their elegant openwork spires, which are shown in the photograph opposite, Cologne Cathedral was dedicated with great pomp and ceremony.

In the nineteenth century, Louis Gonse summed up the opinions of other French art historians when he wrote of Cologne, "The cathedral is a gigantic, terrifying work. . . . To judge by size and visible splendor alone, it is one of the seven wonders of the world." This largest Gothic cathedral in northern Europe, which had taken so many centuries to build, is now the mother of all German cathedrals and the symbol of the city of Cologne and of the entire Rhineland.

The polychromed figure of Christ at right was
completed in 1322 and stands in the
choir, along with a number of similar figures
by German sculptors trained in France.
The group constitutes one of the last—and
one of the greatest—examples of French High
Gothic sculpture in Germany. The choir,
strongly influenced by the architecture
of the Ile-de-France and Picardy, can be
seen in the photograph opposite between the
nave (foreground) and the apse at the rear.

COLOGNE PRAISED AND DAMNED

Cologne Cathedral has always had its supporters and detractors. In this passage, which follows one on the cathedral's art objects, the poet Goethe bewails the building's unfinished state —a state depicted at the right side of the panoramic print of the city below.

However, before the visitor can enjoy such a diversity of remarkable objects, he is irresistibly drawn to the Cathedral. Yet when he has looked at this world's wonder—a wonder, however, as yet only in contemplation—when he has looked at it, within and without, in its incompleteness, he is oppressed by a painful feeling which cannot become in any way pleasurable, unless we cherish the wish, nay, the hope, of seeing the building entirely finished. For it is in a state of completion only, that a grandly conceived master-piece can produce that effect which the extraordinary mind of the master had in view: where the immensity is rendered intelligible. When such a work is seen in an unfinished state, neither has the imagination the power, nor has the understanding the readiness to create the complete image or the idea.

The poet Algernon Charles Swinburne visited Cologne in 1855 at the age of eighteen in the company of an uncle, Major General Ashburnham, who apparently had better things to do than tramp about cathedrals. Young Swinburne was entranced, however, as can be seen from this excerpt from a letter to his mother.

Now I have got the coast clear for the Cathedral here, and really now I am come to it I don't know what to say. Such things are not to be *jabbered* of. The magnificence bewildered me on entering, the large arches and beautiful windows and the enormous size of the whole building; it was worth coming from anywhere to see. Uncle Tom was so good as to come with me to the Cathedral as the guide spoke only German, tho' I don't think he wanted to come: and waited while I saw the relics and crosses, etc., in the Sacristy, and the Shrine of the Three Kings, which on ordinary days like this costs 6 francs to see, which I willingly paid out of my own money and cheap for such beautiful sights.

The crosses of gold and jewels were most beautiful, but the old

Priest who showed them said they were very heavy, and shook his head and smiled at the enormous one of silver which the Bishop carries in Processions. How any one can, I wonder; it is much higher than a man, and the biggest of them all. The tomb of St. Engelbrecht in the Sacristy is one of the most beautiful things I saw there, all the carved work and images silvergilt. But the shrine was best of all. The Priest removed a part at the head, and showed me the 3 skulls crowned and the names written in rubies. The bare dark skulls looked strange, but not, I thought, ugly or out of place in the diadems of gold and pearls. Every pillar of the shrine is of a different mosaic pattern. Down the sides are the Apostles and Prophets; at the foot the Passion in separate groups. The expression of the faces of each figure (one of Our Saviour particularly) looked wonderfully true on so small a scale. The 4 pearls at the top, and some other of the jewels about it were enormous; I never saw such a size. This is the best description I can give of the Shrine; there are, I am afraid, many other things well worth seeing that I had not time for. I grudge especially the view of the whole Cathedral from above, and a closer view of some of the east windows, the choir and the old frescoes. But I trust some day that we may all come here and see everything!

The painter and poet William Morris found the cathedral a disappointment on a second visit made in 1879.

Do you remember how strange and romantic the unfinished Cologne Cathedral looked? How stupid the present completion of it looks I myself can bear witness.

The architectural critic John Ruskin, who on one occasion called Cologne Cathedral "a miserable humbug," delivered himself of some further animadversions in 1859 in the course of a letter to a lady friend of his back in England, Mrs. John Simon.

I find the German Gothic abominable—Cologne Cathedral an enormous failure—the Rhine not half so grand as the Thames at Chelsea. I have, however, two good reasons for admiring the Thames at Chelsea, so I am perhaps partial. But Cologne Cathedral is assuredly good for nothing —old or new, it is all bad.

FROM L HENNE AM RHYN, *Kulturgeschichte des Deutschen Volkes*, 1892

Worms

A CASTLE ON THE RHINE

Like a "mighty castle," the cathedral at Worms, known as the Kaiserdom (the interior of whose dome is seen at left), has loomed over great events in German history. Worms itself is perhaps Germany's oldest city. The date of its founding is unknown, but it was a pre-Christian Celtic settlement and a fortified capital of Caesar's foes in Roman times. In the fifth century it became the capital of the Burgundian kings, and the *Nibelungenlied* is based on events that actually occurred there. Huns later destroyed the city, but it was rebuilt; in Merovingian times it became an episcopal see whose bishop served in the dual capacity of religious and political leader. This situation displeased the city's more-influential citizens, who, after a long struggle, achieved imperial-city status in 1156, making their town the first one in Germany to enjoy that distinction.

The cathedral dates from about 1000 A.D., when its construction was begun by the powerful bishop Burchard, an expert in canon law and the guardian of the future emperor, Conrad the Elder. Set on the foundations of an old Carolingian church overlooking the Rhine, Burchard's building consisted of little more than a choir and two large tower bases. Over the next hundred years, work was continued on the apse and eastern sanctuary (consecrated in 1181), and in the thirteenth century the building was substantially completed in the Romanesque style.

History continued to swirl about the city. The Concordat of 1122, held in the shadow of the cathedral, established a compromise peace between the Holy Roman emperor and the pope, who had been feuding over the rights of episcopal investiture. Emperor Charles V heard Mass at the Kaiserdom in 1521 on the eve of his momentous confrontation with Martin Luther, who had journeyed to the Diet of Worms to defend his doctrines. A little more than one hundred years later, the city suffered greatly in the Thirty Years' War. The cathedral, and especially the choir, were severely damaged, requiring reconstruction that led eventually, in 1741, to the creation of a magnificent Baroque altar designed by Balthasar Neumann. A gilded, festive affair, rising to a crown surrounded by cherubim, the altar seems a bit out of place in the otherwise austere cathedral.

The Kaiserdom underwent its share of vicissitudes during the violent periods of recent German history. French shells struck the cathedral in World War I; and World War II, with its considerably improved engines of destruction, saw serious damage inflicted upon the exterior. Repairs have only recently been made to the historic structure.

HELGA SCHMIDT-GLASSNER

JEAN ROUBIER

The expressive head at left is part of a
Deposition relief by Hans Seifer of Heilbronn,
which was transferred to Worms' baptistery
from the cloisters when the latter were demolished
in 1484. The four slender cylinders that
form the towers of the cathedral can be seen in
the photograph at bottom left, which was taken
from a position to the northeast of the
edifice. The stylized feline below surveys the
city from a window in the cathedral's
eastern façade, while two similar beasts display
a leonine form of gratitude to Daniel in the
relief (opposite) from St. Joseph's Chapel.

LEFT AND ABOVE: HELGA SCHMIDT-GLASSNER

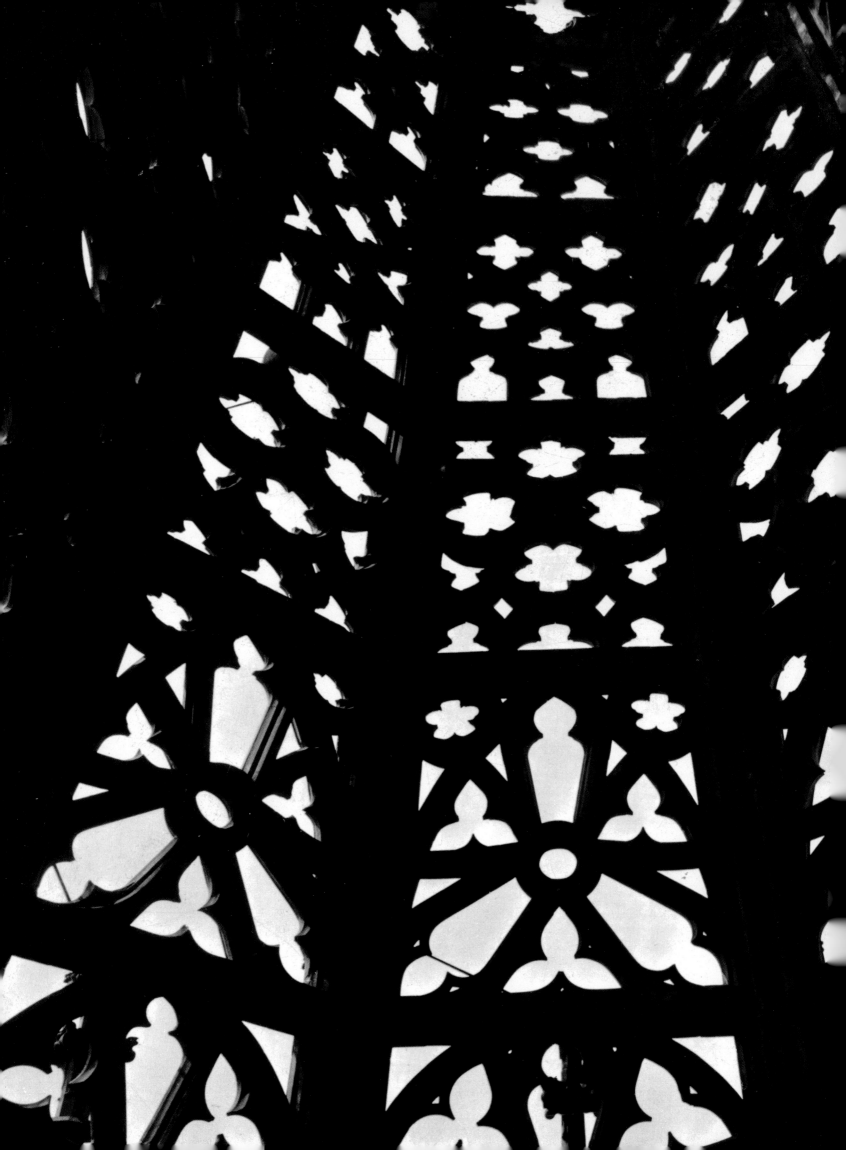

Freiburg

"TRIUMPHANT IN PHOEBUS' LIGHT"

One of the most notable glories of German Gothic art, Freiburg Cathedral's filigree stone spire (seen from its interior at left) is a slender, 380-foot shaft of petrified lace designed by Master Remigius Faesch of Basel in the fourteenth century. Standing beneath it, within the cathedral, one is dappled with sunlight on fair days and exposed to the elements on foul. Practical or not, the spire served as the model for many others on cathedrals built along the Rhine, including the west spires of the great cathedral at Cologne.

As an inspirer of poets, the tower has fared less successfully. An example is a pompous rhymed allegory by an Anglo-German official, one John Andrew Ritschel, who was smitten by its beauty in 1836 and moved to a flash of insight. According to Ritschel's poetic fantasy, the wind, jealous of the effortless grace of Freiburg's spire, launched one night a furious assault from all directions:

> The wind's raging contest with one blow
> Combined at once the structure t'overthrow.

Happily, the structure resisted the onslaught and pointed out a valuable lesson: As Ritschel saw it, man must resist the attacks of jealous forces so that he, like the Freiburg tower, might "emerge triumphant in Phoebus' light."

Over the centuries, the cathedral, built between 1122 and 1252, acquired a large collection of precious works of art, including altar paintings by Hans Baldung Gruen, panels by Lucas Cranach the Elder and Hans Holbein the Younger, and a great variety of French-influenced sculpture (much of which adorns the cathedral's portals and corbels). There is also a celebrated bell, known as "Hosanna," one of the oldest in Germany, and, at five tons, one of the world's heaviest.

An early twelfth-century capital (left) from the portal of St. Nicholas' Chapel shows Alexander the Great making his way toward heaven in a ship drawn by giant birds. The cathedral's south transept (below) is one of the earliest parts of the building. Its twelfth-century Romanesque arches can be seen in the lower right-hand corner of the photograph.
OPPOSITE: *The spire-capped structure seems to leave an earthbound city behind as it soars upward toward the heavens.*

SEEGER

HELGA SCHMIDT-GLASSNER

Aachen

CHARLEMAGNE'S CHAPEL

Charlemagne was so delighted with the charms and natural resources of Aachen that it became his favorite residence. In 798 he established his personal chapel there on the ruins of an ancient Roman bath. The chapel was designed also to serve as his mausoleum, and to endow it with as "holy" an appearance as possible, Charlemagne ordered his architect to model it after the Church of San Vitale in Ravenna, which, in turn, had supposedly been modeled after the Holy Sepulcher in Jerusalem. In the detail (right) from the reliefs adorning his sarcophagus, Charlemagne offers a model of the chapel, with its Carolingian chancel, to the Virgin. The chancel was later replaced by another in the Gothic style, and, indeed, since the chapel's consecration in 805 (nine years before Charlemagne died and was buried there), a series of additions and embellishments have turned the building into what might be called a three-dimensional history of German church architecture.

In 1000 A.D., the young emperor Otto III made a ceremonious pilgrimage to Aachen to open Charlemagne's tomb. The visit and exhumation were described (with questionable accuracy) by a member of Otto's entourage: "We entered in unto Charles. He was not lying down, as is the manner with the bodies of other dead men, but sat on a certain chair as though he lived. . . . But none of his members had corrupted and fallen away, except a little piece of the end of his nose, which he [Otto] caused at once to be restored with gold; and he took from his mouth one tooth, and built the tabernacle again and departed."

Over two hundred years after Otto's pilgrimage—at the time of Charlemagne's canonization—Frederick II ordered a golden reliquary shrine to be created for Aachen and decorated with a portrait of the new saint, seated on his throne as Otto supposedly had found him: robed, holding his scepter, and wearing the bejeweled diadem which became the model for the coronation crown first used by Charles IV in 1349. Charles' crown is now on display at Aachen, as is the *Kaiserstuhl*, the marble throne upon which Charlemagne's body was allegedly found almost a thousand years ago.

In addition to these relics, the cathedral (the chapel became one in 1801) contains some of Christendom's greatest treasures, including the swaddling clothes of the Infant Jesus, the cloak worn by the Virgin at the Nativity, and the loin cloth that Jesus wore when He was crucified. Over the centuries these sacred objects have drawn millions of pilgrims to Aachen Cathedral from all over the world. They are still publicly displayed every seven years for a two-week period.

*The nucleus of the present cathedral, the
octagonal chapel built for Charlemagne
in the Byzantine style by the
master architect Odo, is shown opposite.
The structure served as the coronation chapel
for several German emperors. In the
miniature at right from a fifteenth-century
manuscript, Charlemagne personally
directs the building of his cathedral.
The throne upon which the emperor's
remains supposedly were found is visible
between the central columns in
the photograph of the Palatine Chapel below.*

*In Aachen have I seen the well-proportioned columns
with their fine porphyry capitals of green
and red gutterstone, which Charlemagne . . . had there
installed. . . . I have seen also there all sorts
of magnificent treasures, unlike any . . . which we
living may see today.*

—*Albrecht Dürer*

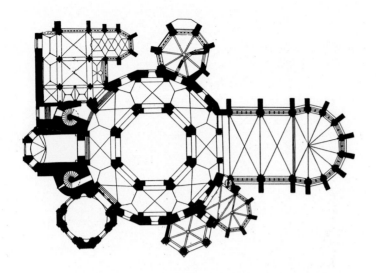

In the floor plan of the cathedral at left, Charlemagne's chapel is indicated by the octagon within the main polygonal structure. The photograph below shows (left to right) the Gothic choir, the Palatine Chapel with its cupola, and the modern Gothic bell tower with its slate-covered spire. The cathedral as it looked in the seventeenth century, before its central spire was replaced by the cupola, is shown in a detail (opposite) from a topographical view of the city by Matthew Merian; the cathedral is at the picture's left.

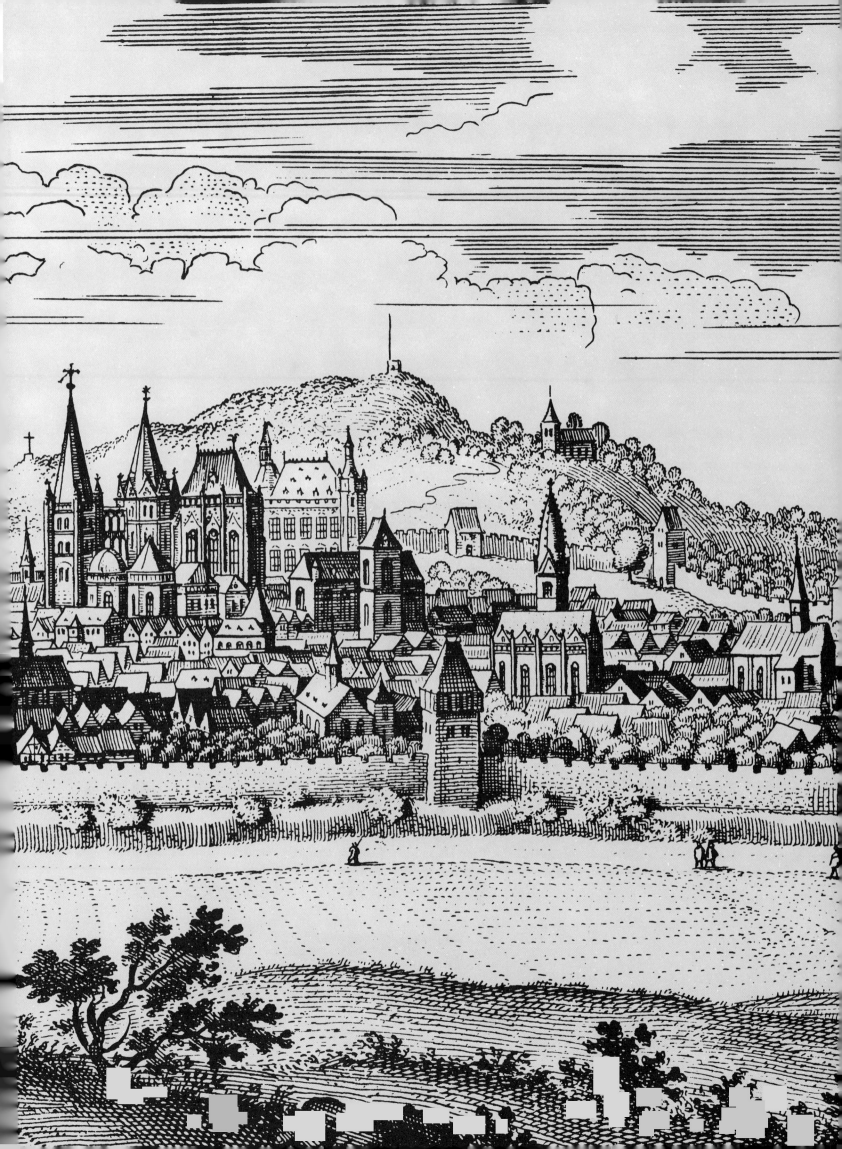

BISHOPS ASSEMBLED

A Portfolio on the Constance Council

The Council of Constance, second of the three great fifteenth-century councils, was convened by Pope John XXIII, called the "antipope," in 1414 at the urging of King Sigismund of Hungary. All forty-five full sessions of the Council were held in the bishop's cathedral in Constance; the *Kaufhaus*, or Merchants' Hall, which had been completely rebuilt inside to accommodate the delegates, was used only once during the three-year period of the Council—and then briefly. The lakeside hall was probably better suited to house the twenty-nine cardinals and more than two hundred bishops who took part in the Council, but the cathedral, built in the eleventh century on the foundations of a Roman fort, was the seat of one of the empire's oldest bishoprics—and, as such, the logical location for a gathering of the church's highest officials. The nave of the minster, twice renovated and enlarged during the eleventh century, was similar in layout to the assembly hall in St. Peter's in Rome—and it was there that the Council met for the first time on All Saints' Day. Like previous councils, this one had its chroniclers—but unlike them, it also produced a journalist who was neither a delegate nor an official scribe. Ulrich Richental was an onlooker, a burgher of Constance who was sufficiently intrigued by the Council's activities to record them in a journal, which he then hired draftsmen to illustrate according to his extensive instructions. The resulting *Chronicle*, although laced with low gossip and fraught with inconsistencies, is nonetheless a unique and highly significant document. It describes the Council as no other great medieval assembly was described, emphasizing its pomp and its display while minimizing political implications.

The vividness of Ulrich Richental's *Chronicle* is due, at least in part, to his deliberate manipulation of dates and data, which reduces the events of those years to a series of spectacular but specious tableaux. Richental's penchant for embellishment and distortion has resulted in a pictorial catalog of the Council's activities that is at once exhaustively detailed (down to the number of horses certain nobles kept) and wildly speculative—as when, for example, Richental puts the number of delegates, tradesmen, and servants arriving in Constance between 1414 and 1417 at close to 100,000. An obvious example of Richental's license can be seen opposite: The outsize umbrella, carried by a knight on a heavily caparisoned horse, is more eye-catching than historically accurate. Less obvious, but no less significant, are the many distortions that occur in scenes illustrating the Council sessions in the cathedral.

OVERLEAF: *Here the draftsman has given his work a striking but contrived symmetry: The enthroned pope is flanked by two cardinals and they, in turn, are flanked by three bishops, each accompanied by a secretary. The general effect is heightened by the use of reverse perspective, which here equates size with rank, and no effort has been made to depict accurately the delegates or, for that matter, the hall itself. Historians know, for example, that the cathedral had a flat, not vaulted, ceiling and that debates were conducted in the center of the hall, not from pulpits in the corners. Yet despite inaccuracies of this sort, which have led critics to condemn Richental's chronology and to question the accuracy of his data, the* Chronicle *remains an exuberant record of the times, as revealing in its occasional falsities as it is in its fidelities.*

Certainly the most lavish of the secular ceremonies held in Constance while the Council was in session was the enfeoffment of Burgrave Frederick of Zollern (below) in 1417. In the formal ceremony on April eighteenth, Sigismund, king of Hungary and Holy Roman emperor (shown seated, flanked by two dukes holding the scepter and orb, insignia of the realm), invested Frederich (kneeling before Sigismund) with the Mark Brandenburg, the territory surrounding and including Berlin, in fief. Richental, whose fascination with heraldry was apparently boundless, has filled his journal with banners and escutcheons—over eight hundred of them. Some are spurious—the result of a willingness to rely on secondhand reports that made Richental the occasional dupe of unscrupulous informants —but most are not, as the illustration below shows. Frederich himself holds aloft the banner of Brandenburg, as do two heralds in the far left corner, and two members of Frederich's own party (one directly behind him and another half-hidden in back) bear the device of the Zollerns.

Nothing altered village life in medieval Europe as much as the convocation of a church council, and no council altered Europe as much as the one held in Constance from 1414 to 1417. In a little over three years, Constance was transformed from a small commercial center on the southern European trade routes into a city of thirty thousand inhabitants, including the most eminent theologians, politicians, and scholars of the day. It became the forum for one of the longest and most controversial debates on ecclesiastical polity in church history—one culminating with the Council's decree, *Sacrosancta*, which asserted the primacy of the Council—and all future councils—over all of the church's officials, including the pope. And while the citizens of Constance were not participants in the Council itself, they were directly involved in feeding, housing, and transporting its delegates and members of their retinues. It is just such a group of elaborately costumed representatives, bearing pennons as they pass under the window of an unidentified duke and duchess, that Ulrich Richental's hired illustrators have pictured above.

No less spectacular—though for quite different reasons—
was the public immolation of the condemned heretic John
Huss on July 6, 1415 (right). Huss, a noted theologian and
twice rector of Prague University, had come to Constance
on a safe-conduct guarantee issued by King Sigismund to
defend his views before the Council. (Like Wycliffe, Huss
refused to recognize any temporal organization of the
church, which he considered simply a spiritual community
of those predestined for salvation.) Soon after his arrival
in Constance, Huss was imprisoned, not by the king but
by the Council, interrogated, and eventually tried. His
plea—"I teach no error; no Czech is a heretic"—was
ignored, and he was condemned. Richental's illustration
shows Huss at the stake, and above him the words: "I die
joyfully for the Gospel." His martyrdom, witnessed by
soldiers, burghers, and priests, touched off the Hussite
Wars, an insurrection in Bohemia that crusading invasions
in 1420 and 1431 could not quell, and one that led eventually to the founding of the first national reformed church.

The election of a new pope, Martin V, on November 11, 1417, was the culmination of almost three years of Council effort to end the Great Schism which had sundered the church and threatened its very survival for almost forty years. There were three popes when the Council convened in 1414: Gregory XII, elected by the Sacred College in Rome in 1406; Benedict XIII, appointed by the College still located at Avignon in 1394; and finally John XXIII, whom the Synod of Pisa had elected in 1410 after first declaring the other claimants heretical and schismatic. By 1417 all three had abdicated or been deposed. Gregory XII resigned without coercion in 1415, and John XXIII, who fled to Schaffhausen in March, 1415, after losing his backing, was brought back under guard and forced to abdicate. In July of 1417, Benedict XIII was deposed for a second time, thus freeing the Council to elect a new pope.

Richental's *Chronicle* quite fittingly devotes considerable space to the election of Pope Martin V, for although the Council's real triumph lay in firmly establishing its primacy within the hierarchy, the public manifestation of that control was not so much the arrest of John XXIII or the forced abdication that followed—for popes had been deposed before—but the election of a new pope who was clearly answerable to the Council. The Sacred College met in the *Kaufhaus* (often erroneously called the Council Hall, simply because it was converted for possible Council use in 1413) in November, 1417, and the announcement of the election of Martin V was made from one of its windows (below) to the delegates kneeling in the street. The plate opposite shows the new pope being led through the streets of Constance by Sigismund himself. Four unidentified dukes carry the baldachin, or pope's canopy.

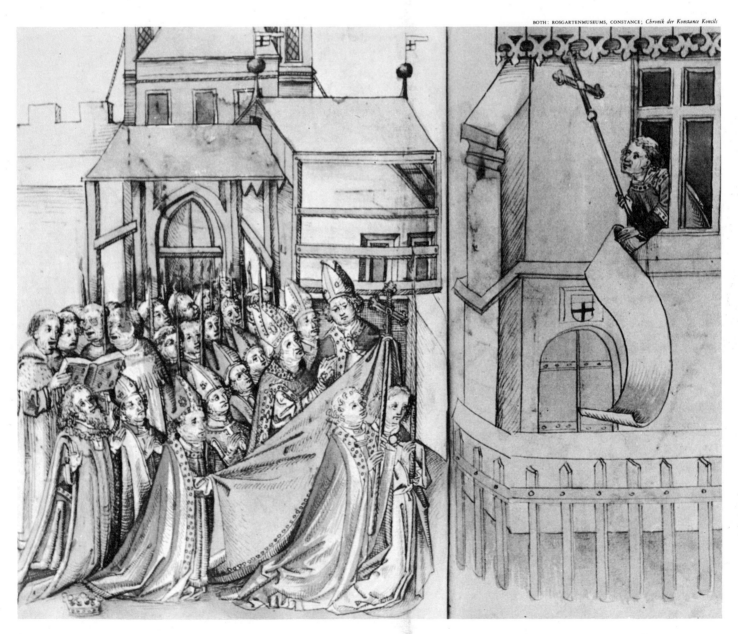

BOTH: ROSGARTENMUSEUMS, CONSTANCE; *Chronik der Konstance Koncils*

SANTIAGO DE COMPOSTELA

BURGOS

ZAMORA

BARCELONA

MADRID

TOLEDO

CORDOBA

SEVILLE

CADIZ

SPAIN

A remarkable diversity of influences fused in Spain to create an architecture that reflects the national temperament as no "pure" style could have done. And in Spain, as nowhere else, the various architectural styles overlapped and mixed to produce some of the most striking cathedrals in Europe. At Seville, the world's largest Gothic church arose above a twelfth-century mosque; at Santiago de Compostela (which played no small role in the spread of the Gothic style), a Romanesque cathedral hides behind one of the most elaborate of Churrigueresque façades; and at Jaén (below), the cathedral is pure Renaissance. If Spain, then, developed no single dominant style—as France, for example, developed the Gothic—the country itself is the macrocosm of its own church architecture: Spain is, as one writer felicitously puts it, "one great cathedral."

Perched on its granite hillside, the multispired Cathedral of Santa María (shown in the photograph opposite and the engraving at right) looms majestically over the ancient and picturesque town of Burgos —center of chivalric literature, birthplace of El Cid, and former capital of Castile, Spain's most important state. Burgos is considered the most interesting of the three major Spanish Gothic cathedrals—the other two are León and Toledo—and, to the nineteenth-century writer Edmondo De Amicis, it was "one of the largest, handsomest, and richest monuments of Christianity."

In 1075 King Alfonso VI fixed the episcopal see at Burgos and offered his palace ground as the site for a cathedral, which was finished in 1096 in the Romanesque style. About twelve decades later the English bishop Maurice, who had come to Burgos in the retinue of the English queen Eleanor Plantagenet, was sent to Germany to convey Princess Beatrice back to Spain as a bride for King Ferdinand III. Maurice not only accomplished this mission, but returned with several European master builders and a taste for the Gothic style that he had discovered during his travels. The marriage ceremony took place in 1219 in the old cathedral, which shortly thereafter was torn down. Two years later Ferdinand laid the first stone for the present Santa María.

Although enough of the building was completed in only nine years to enable services to be held, the final touch, Burgos' octagonal dome, was not finished until 1568. Despite this lapse of time, there is a certain stylistic unity to the towers and pinnacles, largely because the architects during the last stages of construction represented three generations of the same family.

The early cupola above the crossing collapsed in the sixteenth century, coinciding with Burgos' decline as a political center and leading many people to surmise that both events stemmed from the same causes. Although the town's importance waned, its cathedral was later to become the recipient of a most important set of relics. During the Peninsular War in the early nineteenth century, El Cid's tomb in San Pedro de Cardeña was ransacked and some of his bones wound up in Germany. Alfonso XII, however, later secured their return to Spain, and in 1921 they were placed in the cathedral.

The effect of Burgos' profusion of sculptures, considered among the most ornate and perfect in Europe, was flamboyantly described by the aforementioned De Amicis: "On whatever side you turn your eyes, you meet eyes that are gazing at you, hands that are beckoning you, cherub heads that are peeping at you, scarves that seem to wave, clouds that appear to rise, crystal suns that seem to tremble; an infinite variety of forms, colors and reflections that dazzle your eyes and confuse your brain." To the historian John Allyne Gade, this was a bit overdone; to him Burgos seemed "more emotional than sensitive. Riotous excess and empty display take the place of restrained and appropriate decoration." But perhaps the most reasonable description of Burgos Cathedral's impact on the viewer who sees it for the first time comes from one of the leading modern authorities on Gothic architecture, John Harvey, who writes: "The effect of these three groups of pinnacles, pale yellow spires forcing their way upwards into a sky of solid blue, is unforgettable. A distant view of Burgos is a sight of a fairy building from lands of romance and chivalry."

Burgos

A VARIETY OF FORMS

The Florid Gothic façade of the Condestable Chapel (left)—so called because it was built at the expense of the high constable of Castile— dates from the late fifteenth century and was designed by a father-and-son team of German architects. The octagonal chapel's interior (bottom right, opposite page) is adorned with a profusion of sculptures in the Isabelline style (named for the queen during whose reign it flowered), including a single figure of Saint James and a Visitation group, both of which are shown on the opposite page.

BOTH: SCALA

YAN

*The ornate stairway shown in this nineteenth-century engraving bears
the arms of Bishop Fonseca, who had it built in Burgos'
Chapel of St. Nicholas in 1519. Although chiefly the work of the
Spanish architect Diego de Siloé, the double staircase carries a metal
balustrade by a Frenchman named Hilaire.*
OPPOSITE: *The dome of Burgos' crossing, which rises 164 feet above the
floor of the cathedral's nave, shows that Moorish influences were still
affecting Spanish architecture as late as the mid-sixteenth century.*

Zamora

WHERE PRIESTS
AND SOLDIERS PRAYED

On a ridge above the Duero River, the quiet town of Zamora, site of many of the epic events recounted in the chronicles of El Cid, today gives little hint of its tumultuous past. The city dates from the Moorish conquests and, as an important frontier post, was long contested by Moors and Christians. It was first taken from the Moors by Alfonso I in 748 and was later subjected to two tremendous sieges. The alleged loss of forty thousand Moorish warriors there in 939 gave birth to the Spanish saying, "Zamora is not gained in an hour." In 988 Almanzor destroyed the town, but Ferdinand I rebuilt it in 1065. Seven years later it was the site of a bloody battle between Ferdinand's son and daughter, Sancho II and Doña Urraca. The famous El Cid was on Sancho's side, but he refused to fight Urraca, and Sancho lost both the city and his life. That struggle, as well as Zamora's continuing role as a strategic bastion against the incursions of the Moors, required the building of defenses that earned the city the nickname *la bien cercada*, "the well-walled."

Despite its military position as a key border site, Zamora became a strong center of the Christian faith and was known as a town of "priests and soldiers." The cathedral (seen both at left and on the opposite page), built in the twelfth century, was probably the most notable religious structure in León and Castile at the time, harmoniously combining a Romanesque ground plan and an Oriental lantern dome (*cimborio*) over the crossing. The latter was completely new to twelfth-century Spanish Romanesque architecture and is believed to have been an import from either the Latin Kingdom of Jerusalem or the Byzantine Empire. It is found next in the slightly later Spanish cathedrals of Toro and Salamanca and underscores the role of either the Almohades (the Berber Moslems in the South) or the returning crusaders as carriers of Eastern architectural forms and ideas to Spain. Whatever may have been its exact source, the Oriental quality of this dome and its turrets was undoubtedly more pronounced before their exteriors were covered with scalloped, or "fish-scale," tiles.

The cathedral felt another foreign influence in the use of French ogival vaults and pointed arches, devices that may have been introduced into Spain by way of the pilgrimage route to Santiago de Compostela. If not, there were other links with France to explain the importation, among them the marriage of Teresa, the daughter of Alfonso VI, to Henry of Burgundy, whose family thereafter greatly influenced the region of Zamora.

An outstanding feature of the cathedral is the *Puerta del Obispo* on the south façade, facing the bishop's palace. This door with its floral motifs is reminiscent of features of the Cistercian buildings that sprang up in Spain along the pilgrimage trail, notably the nearby Cistercian monastery of Moreruela, completed in 1168. These motifs, as well as the pointed arches in the nave and side aisles, reflect the diffusion of the Cistercian style. Although most of the cathedral is of the twelfth and thirteenth centuries (the main part was built between 1151 and 1174), the three graduated apses were replaced during the reign of Ferdinand and Isabella with a much larger chevet; and during the seventeenth century a wide portico was built onto the north portal in imitation of Roman architecture. Still dominating the building, however, is its massive, three-story, martial tower, a grim, enduring reminder of the turbulent early history of the people of the border city.

ROBERT SOWERS

236

The cathedral's unfinished square tower and its unusual cupola can be seen above the roof tops of Zamora in the photograph on the opposite page. The central dome, a mixture of French and Byzantine influences, is set in a cluster of four smaller cupolas. Its interior (above) is called a medio naranjo, or "half orange," for obvious reasons. The blind door shown at right, one of a pair that flanks the west front's Puerta del Obispo (Bishop's Portal), is surmounted by a particularly fine relief depicting the Virgin and Child with angels.

Córdoba

RAISING THE ROOF

Originally the site of a Roman temple of Janus, the location of the Cathedral of Córdoba (still referred to as *La Mezquita*, "the mosque") was occupied by a Visigothic Church of St. Vincent at the time of the Moslem conquest of Córdoba in 711. From 748 until 785 the Christians shared their place of worship with the Moslems (the Christians being warned not to disturb their superiors with too-loud hymn singing and bell ringing), but in 785 Abd-al-Rahman I purchased the church and within the year built a mosque on the site. This "Great Mosque," which later became the largest Moslem house of worship outside the Kaaba of Mecca, was built to help consolidate the power of the Umayyad caliphate in Spain. Abd-al-Rahman had fled to Spain after the rest of his family lost the throne at Damascus to the rival Abbasid dynasty of Baghdad. He made Córdoba his capital only after overthrowing the Abbasid government there and seizing power for himself. His desire to create a great religious center in Spain, the wish of a benevolent monarch to save his people the long pilgrimage to Mecca, was also part of his plan to abandon the traditional nomadic way of life and to establish an Arab kingdom in Spain completely independent of the ruling dynasty in Syria. The building itself reflects its Western situation, and there is no trace of Abbasid influence in the construction dating from his reign. The structure's approximately 850 columns came from both ancient Roman and Visigothic buildings and include some taken from the ruins at Nîmes or Narbonne, Seville or Tarragona, and Carthage. The decision to use these rather short columns (approximately 13 feet high) necessitated devising another way to heighten the enormous roof. The solution was the use of double rows of horseshoe arches that, although later considered typical of Moslem architecture, is really a Roman technique transmitted via the Visigoths to the Moslems. The way multiple arches are used here to create a space above slender columns, however, produces a fanning-out effect quite the opposite of the slightly bottom-heavy Classical architecture from which it derives its elements.

The mosque was enlarged and greatly elaborated by successive emirs to accommodate the growing population of the city. It finally doubled its original size and (including its forecourt) became one of the largest houses of worship anywhere in the world—one almost as large as St. Peter's in Rome.

With the capture of Córdoba by the Christian King Ferdinand III of Castile, the mosque became the Church of the Virgin of the Assumption, but it was not altered beyond the insertion of a few chapels here and there (the engraving at left shows the celebration of Mass in one such chapel) and the use for Christian purposes of certain areas of the mosque, such as the *maqsura* (right), or royal gallery, in front of the *mihrab* (prayer niche). In 1523, however, Charles V authorized the cathedral chapter to build a cruciform church in the center of the mosque. The construction extended over a hundred years, but by 1526 enough "progress" had been made (construction necessitated the removal of about sixty ancient columns) for Charles to regret his decision and to admonish the chapter: "You have built here what you or anyone might have built anywhere else, but you have destroyed what was unique in the world." Belated though it was, Charles' sudden turnabout preserved at least a part of a great building and resulted in one of the most unusual cathedrals in Christendom.

ALL: YAN

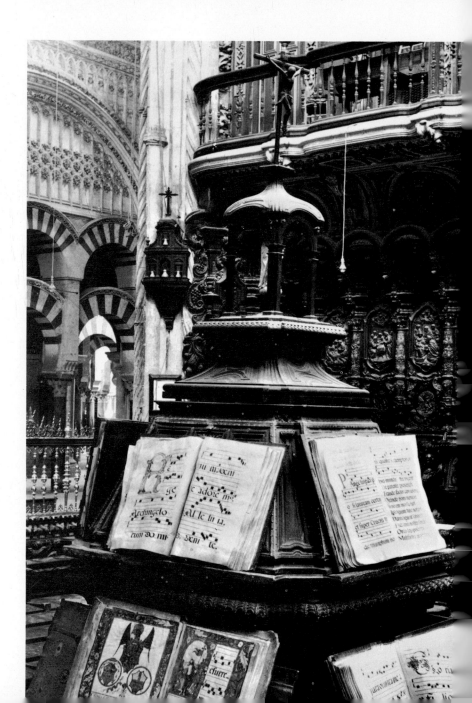

The miniature at right shows Ferdinand III, who liberated
Córdoba from the Moors in 1236, receiving the keys either to
that city or to Seville, which he also freed twelve years later.
Córdoba's peculiar mixture of Gothic and Moorish elements
can be seen clearly in the aerial photograph shown below.
OPPOSITE: The cathedral's Churrigueresque choir stalls (left) by
Pedro Duque Cornejo are located—somewhat anomalously—at
the center of the old mosque. Hernán Ruiz, the architect chosen by a
royal council to Christianize the appearance of the mosque in
1523, was responsible for the vault shown at top right and for the
choir (bottom right), which, with its elaborate music stand, contrasts
rather sharply with the original Moorish architecture.

A succession of Moorish arches (left) in white stone
and red brick spans an aisle leading to
the mihrab, or prayer niche, of the old mosque.
The arches constantly recombine to form new patterns
—as can be seen in the photograph below—
depending on the position of the spectator.
The maqsura, the private gallery of the Moslem
sovereign, is roofed with a mosaic-studded octagonal
dome (opposite) and supported by a magnificent group
of intertwined and superimposed arches (below right).

WIM SWAAN; COURTESY ELEK BOOKS, LTD.

Seville

A FINE MADNESS

"Seen from a certain distance, it resembles a high-pooped and be-flagged ship, rising over the sea with harmonious grouping of sails, pennons, and banners, and with its mainmast towering over the mizzenmast, foremast, and bowsprit." Thus did the nineteenth-century Spanish writer, Ceán-Bermúdez, describe the largest Gothic building in the world and the largest, highest, and richest church in Spain— the Cathedral of Seville. Of this "colossal, incongruous, mysterious, and elusive" pile, even Alexander Pope, a man not easily given to superlatives, wrote, "*There* stands a structure of majestic fame."

When Ferdinand III of Castile liberated Seville from the Moors in 1248, he transformed the city's mosque into a cathedral dedicated to the Virgin. By 1401, age and earthquake had taken their toll of the structure, and the cathedral chapter convened to consider designs for a new church that was to be "so great and of such a kind that those who see it finished shall think we were mad." To hasten the work, begun in 1402, the canons renounced their incomes; but they may have overemphasized the element of speed, for in 1511, only five years after its completion, the great central dome toppled into the vaults below, revealing to everyone's horror that many of the pillars were mere hollow shells carelessly filled with debris.

The vastness of Seville's interior is minimized by its simplicity and the exact proportions of its component parts. Although the main body of the cathedral, surrounded by Roman columns and the pillars of the original Arab mosque, is pure, severe Gothic, the huge edifice also comprises almost every known architectural style: Classical, Late Florid Gothic, Rococo, and Moorish. When the mosque was razed, the citizenry could not bear to see its spectacular twelfth-century tower (right) destroyed, and it was spared, later to become the symbol of the city. In 1568, the tower was crowned with a colossal statue of Faith, mounted so cleverly that it turns in the slightest breeze.

Seville's seven naves, thirty-seven chapels, and eighty altars, celebrating fifty masses each day, teem with life. "In and out of these many entrances," writes the noted historian John Allyne Gade, "the populace stream, to worship, to whisper, to gossip, to rest, to bargain, to beg, and to make love. The great edifice with all the ceremonial of its religious services is woven into their life, as is the sound of the guitars and castanets that echo within its portals and courtyards."

ARCHIVO MAS

YAN

The vast dimensions of the cathedral
are readily apparent in the aerial
photograph opposite. The circular
structure in the background is the city's
Maestranza bull ring, which stands
beside the Guadalquiver river. Seville's
unusual buttressing can be seen in
the photograph at left, which shows the
angle formed by the crossing of the
nave and transept. In the 1895 painting
by Manuel Cabral below, a procession
pauses before the cathedral
during the Feast of Corpus Christi.

MUSEO MODERNO DE MADRID; BRADLEY SMITH

The tympanum of the cathedral's Puerta de las Campanillas
(Portal of the Little Bells) is decorated with a terra
cotta relief (above) depicting the Adoration of the Magi.
The sculpture, which dates from the sixteenth century, is by
Miguel Perrin. The Puerta de los Naranjos (Portal of
the Oranges), shown opposite, opens onto the Orangery
Courtyard (visible behind the Giralda Tower in the photograph
on page 246), which was part of the original mosque.
The sculpture by Joaquin Bilbao of the portal's tympanum
illustrates the Conception in terra-cotta relief.

Santiago de Compostela

THE MOORSLAYER'S SHRINE

It all began one night in 813 when the appearance of strange lights in the sky attracted Bishop Theodomir of Iria Flavia to a spot near his church, where he discovered a tomb that he claimed belonged to the apostle Saint James the Greater (*Santiago* in Spanish) and around which he built a small chapel that was converted to a cathedral later in the ninth century by Alfonso III. According to legend, when the apostle came to Spain eight centuries earlier, he landed near Iria and preached for several years before returning to Judea. After the saint's martyrdom, his disciples placed his stone coffin on a boat that miraculously returned to Iria. There the coffin remained, forgotten until 813. From that date on, however, a city began to grow around the shrine that was later to become, after Jerusalem and Rome, the most famous place of Christian pilgrimage in the Middle Ages. When an image of Saint James appeared during the battle against the Moors at Clavijo in 844, the saint became the spiritual leader of the Reconquest, and from then on troops went into battle with the cry, "Santiago!"

By 997 the city was important enough to warrant the wrathful attentions of the Moorish conqueror Almanzor. In admiration of a certain monk, who alone among the citizenry remained to guard the apostle's tomb, Almanzor spared both monk and tomb but ordered the city and church demolished: "not one stone, it is alleged, being left upon another." The church doors and huge silver bells were carried off to Córdoba on backs of Christian captives. Five years later, according to a Burgos monk, "Almanzor died and was buried in Hell."

In the eleventh century the city was rebuilt and its name changed by Pope Urban II from Iria Flavia to Santiago de Compostela (perhaps derived from *campus stellae*, "field of the star"). Over the saint's tomb a new Romanesque cathedral was begun about 1075, consecrated in 1211, and publicized in the twelfth-century Codex Calixtinus: "In it health is bestowed on the sick, sight returned to the blind; the tongue of the mute is unloosed; hearing is restored to the deaf, normal carriage afforded the lame, relief conceded the possessed; and what is better, the prayers of faithful people are heard. . . ." In 1236, the bells of Santiago, liberated by Ferdinand III at Córdoba, were returned, this time on the backs of captive Moslems.

Although Santiago de Compostela itself is not really large, it is so placed in a group of huge buildings that the whole effect is one of immensity, as can be seen by the photograph at right. Its Baroque west front, added in the eighteenth century, is covered with masterful carvings, and its combination of grayish-brown granite and gold-flecked lichen imbues the cathedral with a somewhat dreamlike air.

250

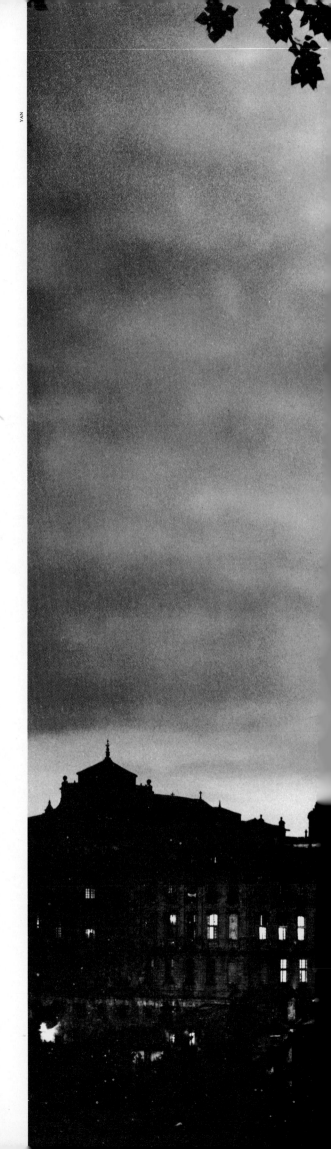

The apostle James, the cathedral's patron saint, stands under an open arch in the gable (left) of the Churrigueresque west front. The entire façade (below) was designed by the eighteenth-century architect Fernando Casas y Nóvoa, although the double stairway leading to the central portal was built in 1606. The cathedral's Romanesque nave (bottom left) is more than three hundred feet long and houses a spectacular Baroque double organ (half of which is shown on the page opposite) attributed to Miguel de Romay (1705–12).

ALL: YAN

OPPOSITE: *Four of a group of twenty-four twelfth-century
granite figures of the prophets that decorate the*
Puerta Santa *on the cathedral's east transept are shown at
top left. The three seated musicians at bottom left
are from the west front's* Pórtico de la Gloria, *the work of
the sculptor Mateo (1168–1217). The figure of Christ in Majesty
is from the twelfth-century* Puerta de la Platerias.
*Also from the same portal is the relief sculpture of Abraham
leaving the sepulcher (below), the work of artists imported
from Toulouse. The column at right—part of the* trumeau
of the Pórtico de la Gloria—*represents a portion
of the tree of Jesse with the Virgin at the top.*

The goal of the Great Pilgrimage: the reliquary containing the remains of Saint James and his disciples, Saint Theodore and Saint Athanasius.

TO BE A PILGRIM

A Santiago Portfolio

"In a wide sense . . . whoever is outside his fatherland is a pilgrim; whereas in the narrow sense, none is called a pilgrim save he who is journeying towards the sanctuary of St. James of Compostela or is returning therefrom." Even though Dante in his *Vita Nuova* first universally defined the word, for centuries men had esteemed the fundamentals of the old French *pèlerinage*—that a journey to a sacred spot could bring the devotee some supernatural benefit or dispensation. Next to building a church, the best way to get to heaven was to go on a pilgrimage, and toward this end men streamed in swelling multitudes to Palestine and Rome. In the ninth century, with the announcement of the miraculous discovery in northern Spain of the tomb of Saint James, a new pilgrimage was born.

The pilgrimage to Santiago had certain advantages. For some travelers, the shrine's relative inaccessibility generated excitement and romance, further kindled by the *chansons de geste*, while the hardships endured in crossing the rugged terrain were rewarded by greater spiritual favor. Furthermore, Saint James had a particularly winning quality—given time, it was said, he answered every prayer.

By the eleventh century the throngs of people who wished, in the words of the Venerable Bede, "to live as pilgrims on earth that they might be welcomed by the saints when they were called away from their earthly sojourn" clogged the highways and were likened to the stars of the Milky Way, Dante's "white circle which the common people call, Way of St. James."

Spiritual rewards, acts of penance, proofs of devotion, and insurance against famine and plague were not the only reasons for a pilgrimage. For some it was a papal command; for others a personal pledge to the saint in exchange for a favor; and for still others it was a chance to seek new work, transport their goods to a distant town, visit new lands, or enjoy a holiday. And many, if asked, might have answered in Montaigne's words: "I know well what I am fleeing from but not what I am in search of."

Special privileges afforded pilgrims also contributed to their swelling ranks. Once he had attained the sacred badge of his shrine, the pilgrim was above all law but that of the church. During his trip he was exempt from taxes, debts, arrest, or confiscation of his property, and often was honored and entertained, the belief being that anyone aiding a pilgrim shared in his grace.

In the number of notables who journeyed there, the cathedral at Santiago outdid all other shrines. William, duke of Aquitaine, arrived in 1137, perhaps to atone for the evils committed in his Normandy campaign; Bishop Nicholas Cambrai in 1153, to be cured of illness; and King Louis VII in 1154, for the slightly less-than-pious purpose of inquiring about his wife's alleged illegitimacy. John of Gaunt's intention in 1386 was to seize the crown of Castile, and in 1488 Ferdinand and Isabella prayed before the saint's tomb (left) for the deliverance of Spain from the Moors.

The effects of the pilgrimage route cannot be overestimated. Markets bustled, building and shipping industries boomed, churches throve, and customs, songs, and tales were exchanged. Souvenirs and art objects carried by the pilgrims helped to spread artistic styles from country to country, and the necessity of accommodating huge crowds of pilgrims gave rise to a series of new churches along the route from southern France to Santiago and impetus to the southward spread of France's Gothic architecture.

DR. HELLMUT HELL

He was the "most worthy and holy Apostle, radiant, gold-glittering leader of Spain, our powerful protector and our own most special patron saint" to Saint Beatus of Asturias in the eighth century. Earlier, Saint Isidore of Seville and Saint Julian of Toledo, however, had scarcely thought of Saint James one way or another, since in their time there was little reason to assume that the apostle had ever been to Spain. Seizing upon a possible scribal error in a list of apostles' mission fields, Beatus identified the saint with Spain instead of Jerusalem (*Hispaniam* rather than *Hierusalem*) and thus labeled Spain in his own *Apocalypse* as "St. James Country." A theologian known to the courts of Europe, Beatus was in a good position to promulgate his views. Europeans, avid for new miracles, pounced upon his theory and were therefore emotionally and spiritually ready for the dramatic announcement of the discovery of the apostle's tomb in 813 at Iria Flavia.

To refuse other ecclesiastical claims to the relics of Saint James, the word went out from Santiago that the tomb's miraculous immovability had necessitated the building of a cathedral directly above it. The apostle, who is shown at left in the illumination from the *Codex Calixtinus* (or, *Liber Sancti Jacobi*), became world-renowned and later was often depicted in pilgrim's attire.

Although masses flocked to his shrine, not everyone was caught up in the mania. A celebrated thirteenth-century preacher, Berthold of Ratisbon, reminded his flock that Saint James was in heaven, not Galicia, and asked therefore what the point was of traveling all the way to Santiago to see some remains. After visiting the cathedral, where he had gone "to see and know of many things," Andrew Boorde, a sixteenth-century English physician, announced that "there is not one hair nor one bone" of Saint James in Santiago. There were also those who believed that, bones or no bones, a pilgrimage was foolish. It was William Thorpe's assertion in the fifteenth century that "such persons . . . do that which is in direct disobedience to the commands of God, inasmuch as they waste their goods partly upon innkeepers, many of whom are women of profligate conduct, partly upon rich priests, who have already more than they need." The archbishop was not amused by Thorpe's indictment and responded, "Ungracious lousel! Thou favourest no more truth than a hound." Although many agreed with Andrew Boorde when he said, "I had rather go five times to Rome oute of England, than one to Compostella: . . . by land it is the greatest iurney that one Englyshman may go," they still braved every obstacle to visit the apostle's shrine.

Whether or not the relics were really those of Saint James, the wisest comment about the pilgrimage to Santiago was probably made by the German Jerome Münzer, who concluded after his visit to the shrine in 1494: "We believe in only one thing, that which saves us man."

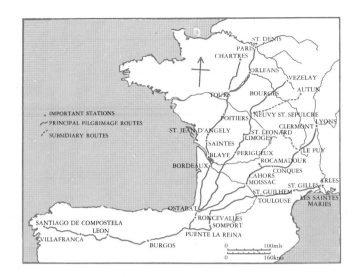

There were four main pilgrimage routes across France, the choice of one over others usually depending on the shrines one desired to visit along the way. The better traveled the road, the better the accommodations, but once across the Spanish border there was only one road to Santiago, mountainous and rugged, where pilgrims faced not only the terrors of a country not yet free from the Moors, but also rugged terrain, illness, and bandits.

Not the least problem for the pilgrim entering Spain was the country's tainted water, so foul that a twelfth-century guide called it instantly fatal—as it later proved to the nine companions of Andrew Boorde, who recorded that his friends "dyed, all by eatynge of frutes and drynkynge of water, the which I dyd ever refrayne my selfe."

Although he was probably more interested in commerce and military pursuits than in the plight of the pilgrim, Sancho the Great of Navarre improved the way as far as Burgos when in the eleventh century he established the *Camino Francés*, the famous road to León and Galicia.

A pilgrimage usually took about a year. Written guide-books advised with questionable accuracy the length of a day's journey and what to carry along. For the Englishman William Wey in 1456, the latter included a barrel of water and "a lytel cawdron and fryying pan, dyshes, cuppys and such nessaryes," but for one Aymery Picaud the mere mention of specific saints elicited "nessaryes" along the way. The returning pilgrim was known by a badge emblematic of a certain shrine. In *Piers Plowman*, an inventory of accoutrements includes "a bowl and bag . . . and on his hat . . . scallop-shells of Spain." Similarly, the shells sewed on their hats identify returning pilgrims in the drawing at right by the sixteenth-century artist Lucas van Leyden. One *departing* pilgrim, Sir Walter Raleigh, also asked for "my scallop-shell of quiet,/My staff of faith to walk upon,/My scrip of joy, immortal diet,/My bottle of salvation,/My gown of glory, hope's true gage. . . ." Having itemized the necessities for *his* journey, the Elizabethan courtier-poet (whose life was not one of uninterrupted piety) was ready to go: "And thus I'll take my pilgrimage."

A pilgrimage to Santiago was also regarded by some as a crusade against the Infidel, and foreign knights, like those shown in the twelfth-century fresco detail below at left, flocked to Spain. The crusaders sometimes inflicted more punishment on themselves than they did on the Moors (who were not much of a threat in northern Spain anyway). John of Gaunt and his knights, for example, arrived in Santiago in 1386 and immediately made for the cathedral, where they were treated royally. Too royally perhaps: Jean Froissart in his *Chronicles* reported that "they founde there flesshe and strong wyne . . . whereof the Englysshe archers dranke so moche that they were ofte tymes dronken . . . they coulde not helpe themselves . . . after."

The miles traversed in pious pursuits were many. With pilgrimage a tradition in her family, Saint Brigid (left) set out in 1341 with her husband and a Cistercian monk and traveled the enormous distance from Sweden to Santiago de Compostela. Many preferred the sea route from England, and the carrying of pilgrims to Spain became a thriving business. Provided the pilgrims first swore "not to take anything prejudicial to England, nor to reveal any of its secrets, nor carry out with them any more gold or silver than what would be sufficient for their reasonable expense," licenses for their transport were granted in 1429 by King Henry VI.

Accommodations were limited and cramped, but for one passenger, Earl Rivers, known as Lord Anthony and most likely a strong-stomached soul, the time on board proved advantageous. To while away the hours he read in French the *Dictes and Sayings of the Philosophers*, and his translation made in 1477 became the first book to be printed in England. Of the sea voyage an anonymous fifteenth-century rhymster wrote, "Men may leave all games,/that sail to St. James!/For many a man it gramys [grieves]/When they begin to sail/. . . For when that we shall go to bed,/the pump is nigh to our bed's head;/A man were as good as to be dead/As smell thereof the stink!"

It is no wonder that many of the pious entrusted their pilgrimages to others, often delegating them posthumously to their heirs. In the drawing below, the earl of Warwick sets out on a sea pilgrimage to Spain in 1475.

The medieval traveler faced daily the chance that he might be not only cheated but attacked, robbed, and even murdered. A major threat in the western Pyrenees was the pass of Puerto de Cisa to the north of Roncevalles (see map, page 259) where bands of Basques were known to lie in wait for pilgrim prey. Below, a miniature from the *Codex Aureus* (*The Gospel of Henry* III) depicts the danger of the roads in illustrating the parable of the Good Samaritan.

A traveler of whom it could be said that he was less than enchanted with his Spanish sojourn was Arnold von Harff (right), a twenty-five-year-old German aristocrat who visited Santiago in the course of a long pilgrimage between 1496 and 1499. For the benefit of future pilgrims, von Harff detailed his experiences. "From Ortes there is no good inn for you and your horse until St. James," he advised. "You will find neither oats, hay or straw for your horse.

You must sleep on the ground and eat barley." The situation apparently did not improve between Ortes and Salva terra, for at that stop he emphasized, "You must pay [duty] for each piece of gold . . . under your sworn oath, or you are searched, and if they find that you have more, you are in danger of life and goods." His impressions were no more favorable when he reached the small town of Fromeste, where "The inns are bad. Whatever you want to eat and drink you have to buy on the roads," or on the return trip from Santiago when, near León, two of his friends were killed by highwaymen from whom he himself only narrowly escaped. Von Harff's opinions concluded with "*Summa Summarum* . . . Spain is an evil country."

Another celebrated visitor to the shrine at Santiago was Francis of Assisi, the thirteenth-century saint and poet, known for his joyous spirit, humility, and concern for the poor, shown receiving the stigmata in van Leyden's painting below.

Along his route Francis befriended many *Juglares*, minstrels of the common people, with whom he closely identified. Music, he said, aided prayer, and he termed his traveling friends *Joculatores Domini*, minstrels of the Lord, who united people in love and friendship as they journeyed from town to town chanting "*Buon giorno, buona gente.*"

"'Tis the belly's call compels these men to be travelers, always wiping off their sweat with the straw of a stranger's bed," wrote an anonymous eighth-century author. No matter what his pious intention or anticipated spiritual reward, the pilgrim clearly expected to have a good time along the way. "Every man in his wise made herty chere," wrote Chaucer of his Canterbury pilgrims, "Telling his fellows of sportes and of cheer,/And of mirthes that fallen by the waye,/as custom is of prilgrims,/and hath been many a daye." Good cheer (and one overindulgent pilgrim fallen by the way) is shown below in a detail from a sixteenth-century drawing by Unton Möller.

Upon arrival at their shrines pilgrims sometimes failed to remember the purpose of the trip; Sir Thomas More remarked that "there be cathedral churches into which the country come with procession, and the women following the cross with many an unwomanly song." Travelers of the period often described the chaotic conditions at Santiago, where mobs of unruly pilgrims stumbled over worshipers and fought one another for space near the apostle's tomb. No matter what the discomforts, though, a pilgrimage was usually a happy time. At the end of the journey," wrote J. J. Jusserand, ". . . [one] tasted fully of the pious emotion he had come to seek, the peace of heaven descended into his bosom, and he went away consoled."

Returning to England from Rome in 1151, Henry of Blois, brother of King Stephen as well as the abbot of Glastonbury and bishop of Winchester, altered his itinerary to allow a stop at Santiago. His twofold purpose was to thank Saint James for the absolution Henry had received on his pilgrimage to Rome and to enlist the apostle's aid against troubles he feared would arise at home.

This wealthy landowner and financier, who consecrated Becket archbishop of Canterbury, typifies the tremendous power wielded by church officials, who supposedly viewed all penitents as equal but were decidedly sympathetic to the causes of gold givers. In the rendering, above at right, of an enamel plaque, Henry kneels, holding a reliquary that he may have donated to his own cathedral, but his humble posture clashes with the rim's inscription (not shown) which describes him as "equal to the muses in intellect and greater in eloquence than Marcus" [Cicero].

MME. A. GATACRE-DE STUERS COLLECTION

It was traditional advice that "if ye owe any pilgrimages, pay them hastily," and those who could muster the necessary funds rushed to don pilgrim's garb like that in Brueghel's drawing at left. If funds were not forthcoming, however, all was not lost. In medieval times the tremendous awareness of sin and punishment evoked great sympathy for the penitent from his friends, who considered it their duty to aid his pilgrimage. For this purpose guilds sprang up, and two in England declared the following rule: "If any brother or sister wishes to make a pilgrimage to Rome, St. James of Galicia or the Holy Land, he shall forewarn the guild, and all the brethren and sisters shall go with them to the city gate and each shall give him a halfpenny at least." Not only the pilgrim's friends but also the church and state joined forces for his protection. Laws laid down in the twelfth century threatened excommunication to anyone accused of cheating, attacking, or robbing a pilgrim; toll fees were abolished; guide service was made available; and a charitable system of shelters and hospitals developed where the voyager could receive free benefits ranging from a haircut or shoe repair to qualified assistance with his will.

Although much of their time and energy was spent on the adornment of churches, guilds such as the Brotherhood of St. James and St. James' at Ghent did much to improve the pilgrim's welfare, and by the fourteenth century the average traveler to the shrine at Santiago de Compostela carried for his protection as many passes, licenses, and letters of recommendation as a modern American tourist carries.

With the huge traveling groups of royalty, clergy, and citizens, rich and poor, went also professional minstrels, wastrels, beggars, debtors, and even some hunted criminals, all of whom shared in the benefits if not the blessings. On the strength of numerous accumulated badges and the sanctity represented thereby, beggars received alms from the devout, and in Chaucer's time, retail sellers of indulgences were well-known ecclesiastical officials called pardoners: "But of his craft, from Berwick unto Ware,/Ne was there such another pardonere,/For in his mail he had a pillowbere,/Which, as he saide, was our Lady's veil/He said, he had a gobbet of the sail/That Saint Peter had . . ./A cross of laton full of stones."

Pilgrimage became so popular that almost any cause was sufficient for departure. Peter the Hermit, it is said, went to escape matrimony, and Louis VII, scarcely home from a pilgrimage of thanks after shedding a bad wife, immediately set out on another in gratitude for getting a good one.

The pilgrimage to Santiago de Compostela had a universal effect on men of the medieval world. As far away as Germany, a fresco from Uberlingen (right) depicted the parents of a redeemed youth giving thanks to Saint James.

Toledo

GLITTER AND GOLD

264

"Never was there an ancient queen, not even Cleopatra who drank pearls, nor a Venetian courtesan of the time of Titian, who ever had a more glittering jewelbox or a richer trousseau than Our Lady of Toledo." Preserved as national monuments, both the city—dating from pre-Roman times and formerly the capital of the wealthy Spanish Empire—and its art-laden cathedral still retain the richness described above by the nineteenth-century French author, Théophile Gautier.

Although legendarily constructed during the lifetime of the Virgin herself, the first church on the site can be more realistically traced to the year 587 when King Reccared, by his public conversion to Catholicism, altered the course of Spanish history and made Toledo one of the first Spanish cities to embrace Christianity.

During nearly four hundred years of Moorish rule, both the church and the state adopted their conquerors' ways: Spanish and Jewish inhabitants—called "Mozarabs"—adopted Arab customs, and the church, modified, served as the principal mosque. As a condition of Moorish surrender in 1085, Alfonso VI, when he reclaimed Toledo, granted the Arabs permission to carry on worship in the mosque, a promise quickly broken by his wife and Toledo's archbishop during the king's untimely absence from the city. Alfonso's threat to avenge this insult to his royal pledge by burning wife and archbishop was averted only by the Moslems' offer to relinquish the mosque, which was razed in 1227 when the new cathedral was begun.

Previously too preoccupied with internal problems to concentrate on the building of cathedrals, the Spaniards made up for lost time at Toledo by importing hoards of workmen from Germany, Italy, Flanders, and France—a circumstance that accounts for the incongruity of architectural styles in which the cathedral was constructed. Although it was begun in pure Gothic by "Petrus Petri," probably a Frenchman, the massive building was subjected to additions and alterations over a period of nearly six centuries, during which time it benefited from donations of jewels, relics, and priceless paintings, as well as the first gold brought from America by Columbus.

Asymmetrical, wide, and squat, the exterior of Toledo (which is shown in the nineteenth-century engraving at left) is dominated by a unique 300-foot, three-storied tower that supports the 17-ton *Campana gorda* (big-bellied bell) for which the city is famous and under which, it is said, fifteen shoemakers could work without touching one another. According to legend, Saint Peter (who had died centuries before the bell was installed) flew into a jealous and most unsaintly rage upon discovering it to be larger than his own bell at the Vatican in Rome and hurled his symbolic keys at the *gorda*, causing the crack which still can be seen.

Although the cathedral may be entered by any one of eight doors, the most celebrated entrance is the *Puerta del Perdón*, whose steps for centuries have been ascended and descended by Toledo's pregnant women to ensure easy childbirth.

In the late fifteenth century, the Cathedral of Toledo was the site of a splendid procession honoring King Ferdinand of Aragon and his queen, Isabella of Castile. "Dignitaries of the Church," wrote a contemporary chronicler of the impressive rite, "the archbishop . . . the canons and the clergy, in their pontifical garments, preceded by the Cross, came forth from the Puerta del Perdón to receive them."

One of the most richly furnished churches in the world, Toledo Cathedral long has been the target of plunderers. The cathedral was looted in 1521 during a citizens' uprising against Charles V and again by the French in 1808 during Napoleon's Peninsular War. More treasures were lost in 1936 during the Spanish Civil War; most of the latter, however, were subsequently recovered. Three of the cathedral's finest works of art are reproduced here: Alonso Berruguete's sixteenth-century figure of John the Baptist (opposite); one of a series of fifty-four late fifteenth-century reliefs (below) by Rodrigo Alemán, illustrating the conquest of Granada; and a thirteenth-century Madonna and Child (right).

YAN

SKIRA

267

OVERLEAF: *The cathedral's spire dominates the city.*
EVELYN HOFER

MILAN
ST. MARK'S
PARMA
LUCCA
PISA
FLORENCE
SIENA
ORVIETO
ROME
MONREALE
CEFALU

ITALY

"Your dragging of stones is well deserved. Pull, you villains!" Thus reads an eleventh-century Italian inscription that sheds considerable light on medieval Italy's apparently inexhaustible capacity for cathedral building. Cheap (even unpaid) labor was always available, and this factor, along with immense community pride, fierce intercity rivalries like the one between Orvieto (below) and Siena, and a native genius for stonework, led almost every Italian town worthy of the name to put up the most splendid churches that its resources could provide. Unlike France and England, Italy developed no single dominant style, and little in medieval Italian architecture approaches the purity achieved elsewhere. Instead, Byzantine, Saracen, Romanesque, Norman, and Gothic influences combined and fused to produce cathedrals like sets from an enchanted theatre.

Monreale

SICILIAN VESPERS

The brief glory of the Norman rule in Sicily was largely the result of the Norman genius for assimilation. In southern Italy and Sicily, as well as in England and France, Norman rulers showed what one historian has called "the Norman talent of conciliating the native elements." Religious freedom was guaranteed not only to Greek Christians but also to Moslems and Jews, local rights and customs were respected, and Byzantine and Arabic offices and officials were retained. This conciliatory tendency obtained in architectural matters as well, and the Cathedral of Monreale, seen in the aerial view below, is one of many testaments to it. Scholars may argue whether the designers and workmen were Sicilians or imported specialists, but certainly Monreale represents a fusion of diverse styles: The plan is early Christian and quasi-Byzantine, the ceiling and the exterior are decorated in the Arabic manner, and the interior is covered with glittering Byzantine mosaics. The cathedral, begun in 1174 by William II, was substantially complete by 1182. This haste doubtless accounts for the uncommon aesthetic unity of the cathedral, for, although many styles were employed, the accord between sculpture and decoration is so complete that one scholar has concluded that the architecture was designed as a framework for the mosaics. These mosaics, which have been called "the swan song of the Norman era," far surpass in quantity (if not always in quality) the mosaics of earlier Norman churches in Sicily, including the Royal Chapel in Palermo, which served as their iconographic model. There is evidence that in building Monreale and its cloister (two capitals of which are shown at right), William was trying to outdo, or at least to rival for prestige, the cathedral of his grandfather, Roger II, at Cefalù and to fulfill that monarch's dream to build a burial church quite literally fit for a king.

No art—either Greek or
Byzantine, Italian, or Arab—has ever created
two religious types so beautiful, so
serious, so impressive, and yet so different,
as Mont-Saint-Michel watching over
its northern ocean, and Monreale, looking
down over its forests of orange and
lemon, on Palermo and the Sicilian seas.
—Henry Adams

An astonishing variety of themes
is represented in the more than two hundred
stone columns in the cloister (opposite) of
Monreale. Scenes from the life of Christ are
juxtaposed with key episodes in the lives
of the Norman princes, and with biblical motifs,
grotesques, stylized classical devices, and forms
derived from nature. The columns (below
and bottom right) are also decorated
with Arabic zigzags and Byzantine reliefs.
After the death of William II, the cloister was
finished by Benedictine monks, who called
in sculptors from every part of Sicily and allowed
them complete artistic freedom.

OVERLEAF: Mosaics in the cathedral's interior
depict Rebecca's journey to Canaan (left) and
Esau hunting game to earn his father's blessing (right),
while Jacob and Rebecca scheme against him.

SCALA

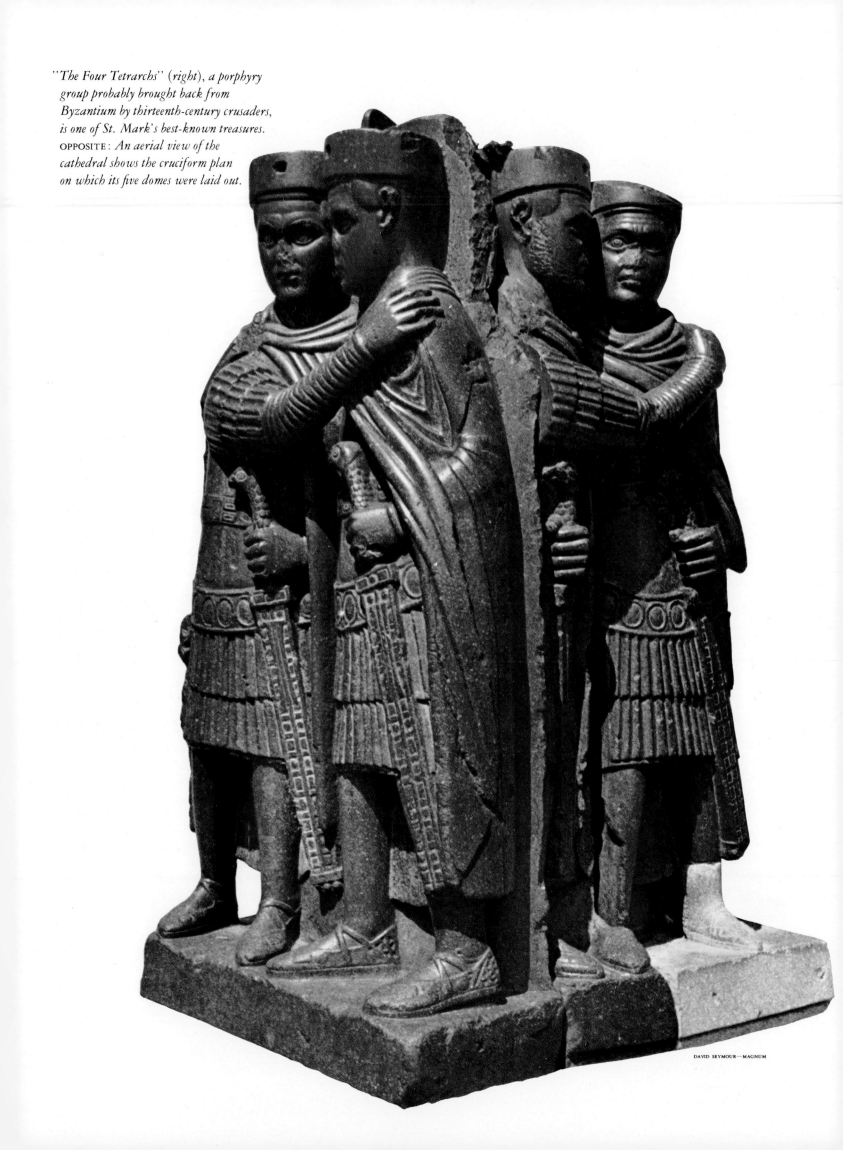

"The Four Tetrarchs" (right), *a porphyry
group probably brought back from
Byzantium by thirteenth-century crusaders,
is one of St. Mark's best-known treasures.*
OPPOSITE: *An aerial view of the
cathedral shows the cruciform plan
on which its five domes were laid out.*

St. Mark's has always inspired artists, from the anonymous painter of the fourteenth-century miniature at left to the masters of modern art. Antonio Canaletto (1697–1768), whose view of St. Mark's appears at center below, was a native Venetian; but J. M. W. Turner, who in 1836 painted the church into the background of his Juliet and Her Nurse (*right*), was an Englishman spellbound with the effects of light on the city's canals and buildings. Francesco Guardi (1712–93), another native, painted the interior shown below, and the American James A. Whistler executed the atmospheric view at bottom right around 1880.

OSVALDO BOHM

Successive crews of mosaicists devoted almost the entire thirteenth century to the depiction, in the atrium of St. Mark's, of Old Testament episodes. These begin with the Creation and end with Moses leading the children of Israel through the wilderness. The details from this great work shown here portray one of the Angels (left) who witnessed the Creation, several of the beasts created by God on the sixth day (below left), and the creation of Adam (below right). The cycle of the Creation appears in its entirety opposite.

ALINARI

OSVALDO BOHM

Cefalù

AMBITION
AND THE PRIDE OF KINGS

Mountainous waves were battering the flimsy ship, threatening to capsize it, and a badly frightened would-be king vowed that should he by some miracle reach any part of the Sicilian coast alive, *there* would he build a cathedral for San Salvatore. Somehow the craft limped into the harbor of Cefalù; two years later Roger II, now king of all Sicily and true to his word, laid the foundation stone for his cathedral. Or so the legend goes. As it happens, there are almost as many such legends as there are churches along the seacoasts of southern Europe, and there is no particular reason to think this one more credible than the rest. Roger himself, a second-generation Norman administrator in Sicily, threw little light on the matter, merely remarking with pious ambiguity, "A worthy and reasonable thing it is to build a house for our Lord, and to found a refuge in honor of Him who has so benefited us and has decorated our name with the ornament of Kingship."

Whatever Roger's motivation may have been, seldom has so unprepossessing a community been chosen for so superb a monument. Cefalù was an obscure fishing village in 397 B.C. when history first noted its existence; it was an obscure fishing village in 1129 when Roger's ship arrived there; and it is an obscure fishing village today. Its cathedral nonetheless is an ornament far more dazzling than the ornament of kingship bestowed from on high upon its founder.

Roger built his church on a site first occupied by a pagan temple and later, during the Saracen occupation, by a mosque. Whether he was really giving thanks to God or to God's vicar on earth (the pope, it seems, happened to be looking elsewhere while Roger employed questionable means in obtaining his crown), the king spared no expense on the project. The best Saracen and Norman architects were brought to Cefalù for consultation; the finest Byzantine mosaicists were employed on the decoration of the cathedral's interior. The resultant structure is one of the world's great examples of Norman-Arabic architecture, and the enormous mosaic (right) of Christ Pantocrator in its apse is one of the world's most magnificent works of art.

Besides all this, Roger built himself a massive sarcophagus and had it installed in the cathedral. In the next century, however, his successor, the Holy Roman Emperor Frederick II, sent the bishop of Cefalù away on a wild-goose chase and, in his absence, evicted Roger's remains and transferred the coffin to the Cathedral of Palermo, there to await the reception of his own mortal dust. *Sic transit gloria mundi.*

The arches crowning the columns of Cefalù's
nave (below) show the influence of
Arabic architecture, but the carved decorations on
the capitals are the work of Sicilian artists.
The nave has three aisles that terminate at the
cathedral's east end in three apses, two of
which—the central apse and a smaller one to
the north—are visible in the photograph opposite.

SCALA

Siena

THE IMPOSSIBLE REALIZED

"In the name of the Lord our God, Amen. We, Lorenzo son of the Master Mason Maitano, and Niccola Nuti of Siena, Cino son of Francesco, Tone son of Giovanni, and Vanni son of Cione of Florence, being consulting masons, have been called in consultation by the . . . Guild of Masons of the Cathedral of the Holy Virgin in Siena."

Thus began a committee report submitted early in 1321 to Siena's alarmed city fathers. The committee's chairman, Lorenzo Maitani, was renowned throughout Umbria and his native Tuscany as *capomaestro* of Orvieto and the designer of that city's cathedral façade. He and his colleagues had been summoned to determine what, if anything, could be done to salvage a grandiose project now threatened with imminent collapse. The great enterprise was the enlargement of Siena's cathedral to almost twice its existing size. The threat to its completion was all too apparent in the gaping fissures that had appeared where the old and new walls joined. The committee presented a splendidly reasoned paper on the project's structural and aesthetic defects and advised immediate demolition of the edifice before its buckling foundations gave way altogether. The advice was ignored.

Late medieval Siena was a prosperous republic, proud of its magnificent school of painters, contentious in its rivalry with Florence, Orvieto, and Pisa, and unique in its determination to impose unity and order on its own processes of physical growth. The Sienese visualized their earth-red city as a single, balanced, wondrous work of art, an unprecedented exercise in city planning that altogether or in its component parts would have no parallel anywhere. Their cathedral perforce would have to outdo the great *duomo* then under construction at Florence, the white marble cathedral at Pisa, and the superb limestone and basalt cathedral at Orvieto. Siena's own Tuscan Gothic cathedral, which straddled a hilltop site once occupied by a temple of Minerva, was conceded to be a fine piece of architecture, but it was not of sufficient grandeur to satisfy the ambitions of the Sienese. An audacious plan was therefore adopted in 1316: The original façade and dome would be retained, but the chancel would be lengthened enormously to extend over a steep slope in an acrobatic arrangement supported only by the Baptistery of San Giovanni at the foot of the hill. Inevitably, the stunt was something like trying to train a goat to carry an elephant, but the Sienese pressed on despite Maitani's advice on the manifest folly of continuing. Indeed, by 1339 the city authorities were toying with the idea of expanding the scheme even further: Everything then under construction would become merely the choir and transepts for a cathedral of stupefying proportions. This notion was dropped when the Black Death struck in 1348.

Faith has been called an illogical belief in the occurrence of the improbable. Perhaps faith alone has enabled Siena's superbly misproportioned cathedral (right) to defy the laws of gravity for six centuries.

In 1266 Nicolo Pisano, who had just completed
a magnificent pulpit for the cathedral at
Pisa, was summoned to Siena, where he designed an
even more elaborate pulpit (left) with an
octagonal parapet. A century later Mino del
Pellicciaio submitted the design above for
the façade of Siena's Baptistery of
San Giovanni. Only the lower half of Mino's
design was executed, however.

*Siena was known in the Middle Ages as the City of
the Virgin. In the miniature above, which
embellishes the cover of a fifteenth-century account
book, Siena's magistrates present the city's
keys to the Madonna, before the high altar of the
cathedral. The cathedral's nave, with its black-and-
white marble pillars, joined by round
arches, is shown in the photograph opposite.*

A Baroque engraving depicts Christ's Coronation of the Virgin—the Heavenly Queen—as cherubim and a dove look on.

SAINTS ABOVE

A Portfolio of Cathedral Protectors

The cult of the saints (those souls residing in heaven, often after martyrdom) was defined in an early Christian manuscript: "We worship Christ, as the Son of God; as to the martyrs, we love them as the disciples and imitators of the Lord"; and it spread rapidly, until in 787 the Second Council of Nicaea decreed that no church that did not contain some relic should be consecrated. Cathedrals named patron saints, pilgrims flocked to their shrines, and for a particular favor, an individual could choose from a wide variety of saints, some of whom appear on the following pages.

By the eleventh century, the monastic asceticism and misogynist traditions that had previously regarded woman as an evil temptress began to give way to new ideals of chivalry and courtly love. At the same time men, increasingly obsessed by the theme of the Last Judgment and the terrors of hell, were dominated by the need for salvation. Fear and awe of God precluded a small man's asking His favor directly, but with the rebirth of respect for Woman, why not approach God through the greatest woman of them all, His mother? The cult of the Virgin was born.

Based on man's instinct for self-preservation, the cult flourished upon his belief that, unlike the Trinity, terrifying and intolerant of human frailty, Mary, the universal Mother, represented Love and would protect and forgive her children. The guardian of farmers, knights, sailors, and women in childbirth, she considered sin a normal human condition and, trampling on convention, absolved the sins of those who appealed to her.

Architectural styles accommodated her whims; her feminine preference for light and color was answered by Gothic raised vaults and windows; she was accorded privacy in her Lady Chapels, interior space for her devotees, and statuary for her pleasure. Feast days, even some of those formerly ascribed to others, were set aside in her honor; the months of August in the East and May in the West were dedicated to her; and untold sums of money were spent on her adulation, the conviction being that money deposited with the Queen of Heaven in this life would be repaid with interest in the next. With the exception of Christ Himself, no other figure was more often portrayed in art and sculpture, and so many cathedrals were named for the Virgin that "Notre Dame," like "Kleenex," became something very like a generic term. Belief in the Madonna's presence inspired masons at Chartres, a "toyhouse" in Henry Adam's opinion, "to please the Queen of Heaven—to please her so much that she would be happy in it— to charm her till she smiled."

By the thirteenth century, the Virgin was regarded not only as the Mother of God but as the very personification of the church. The humble servant of the Lord had eclipsed her son. "God changed sex," wrote the romantic historian Jules Michelet. But it was a prior and poet of the times, Gaultier de Coincy, who perhaps best captured the full extent of the medieval cult of the Virgin: "In heaven and earth she makes more laws/ By far, than God Himself can do,/ . . . There's nothing she can do or say/ That He'll refuse, or say her nay./ Whatever she may want is right,/ Though she say that black is white,/ And dirty water clear as snow:/ My Mother says it and it's so!"

297

SAINT MARK

To avoid entering the Jewish rabbinate, Saint Mark cut off his thumb. After his conversion, however, he mastered writing implements sufficiently to become Saint Peter's secretary and dutifully recorded the Gospel as dictated. Once while shipwrecked on a mission to the Adriatic, an angel consoled, "On this site a great city will arise in your honor." When Venice was founded four centuries later by refugees fleeing the Huns, Saint Mark became the patron of the city as well as of its cathedral. A guardian of glass-makers and basket weavers, Saint Mark was also made the patron of scribes, as shown at left with his emblem, a lion.

SAINT ANDREW

Saint Andrew, among the first to receive an apostolic calling, was little known for his earthly exploits, which were largely eclipsed by those of his brother Saint Peter. After evangelizing as far as Russia, Andrew ventured to Greece and proved so popular there that the Roman governor decided to eliminate the apostle. Unlike the ordinary Latin cross used in Peter's crucifixion, Andrew met his martyrdom upon an X-shaped cross, illustrated below. His bones were brought to Amalfi Cathedral in 1210. According to believers, they secrete a curative oil.

SAINT MATTHEW

When Levi the tax collector became Matthew the Apostle, the other disciples in the Apostolic College would not trust the former publican to be their treasurer. Matthew thereupon wrote a Gospel and carried it to Ethiopia, Egypt, Persia, and India—whence the turban in the engraving below, where an angel supplies the saint with ink and inspiration. According to conflicting reports, Matthew died by decapitation, stoning, or being burnt alive. The recovered remains were eventually brought to the cathedral at Salerno, which city, appropriately enough, soon became known as the "city of Saint Matthew."

SAINT PETER

Heeding Jesus' exhortation, "Follow me, and I will make you fishers of men," Saint Peter and his brother Saint Andrew left the shores of Galilee to preach the Saviour's word. Saint Peter (whose name literally means "rock") was also told that he was the living foundation of the church, and he was promised the keys to heaven. Jailed in Jerusalem for performing such miracles as curing the maimed with his shadow and resurrecting the dead, Peter was finally rescued by an angel who removed his chains and illuminated the way for the nocturnal escape, shown at right. After establishing the Christian community in Rome, he was condemned by Nero. So as not to belittle Jesus' demise, Peter elected to lie upside down on the cross. In 336, his remains were interred in the Vatican.

SAINT AGATHA

In third-century Sicily, a comely Christian maiden named Agatha resisted the governor's advances by swearing that Christ alone was her "Heavenly Bridegroom." Although Saint Agatha's virginity remained intact, as a result of this rebuff her breasts were removed, as shown below, and she was condemned to perish by fire. Saint Peter, however, gently salved the distressed damsel's wounds, and an

earthquake heaved her out of the fire's reach. Years after Agatha's death, when her veil miraculously prevented Mount Etna from spewing molten lava over Catania, the saint became the city's patroness, and a chapel in her honor was added to the cathedral. Wet nurses understandably enlisted Agatha's aid, and she was invoked to cure breast cancer and prevent volcanic eruptions and fires. She is also protector of bell makers, supposedly because a bell's shape is evocative of a severed breast.

SAINT MARTIN

Fortunatus, the sixth-century Latin poet, wrote of France's most popular saint, "Wherever Christ is known, Martin is honored." Sainthood came relatively cheaply to Saint Martin, who neither suffered martyrdom nor performed miracles to win Christ's affection, but merely shared his cloak on a wintry night with a beggar, as shown in the equestrian scene below. One miracle attributed to Martin was his conversion of water to wine, a feat which may have particularly endeared him to the wine-loving Italians who erected the Cathedral of Lucca in his memory.

SAINT GEORGE

Although a third-century tribune hardly had shining armor or a garter inscribed with the motto, "*Honi soit qui mal y pense*," as depicted at left, Saint George astride his white charger still managed to cut a gallant caper by saying a prayer, rescuing a princess from a dragon's clutches, and dealing a mortal blow to the monster. Yearning for the return of such chivalrous saints, William Wordsworth wrote: "Let not your radiant shapes desert the land!/ . . . thou St. George, whose flaming brand/ The Dragon quell'd." In his later years, Saint George fared less fortunately. After defying Diocletian by proselytizing in Palestine, George finally gave up the ghost after being branded with red-hot irons, stuck with thorns, force-fed poison, dragged through the streets by a horse, and decapitated. This undignified martyrdom did not tarnish George's image in Italy, however, where he not only became patron saint of Ferrara's cathedral, but allegedly was able to cure syphilis, leprosy, and plague.

SAINT LAWRENCE

Pope Sixtus II took a fancy to a youth named Lawrence whom he had met in Saragossa, Spain, and paid for his journey to Rome, where the youth became deacon in charge of the Holy Library. After Sixtus was sentenced to death in 258, Lawrence wanted to die alongside his benefactor, but Sixtus advised him to wait three days before joining him and meanwhile to disperse church funds to the needy. When a prefect demanded to see the church treasury, Lawrence pointed to the poor. Enraged at being duped, the prefect ordered that Lawrence be roasted alive on a gridiron with an attendant continually fanning the the coals, as seen below. Lawrence, a rare individual, is supposed to have said, "I am roasted on one side. Now turn me over and eat!" Though he left few relics except several pieces of charred flesh, Genoa Cathedral was dedicated to the saint, who had acquired a large following of librarians, users of fire, and sufferers from lumbago, an ailment that is characterized by a burning sensation.

SAINT JOHN THE BAPTIST

Rugged desert life seemed to agree with John the Baptist, who did not mind the "raiment of camel's hair, and a leathern girdle about his loins" or the fare: "His meat was locusts and wild honey." Preaching baptism as a means of repenting sins, the saint, pictured at right, would duly douse his listeners in the river Jordan. Once in an instance of mistaken identity, John was referred to as Christ, and he humbly explained, "I indeed baptize you with water; but one mightier than I cometh. . . . He shall baptize you with the Holy Ghost and with fire." Beheaded in the year 29 at the whim of Herod's daughter, John's remains were burned much later. Since the growth of a saint's cult depends on the number of his relics or on miraculous performances, and since John could meet neither qualification, the martyr's followers supposedly abetted his cause by rescuing his bones from the furnace. On their worldly travels these relics appeared to possess miraculous regenerative properties. By the late Middle Ages, the church claimed twelve heads (the most coveted relics) and sixty fingers. Baptisteries alongside cathedrals were consecrated to John, as was the cathedral at Turin. The faithful invoked the saint's assistance to cure throat maladies and epilepsy and to prevent suffocation. Carrying a plate decorated with an engraving of Saint John's head was considered an effective antidote for migraine headache.

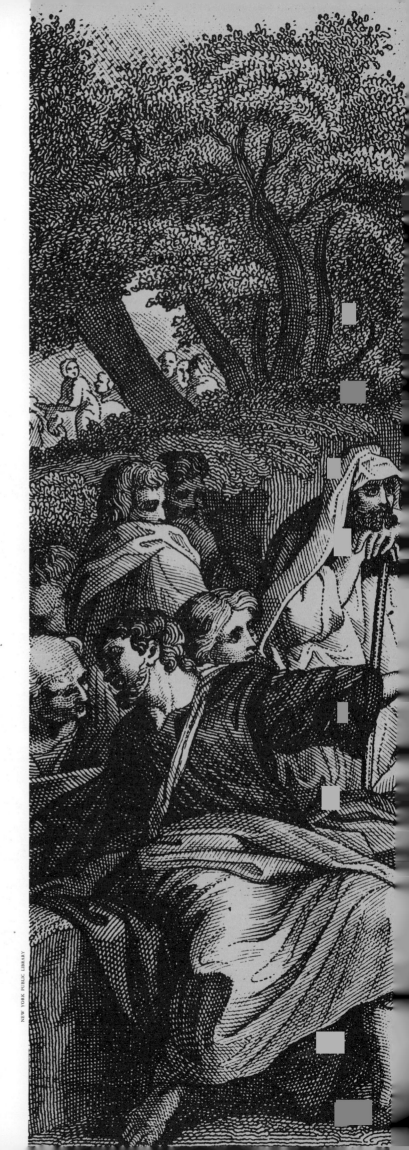

Florence

"A STYLE
OF MAGNIFICENCE"

Much of the history of thirteenth-century Florence is a history of factionalism and bloodshed, of popular revolt, of frequent clashes between the Guelph and Ghibelline parties, and of open warfare with such rival cities as Pistoia, Siena, Pisa, and Arezzo. The closing years of the century, however, were a time of peace, prosperity, and intense creativity. Dante was at work on *The New Life*, Giotto was embarking on his career, and Cimabue and the architect Arnolfo di Cambio were at the height of their powers. By the turn of the century, the city fathers, not to be outdone by the ambitions of Pisa and Siena, projects for whose cathedrals were then under way, issued a typically Florentine proclamation, full of grandiloquence and lofty aspiration: "The Florentine Republic, soaring ever above the conception of the most competent judges, desires that an edifice should be constructed so magnificent . . . that it shall surpass anything of the kind produced in the time of their greatest power by the Greeks and Romans."

The site chosen for the new cathedral was the one occupied by the ancient Church of Santa Reparata, and Arnolfo, *capomaestro* of the commune, was ordered "to make a design . . . in a style of magnificence which neither the industry nor the power of man can surpass."

Arnolfo died after a decade and a half of intermittent work on the new cathedral (during which he completed three bays and a façade); he was followed by a succession of *capomaestri* that included Giotto, Andrea Pisano, Francesco Talenti, and, finally, the first of the great architects of the Renaissance, Filippo Brunelleschi. During the thirteen decades that elapsed between the drawing up of Arnolfo's original designs and Brunelleschi's appointment, the building of the cathedral proceeded piecemeal, with frequent interruptions and incessant controversy. Plans were altered, committees were formed and then dissolved, models were submitted and rejected; even Arnolfo's façade was demolished and eventually replaced by a Gothic front of Talenti's design. In the midst of all this commotion an enclave of burghers lived, procreated, and died in their homes within the cathedral walls until the work had progressed to the point where the encircled buildings had to be razed. Gradually an immense edifice (floor plan at left) emerged from the rubble, and only one problem remained: Not an architect in Italy had the foggiest notion how to construct the cathedral's crowning glory—a dome twice as wide and far higher than Arnolfo's great cupola atop Florence's basilica.

Among the various desperate schemes set forth as possible solutions was one whereby a mountain of earth, liberally spiced with gold coins, was to serve as a supporting mold during the dome's construction and then be removed by a presumably avaricious public. Brunelleschi's own scheme struck many of his contemporaries as no more feasible than any of the previously rejected plans, but the supremely self-confident architect finally sold himself to a somewhat reluctant building commission and was appointed *capomaestro*.

By buttressing the octagonal substructure of the crossing with a series of half-domed apse chapels and creating a kind of external skeleton of eight gracefully curving stone ribs, Brunelleschi at long last carried out the orders given to Arnolfo a century and a half earlier. His majestic dome (opposite), which made all subsequent domes in Europe possible, was indeed built "in a style of magnificence which neither the industry nor the power of man" has ever surpassed.

MUSEO DI S. MARIA DEL FIORE, FLORENCE

*Florence's unfinished façade, shown in
the sixteenth-century drawing at
left, was demolished in 1587 when some
of its sculptural embellishments
were placed inside the cathedral and
others found their way into private
collections. In the bird's-eye view of
the cathedral at bottom left,
Brunelleschi's dome can be seen in the
right foreground; the cathedral's
campanile, begun by Giotto in
1334, continued by Andrea Pisano, and
completed by Francesco Talenti
around 1359, stands beside the main
building's west end.*
OPPOSITE: *Lorenzo Ghiberti's "Gates of Paradise,"
the east doors of Florence's baptistery.
Ghiberti's earlier north doors
resulted from a design competition held in 1402.*

STATO MAGGIORE AERONAUTICA MILITARE ITALIANA, ROME

Orvieto

ALL APPROPRIATE MASTERIES

In 1263 a young, doubt-ridden priest from Bohemia celebrated Mass in the Church of St. Christina at Bolsena, an undistinguished town some 20 miles southwest of the proud city of Orvieto. The youthful celebrant, it seems, was not at all convinced of the validity of the doctrine of Transubstantiation, according to which the Eucharistic bread and wine actually are transformed into the flesh and blood of the Saviour. His doubts, however, were abruptly and spectacularly resolved when blood began spurting from the Host. News of the extraordinary event soon reached Pope Urban IV, who decided to commemorate the miracle by instituting an annual Feast of Corpus Domini and by building a magnificent cathedral—not, to be sure, in little Bolsena, where it rightly belonged, but in Orvieto, which was a favorite haunt of thirteenth-century popes, possibly because of the excellence of the local *vino bianco*.

Work on the cathedral was begun in 1290 under Fra Bevignate, a Benedictine monk who had overseen construction of the celebrated Maggiore Fountain in the allied city of Perugia some years earlier. By 1309, the first roof beam had been raised, at which point the Orvietan authorities began to view the entire project with considerable alarm. Somewhere along the line ambition had outstripped practicality and neither the Romanesque style nor the traditional construction techniques appropriate to it could safely accommodate the vast dimensions of the ground plan or the inordinate height of the nave. The unfinished structure's collapse seemed imminent and so seemed the aspirations of the Orvietans.

At this juncture the Sienese architect Lorenzo Maitani was summoned to Orvieto and appointed *universalis caputmagister*. Almost nothing is known of Lorenzo's activities before 1310, but he must have made quite a name for himself at some point, for he was immediately granted Orvietan citizenship, given the privilege of bearing arms at will, and assured of a lifetime job, not only as *capomaestro* of the cathedral, but also as overseer of bridges and other municipal structures. Besides being beautifully (and safely) roofed over in a more feasible Gothic style, the cathedral, Lorenzo was advised by his new employers, must have a "wall figured with beauty . . . on the front part, and with all the other masteries and ornaments appropriate to this same fabric."

Exactly how much of Orvieto's façade is actually Lorenzo's handiwork and which portions of it can be ascribed to his successors, Andrea Pisano and Andrea Orcagna, are matters of conjecture (Pisano almost certainly was the author of a marble statue of the Virgin, and Maitani of four bronzes symbolizing the Evangelists—one of which, a figure of Matthew, is shown at left); but there is no arguing that the Orvietan city fathers got exactly what they had bargained for. The west façade of the cathedral (right) is indeed a wall figured with beauty and all other appropriate masteries and ornaments. A dazzling encrustation of mosaics, reliefs, bronzes, pillars, stained glass, carved embellishments, and statuary have been subordinated to the overall design in the interests of a transcendent harmony. The complexity—even prolixity—of its parts in no way interferes with the unbroken unity of the whole, and Orvieto's magnificent "wall" seems to stand free of any visible means of support, taking the sunlight like a gigantic, exquisitely wrought altarpiece brought outdoors for an airing.

The Nativity of the Virgin *is depicted in mosaic (right) above one of the doors of the west front. The relief shown below is part of a* Last Judgment *carved by a team of sculptors after* 1310, *in which various saints—male on the left, female on the right—are represented. In the photograph opposite, a statue of Sibyllina Biscossi, a blind orphan who was adopted by Dominican tertiaries, stands outside the north aisle while an elderly worshiper mounts the stairs of the west front of the cathedral.*

OVERLEAF: *Frescoes on the ceiling of the* Cappella Nuova, *depicting the* Apocalypse, *were begun by Fra Angelico in* 1447, *continued by Benozzo Gozzoli, and finished by Luca Signorelli in* 1499.
SCALA

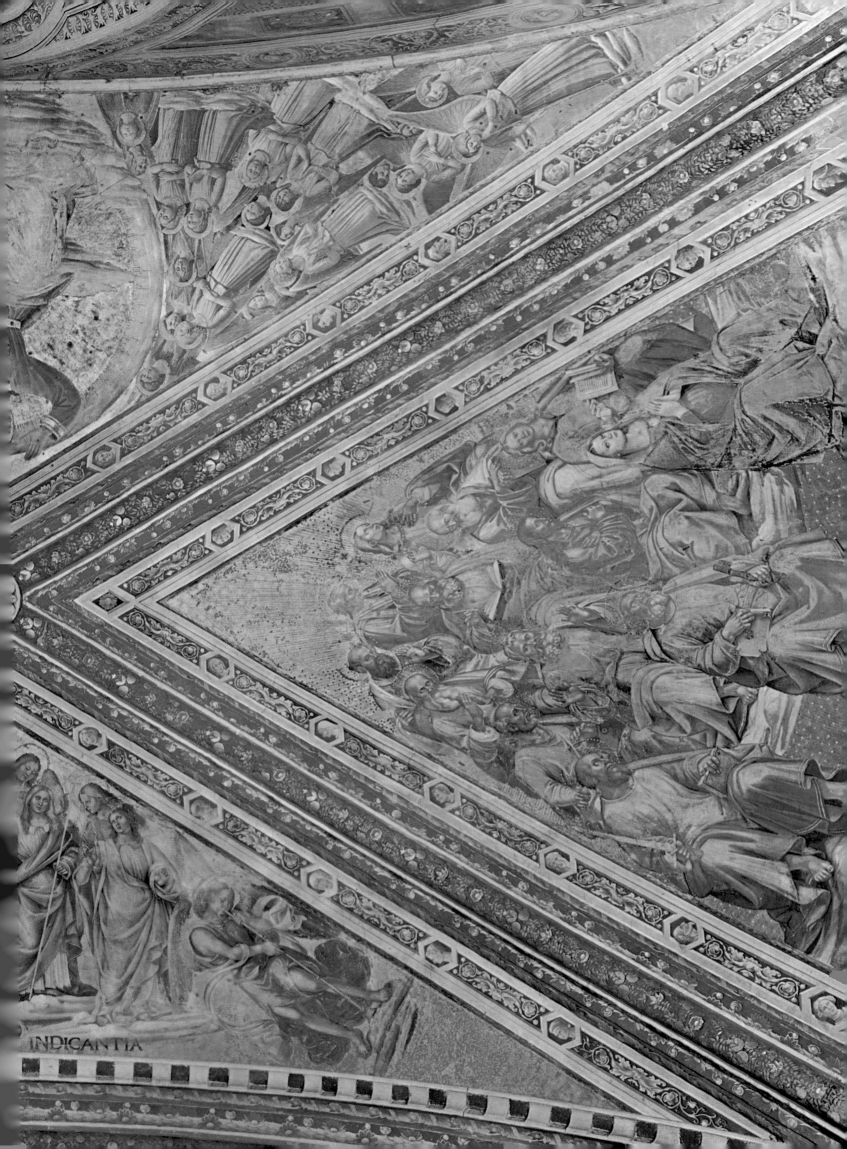

INDICANTIA

Milan

GOTHIC WITHOUT DEATH

"A transparent marble mountain," the nineteenth-century Swiss historian Jacob Burckhardt called it, "hewn from the quarries of Ornavasso and Gandoglia, resplendent by day and fabulous by moonlight." The effect, Burckhardt admitted, could not "be matched elsewhere in the world," but, he lamented, it was *only* an effect, and "he who seeks permanent worth in its forms, and knows *which* designs remained unrealized while with gigantic resources Milan Cathedral was being finished, will not be able to contemplate this building without grief." Earlier, the novelist Stendhal had conceded that the architecture was "brilliant," but he called the cathedral "Gothic minus the idea of death."

The Cathedral of Milan (left), a stone wedding cake whose myriad white marble stalagmites have been described as bristling "as though with a forest of lances," is by far the best illustration of the influence of the northern European Gothic style on Italy. Begun in 1386 and not finished until the era of Napoleon, the cathedral was beset by controversy during the late fourteenth and early fifteenth centuries. The French architect Nicolas de Bonneaventure was brought to Milan to work on it in 1389 and dismissed a year later, to be succeeded by a German, Johann von Freiburg. Freiburg, too, lasted but a year, at which point a native son, Giovanni dei Grassi, was put in charge of the works. Grassi lasted about a month and was supplanted by Gabriele Stornaloco, who was in turn ousted in favor of another German, Heinrich Parler. Parler in his turn gave way to a succession of Flemings and Normans, and finally a Parisian was hired: Jean Mignot, who spent the next few years debating with Milanese architects about the proper procedures for the construction of the cathedral. The disagreement between Mignot and his Italian confreres centered around their conflicting views concerning proportion, with Mignot plumping for an aesthetic ideal while his rivals favored more practical solutions. (Mignot, for example, advised that the gargoyles on the sacristy be raised 5 *braccia* to conform with the dictates of classical mathematics; the Italians countered by pointing out that the gargoyles were *already* spewing water against the windows and that they should—if anything —be lowered.)

Like the cathedrals at Bourges and Paris in France, Milan's is in essence a basilica, consisting of a double-aisled nave, transepts, and a choir and ambulatory. It is a relatively squat edifice, however, and seems even squatter because whatever Gothic verticality it retains is obscured by a wealth of horizontal detail.

If Milan's cathedral lacks the Gothic idea of death, so did Milan itself, one of the liveliest of the flourishing commercial centers of the late Middle Ages. And if its exterior presents us only with an effect, it is an effect that still cannot be matched anywhere in the world.

315

RIGHT: *Gargoyles and other statuary adorn the cathedral's ornate south façade. Inside and out, Milan is decorated with no fewer than 2,245 sculptural figures, not to mention an endless profusion of purely decorative embellishments. The three drawings on these pages show, from left to right, a 1521 transversal section of the cathedral's original design; the interior as it looked to an artist of the nineteenth century; and a cutaway view of the church as seen from the west front.*

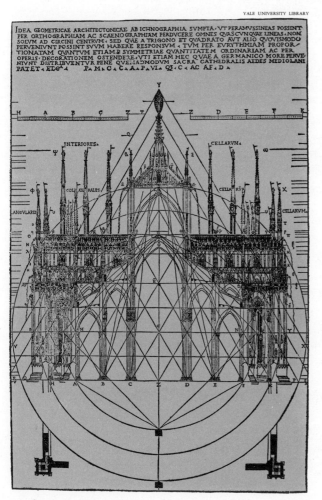

Parma

DELAYS, DISPUTES, AND FROG HASH

Construction of Parma's Santa María Assunta, the largest of all the Lombard Romanesque churches, was begun in 1058 but, because of a series of interruptions caused by an earthquake, the Guelph-Ghibelline wars, and a subsequent ban on the quarrying of marble, the cathedral remained unfinished until around the middle of the thirteenth century; and, although the edifice was substantially rebuilt by 1076, it remained unconsecrated until 1106 because of an extended dispute between Parma's Bishop Cadalo (who was backed by the Parmese) and the pope. Ninety years after the delayed consecration, Benedetto Antelami's baptistery with its splendid Portal of the Virgin (opposite) was begun; when a red brick campanile (to the left of the cathedral's apse in the photograph below) was erected in 1284, a particularly harmonious architectural grouping was at last complete.

In the sixteenth century, the painter Antonio Allegri, known to posterity as Correggio, was commissioned to decorate the interior of Parma's great dome with an *Assumption of the Virgin*. Correggio's extreme foreshortening gave his figures an unusual buoyancy, making them seem almost to force their way from the church walls into the sky, but it also left more limbs than bodies visible from the floor of the crossing below; this circumstance led the Parmese, when the work was finished in 1530, to express their admiration and gratitude by calling it *un guazzetto di rane*, "a hash of frogs," and by paying the artist a much smaller fee than they had originally agreed to pay him.

Besides his relief decoration of the tympanum of
the baptistery portal, Benedetto Antelami
was responsible for a number of other sculptural
works at Parma. In the cathedral's right
transept, for example, there is a superb Descent
from the Cross, *a detail from which,
showing the dead Christ being supported by
Joseph of Arimathea, appears in the photograph
opposite. The figure at right, which
represents September, is one of a series executed
by the sculptor for the interior of the
baptistery—a series that symbolizes the
months and seasons in a free, sinuous style that
influenced such later Italian artists as
Lorenzo Maitani, the designer of Orvieto's façade.*

SADEA/SANSONI EDITORI

Pisa

A PRECARIOUS BALANCE

Elated by their naval victory over the Saracens at Palermo in 1063 and exultant over the rich booty that was theirs as a result of that victory, the inhabitants of the city of Pisa, wrote a contemporary chronicler, "declared with unanimous consent that a splendid temple should be erected, worthy of the Divine Majesty, and also such as to command universal admiration."

In 1153, ninety years after their white marble Romanesque cathedral was begun, the Pisans celebrated another victory—this time over the city of Amalfi—by beginning a circular marble baptistery (right). Unfortunately, their enthusiasm was not matched by funds, and work was suspended until 1278. When the project was resumed, however, it was taken over by the redoubtable architect and sculptor, Nicolo Pisano, who with the help of his son brought the building, with its conical lead-and-tile-covered dome, to completion in a style that complemented that of the cathedral itself.

The third—and best-known—structure in the group, the campanile, was begun in 1172, but its construction, too, was interrupted when the architects became aware that their tower was a bit out of plumb; it had in fact sunk 6 feet into the ground on its south side. When work was resumed sixteen years later, no attempt was made to correct the matter. Instead, the weight of the upper stories was distributed in such a manner as to maintain a precarious equilibrium— much to the delight of future generations of tourists, including Charles Dickens, who called the Leaning Tower, the cathedral, and the baptistery (all three of which are shown in the photograph below) "perhaps the most remarkable and beautiful in the whole world."

JEAN ROUBIER

Giovanni Pisano's elaborate pulpit is shown in the photograph opposite and in a detail below. Pisano was one of the first medieval artists to emerge as a distinct, individual personality. In addition to the pulpit he created for his native Pisa, he designed at least two others: one at Siena, while he was still in his teens, and another at Pistoia, which he signed. Pisano, who had a rather fair opinion of his own abilities, challenged any who wondered at his "noble sculptures" to "test them by the proper laws."

SCALA

Lucca

A RIVALRY WITH PISA

Although it was frequently caught up in the fighting between the Guelph and Ghibelline factions and was involved in wars of its own with Florence and Pisa, the city of Lucca prospered during the Middle Ages. Lucca's rivalry with nearby Pisa was particularly intense, and when the Pisans erected their magnificent *duomo* in the eleventh century, the citizens of Lucca set about to outdo them. Their choice of method, however, turned out to be no insult to Pisa.

"On top of the forms of ancient times" wrote the philosopher Hippolyte Taine, the Pisans added "their own invention: a facing of little columns topped by arches." Words, Taine added, could not "convey the originality and grace of the architecture revived in this way." Words, perhaps, could not adequately reproduce the Pisan columns and arches, but builders in Lucca could and did—and, if imitation is indeed the sincerest form of flattery, it is possible that the Pisans derived more satisfaction from the cathedral built at Lucca than did its builders.

Lucca's cathedral, San Martino, was founded by Bishop Anselmo Badagio (later Pope Alexander II) on the site of a sixth-century church, but major rebuilding in the fourteenth century did away with all of Anselmo's Romanesque structure except the choir-apse and the aisles. The impressive façade, a portion of which is shown in the photograph at right, was begun sometime after 1204 by the architect Guidetto da Como and several Lombard sculptors who were also responsible for a group (a copy of which is visible in the lower right-hand corner of the photograph) depicting the cathedral's patron, Saint Martin, with a beggar. Although Lucca's façade *is* closely patterned on that of Pisa, it is notable in its own right for its rich embellishment, its intricacy of detail, and its inlaid marble of various colors, among which a deep green predominates.

Like its exterior, Lucca's three-aisled interior successfully combines subtle color harmonies with lavish ornamentation. A solid-gold candelabrum, the propitiatory gift of nineteenth-century townsmen who feared an imminent cholera epidemic, hangs above the entrance to the Tempieto, the cathedral's octagonal chapel. The cathedral's most sacred treasure, however, is the *Volto Santo* (Holy Face), a wooden crucifix with a robed figure of Christ which, according to legend, was carved by Saint Nicodemus, finished by an angel, conveyed from Palestine to Italy in a crewless boat, and then brought to Lucca in a chariot drawn by wild bulls. This relic (which probably dates from the eleventh century) was placed in the cathedral—at least, according to more prosaic accounts—by Alexander II. It is adorned with jewels and a crown on feast days and was the inspiration for a favorite expletive of Plantagenet kings: "by the Saint Vult of Lucca!"

A detail from a thirteenth-century arcade
column on the façade of Lucca
Cathedral is shown in the photograph at
left. The engaging little angel
below is part of a fifteenth-century
monument to Ilaria del Carretto, the
second wife of a prominent townsman, Paolo
Guinigi, and was carved by the early
Renaissance sculptor Jacopo della Quercia.
OPPOSITE: The arcades of the nave,
which was built during the fourteenth and
fifteenth centuries, are supported by
massive square pillars and surmounted by
an elegant triforium. The pavement is
laid in polychrome marble.

St. Peter's

THE HAND THAT ROUNDED PETER'S DOME

"If one loses his companion in that church, he may seek for a whole day, because of its size and because of the multitudes who run from place to place, venerating shrines with kisses and prayers." Thus did a fourteenth-century English pilgrim describe St. Peter's, the world center of Roman Catholicism, *before* it became the vast edifice that it is today.

On Vatican Hill in Rome, over what was believed to have been the tomb of the martyred apostle Peter, Emperor Constantine began construction in 324 of a huge, lavishly embellished basilica that was proclaimed by the pope to be "the mother church and head of all churches of the city and of the world." In that church in the year 800, Pope Leo III founded the Holy Roman Empire by crowning Charlemagne Emperor of the West, thus beginning the tradition whereby emperors journeyed to Rome to be crowned by the pope.

During the following years, St. Peter's gradually fell into decay, despite the efforts of various popes to effect repairs. In the early sixteenth century, Julius II, one of the outstanding art patrons of Renaissance Italy, considered building a chapel to house his tomb. After mulling over the subject at some length, however, he decided on a more grandiose plan and accepted designs by the architect Donato Bramante for an entirely new church. On April 18, 1506, the first stone of the present St. Peter's was laid—crooked, the result of Julius' haste to escape the crowds pressing around him. Bramante's actions, too, were hasty—he had begun the project at the age of fifty-five and hoped to complete it during his lifetime, and his precipitate destruction of the old basilica earned him the sobriquet *Il Ruinante*. Bramante's design, a Greek cross covered by a huge central dome with four smaller domes at the sides, was notable for its majestic simplicity, but it was complicated by his successors, Raphael, Baldassare Peruzzi, and Giuliano da Sangallo, who, while vacillating between a Greek cross and a Latin cross, added a succession of chapels, monuments, and treasures that considerably cluttered up the premises.

It was Michelangelo who was finally chosen to design Julius' tomb and, in 1508, to paint the ceiling of the Sistine Chapel. Although popular literature has dwelt lovingly on the physical agonies endured by the artist in the course of his labors, his major anxiety during his six years of effort at St. Peter's was the pope's delinquency in paying him his fees. Disagreements over money finally led to the abandonment of the tomb project, and in the end, Julius' remains were shoveled unceremoniously into the grave of his uncle.

Eventually a man of real decision happened upon the scene: Pope Paul III, who in 1534 told Michelangelo: "I have longed to employ you, and now that I am pope shall I deny myself the fulfillment of my wish?" It appeared at first that any denial would come from the artist himself, who was still rankling over his treatment by Pope Julius, but Michelangelo relented and, in 1547, began designs for the dome that, upon its completion, was generally conceded to be one of the supreme masterpieces of world architecture.

By 1606 the church's final touches were added by Pope Paul V, who, by lengthening the nave and the eastern arm of the transept, reverted to the plan for a Latin Cross. Later in the century the approaches to the church were greatly enhanced by the addition of the splendid piazza by Lorenzo Bernini shown in the Piranesi engraving at left.

The *immense nave of the mother church of Roman Catholicism easily accommodated more than two thousand ecclesiastical dignitaries from all over the world during the final session of Vatican* II, *the ecumenical council held in December,* 1965. *In the photograph opposite, taken while the council was in session, the view is toward the cathedral's west end, with Bernini's* 95-*foot-high baldachin (beneath which only the pope himself can celebrate the Mass) standing in the light of the great cupola. An earlier—but historically no less important— ceremony, the crowning of Charlemagne in the old basilica, is shown at right in the painting by Fouquet. In the drawing below, made by an unknown artist sometime after the middle of the sixteenth century, the circular walls that were to support Michelangelo's great dome are shown in the process of construction.*

STENDHAL ON ST. PETER'S

After Napoleon's fall a French soldier, Marie Henri Beyle, went to Italy, where, under the pseudonym Stendhal, he wrote such novels as The Red and the Black *and* The Charterhouse of Parma *and kept a diary in which he described St. Peter's:*

ROME, November 24 [1827] / This morning when our barouche had crossed the Sant'Angelo bridge, we perceived St. Peter's at the end of a narrow street. . . .

We followed this straight street, opened by Alexander VI, and reached the Piazza Rusticucci, on which the pope's guard parades every day at noon with a fanfare of music and drums, but without ever being able to keep step. This square opens on the immense colonnade forming two semicircles on the right and on the left which so effectively announce the most beautiful temple of the Christian religion. The spectator perceives to the right, above this colonnade, a very tall palace: this is the Vatican. . . .

The square comprised between the two semicircular parts of the colonnade of Bernini (but I beg you to cast your eyes on a lithograph of St. Peter's) is to my mind the most beautiful in existence. In the middle, a great Egyptian obelisk; to right and left, two ever-spurting fountains whose waters, after rising in a spray, fall back into vast basins. This tranquil and continuous sound echoes between the two colonnades and induces revery. This moment admirably disposes one to be moved by St. Peter's, but it escapes sightseers who arrive by carriage. One must descend at the entrance to the Piazza Rusticucci. The two fountains adorn this charming spot, without in any way diminishing its majesty. This is quite simply the *perfection of art*. Imagine a few more ornaments, and the majesty would be diminished; a little less, and there would be bareness. This delightful effect is due to the cavalier Bernini, and this colonnade is his masterpiece. To Pope Alexander VII belongs the glory of having it erected. The vulgar said that it would spoil St. Peter's.

Bernini's two circular porches are composed of two hundred eighty-four great travertine columns and sixty-four pilasters; these columns form three galleries. In the course of certain solemnities, the cardinal's carriages pass beneath the middle one. . . . St. Peter's has five doors. One of them is walled up and is opened only every twenty-five years, for the ceremony of the jubilee. The jubilee, which once brought 400,000 pilgrims of all classes together in Rome, assembled only 400 beggars in 1825. One must hasten to see the ceremonies of a religion that is going to undergo change and die out.

With difficulty we push open a great leather door, and here we are in St. Peter's. One cannot help worshiping the religion that produces such things. Nothing in the world can be compared to the interior of St. Peter's. After a year's stay in Rome, I still went and spent whole hours there with pleasure. Almost all travelers have this experience. One may be bored in Rome in the second month of one's stay, but never in the sixth; and if one remains to the twelfth one becomes possessed with the idea of settling here.

Nothing in the architecture of St. Peter's betrays effort, everything seems naturally great. The presence of the genius of Bramante and of Michelangelo makes itself so felt that things which are ridiculous are no longer so here, they are merely insignificant.

. . . I should be unjust if I did not add the name of Bernini to those of these two great men. Bernini, who in his life attempted so many things heedlessly, succeeded perfectly with the altar canopy and the colonnade.

In lifting one's eyes when one is close to the altar one perceives the great cupola, and the most prosaic being can form an idea of the genius of Michelangelo. If one possesses ever so little of the sacred fire, one is dazed with admiration. I advise the traveler to sit down on a wooden bench and lean his head against the back; there he will be able to rest and contemplate at leisure the immense void suspended above his head.

PLANS FROM THREE GIANTS

When in 1505 Pope Julius II decided to undertake the complete rebuilding of St. Peter's Basilica, he had three master plans from which to choose. The first, worked out half a century earlier by the Florentine sculptor Bernardo Rossellino for Pope Nicholas V, was similar in plan to the Basilica of Constantine, though with a deeper apse and the addition of flanking, rather than radiating, chapels. The similarity between it and the surviving original was probably a reflection of the designer's acquiescence to the Roman populace's tender and possessive feelings toward the old monument. Whatever the reason, the plan, out-of-date for the High Renaissance, was conservative even compared with Late Gothic, and Julius rejected it. The second plan was submitted by Giuliano da Sangallo, who was at the time supervisor of the work being done on the round Vatican tower, a legacy from Nicholas' reign. Giuliano, an old friend of the pope's, was much insulted when Julius rejected his plan. (It is assumed that this layout was also out-of-date, although no record of it survives.) The third presentation, that of Donato Bramante, was the plan that Julius accepted.

Bramante's design (below at left) was based on the central plan—the shape of a Greek cross—that was essential in Renaissance thought to a humanistic approach to religious architecture. Unlike the rectangular basilica with transepts, the central plan consisted of a domed crossing and four projections of equal length and breadth that were symbolic of the universality of Christ: From His central position, in other words, all parts of the universe remained within reach. Radiating from the large central dome were also a number of smaller domes that helped to define the circular universe.

Bramante died in 1514, shortly after Julius, and was replaced by a triumvirate appointed by Pope Leo X. The most important member—and indeed the only one whose decisions counted—was Bramante's nephew Raphael. Unfortunately, Raphael's heart was not really with the architecture of St. Peter's, for he was much more deeply involved with other commissions. Moreover, Leo was neither the visionary nor the inspiration that his predecessor had been; the pressures exerted by conservative and less philosophical churchmen were brought to bear on the new pope and Raphael as they never could have been brought to bear before. The main difference in the plan that resulted from this new state of affairs was an important one: One limb of the cross, extended to allow a greater capacity, thereby negated the entire philosophical basis for Bramante's plan. The layout designed by Raphael (bottom at right) was thus a compromise between a centrally planned Renaissance structure and the traditional Latin-cross shape of the Gothic basilica.

Raphael died within six years and was replaced by a series of competent chief architects who, on the whole, retained the Raphael shape of St. Peter's. In 1546 Michelangelo was appointed by Pope Paul III to determine the future design of St. Peter's. Michelangelo (whose design is shown at center below) reintroduced the central plan, superimposing a Greek cross on Raphael's design. Thus both the philosophical reason for the layout and the additional space that Raphael had had to account for were retained. But the principal virtue of Michelangelo's plan was that it incorporated all parts of the edifice into an artistic whole —all the various chapels and towers and portals, done separately over a century by many popes and many artists. Michelangelo suffered constant criticism and harassment and had to justify his decisions from time to time to important clergymen. But, although the completed St. Peter's is hardly the work of Michelangelo alone, or of any other single artist, it owes much of its unity and grandeur to the influence of his long years as chief architect.

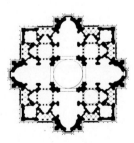
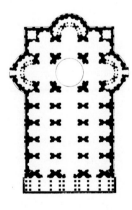
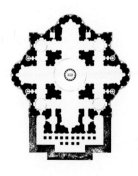

AFTER PAUL LETAROUILLY, *Le Vatican et la basilique St. Pierre*

A Cathedral Tour

113 GREAT CATHEDRALS
OF WESTERN EUROPE

. . . But every nation of Christendom rivalled with the other,
which should worship in the seemliest buildings.
So it was as though the very world had shaken herself
and cast off her old age, and were
clothing herself everywhere in a white garment of churches.
—Ralph Glaber (c. 1040)

A FEW GENERAL REMARKS—*A cathedral, by definition, contains the cathedra, or bishop's throne, and is the principal church of a diocese. For the sake of manageability, the term "cathedral," as it is used throughout this book, denotes only a church currently definable as such. Consequently, a number of historical and architectural landmarks have had to be omitted because they do not fit this definition (the abbey churches of St. Denis and Vézelay, for example), as have several former cathedrals that no longer fit (St. Trophime at Arles, to name one). In only one case, that of St. Peter's in the Vatican, has strict definition been stretched to accommodate a church of such overwhelming historical, ecclesiastical, and architectural importance that it could not be neglected. The purpose of this book is to present a representative sampling of cathedrals that either have figured prominently in history or are architecturally important, or both. We have concentrated on the Gothic style because it represents the great age of cathedral building, but we have included a number of pre- and post-Gothic monuments to place the Gothic in proper historical perspective.*

KEY TO MAPS—*Locator numerals preceding place names correspond to those on maps.*

FRANCE

1 AIX-EN-PROVENCE

The cathedral is notable more for its beauty of detail than for its overall construction and design. Partly Romanesque and partly Gothic, it contains elements of practically every phase of Provençal architecture. Although its beginnings are obscure, the south aisle probably dates from the eleventh century and the cloisters from the twelfth. The nave is an excellent example of thirteenth-century Gothic, and the facade dates mainly from the fifteenth century. The two wooden doors of the main portal bear the strong, sensitive carvings of Guiramand de Toulon, and the interior is a treasure trove of ecclesiastical art. Fifteenth- and sixteenth-century Flemish tapestries adorn the walls; those in the choir depict the Passion and life of the Virgin. Among the most important art works to be found in the cathedral is a triptych of Moses and the burning bush, painted by Nicolas Froment in 1475–76.

2 ALBI *(see pages 78–83)*

3 AMIENS *(see pages 40–47)*

4 ANGERS

Angers Cathedral is particularly impressive in the bold proportions of its interior (296 feet long and 54 feet wide). In the twelfth century, the aisles of the eleventh-century church were removed and

a single wide nave, domed with three high-arched, cross-ribbed vaults that increase the sense of spaciousness and light, was built. The choir and transepts, completed in the next century, also have high domes and are decorated with two fifteenth-century rose windows. The portal of the west front is notable for its statue-columns representing eight biblical figures and for its tympanum, which depicts the Apocalypse.

5 AUCH

High on a hill overlooking the valley of the Gers, the cathedral at Auch (1489–1678) dominates the surrounding countryside with its massive Greco-Roman facade. Incongruously combined are the cold, bare expanse of its naves and the rich interior detail of red marble, painted wooden altars, and stucco statues. The huge choir, with its 18 famous stained-glass windows and 113 oak stalls, was completed through the dual efforts of the glass painter Arnaud de Moles, whose signature, dated June 25, 1513, appears on the last of his windows, and Cardinal François de Clermont-Lodève, an Italophile who brought to France a feeling for the Renaissance. The windows, representing patriarchs, prophets, apostles, and sibyls, are considered among the best Renaissance windows in France; they were so much appreciated by Catherine de Médicis that it took considerable canonical pressure to prevent her from removing them to Paris.

6 AUTUN *(see pages 114–21)*

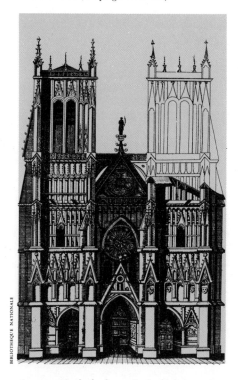

Auxerre Cathedral as it looked in 1670

7 AUXERRE

From the fifth through the eleventh centuries, additions were made to the sanctuary founded by Saint Amâtre at Auxerre. The entire structure, however, went up in flames in 1023, and Hughes de Chalon immediately undertook to rebuild it in the prevailing Romanesque style. In 1215, however, Bishop Guillaume de Seignelay, intrigued by the new "French style" (later termed Gothic), tore down Chalon's choir and constructed a new one of great elegance and purity, which was completed in 1234, a

century before completion of the nave. The huge Flamboyant façade, composed of four stories of arcades, three portals, and a rose window, appears slightly lopsided as a result of its unfinished southern tower. Although the limestone portals were mutilated in the religious wars of the sixteenth century and subsequently have suffered considerable erosion, the sculptures are still interesting, particularly those on the central doorway, where Christ is enthroned between the Wise and Foolish Virgins. The imposing and well-proportioned interior contains some colorful stained glass from the late thirteenth century. In the south transept are four consoles with particularly realistic sculptures, including a courting scene and a somewhat spicy tableau featuring a wanton girl and a wily goat, a popular fifteenth-century theme believed to have originated at Auxerre.

8 BAYEUX

Considered one of the finest examples of Norman architecture, the cathedral at Bayeux was dedicated in 1077 by Bishop Eudes (Odo) de Conteville, half brother of William the Conqueror. In contrast to the somber exterior, the Romanesque nave is exceptionally well lighted by a group of high windows above the triforium. The chapter house's twelfth-century arches were rebuilt in the fourteenth century and are supported by brackets decorated with monsters. The cathedral contains twenty-two chapels, one of which houses a very fine stone altar. Unfortunately, the west window of fifteenth-century glass, presented to Bayeux by the Guild of Cooks, is obscured by the organ. The façade is flanked by Romanesque towers reinforced by large buttresses in the thirteenth century when Gothic spires were added. A fifteenth-century central tower with an incongruous nineteenth-century top is known as "the Bonnet." The carving on the tympanum of the south portal depicts the history of Saint Thomas Becket, and those of the two side portals, the Last Judgment and the Passion. Facing the south door is the bishop's palace containing the Bayeux Tapestry, the famous embroidery tracing in fifty-eight scenes the history of the Norman Conquest.

9 BAYONNE

When a fire destroyed the cathedral at Bayonne in 1213, seventy-three years after its foundation, reconstruction began with the choir. Work continued until 1544, when it was abandoned with the great portal left unfinished. In 1847 a Bayonne resident named Lormand, perturbed by the unfinished façade, bequeathed 35,000 francs per year to complete the work, which was finished by the early twentieth century. The architects successfully met the problem of the cathedral's uneven site by the use of steps which ascend to the door of the north transept and descend to the nave portal. These two portals, already cumbersome and uninspired, were further debased during the Revolution when their sculptures were destroyed. Bayonne's interior is far more beautiful than its exterior, which is of uneven design and so closely hemmed in by houses that only its spires are visible at any distance. The combination of height, bold proportions, and the perfection of detail in its tall clustered columns makes the nave spectacular. Although some fine stained glass from 1575 remains, many panes unfortunately were replaced with clear glass in the eighteenth century by canons who had difficulty in reading their breviaries.

10 BEAUVAIS *(see pages 110–13)*

11 BESANÇON

The Cathedral of St. Jean was built during the early twelfth century on the foundations of a fourth-century church and consecrated in 1148. Destroyed by the usual fire in 1213, it was restored around 1258 and occupies a site that today, unfortunately, is crowded by other buildings. The nave's Romanesque arches combine with Gothic galleries. The columns under the main arches were rebuilt in the thirteenth century, at which time cross-ribbed vaults were added over the nave and aisles. St. Jean is one of a very few double-apsed cathedrals. In 1729 the north bell tower collapsed but was rebuilt. The cathedral contains a number of valuable paintings, among which are Fra Bartolommeo's *Virgin and Child with Saints*, Natoire's four scenes of the Passion, Van Loo's *Resurrection*, and *The Death of Sapphira*, by either Sebastian del Piombo or Tintoretto. Other interesting features include the stone pulpit donated in 1469 by Pierre Grenier, archdeacon of Luxeuil; the circular altar of the old Church of St. Etienne, carved from gutter stone; and an astronomical clock with seventy-two dials made by Vérité in 1860.

12 BEZIERS

The massive Gothic cathedral dominates the other buildings of Béziers by its sheer weight and size. Founded in the twelfth century, it was constructed over the next two hundred years in more-or-less uniform austerity, if not in uniformity of style. The rose window and Gothic portal of the façade are flanked by two square towers with thick walls and crenellated tops. Judging from the history of the town, this martial embellishment probably was more than mere architectural whim. In the twelfth and thirteenth centuries Béziers was a haven for non-Catholics, and during the Albigensian wars the southern "heretics" sought refuge from Catholic "crusaders" within the walls of the cathedral. In 1209 the city was burned and its inhabitants put to the sword in a frenzy of antiheretical zeal. The cathedral was burned as well, but it was later restored.

13 BORDEAUX

Combining Romanesque foundations and Gothic superstructure, St. André (12th–15th centuries) is the cathedral where Richard II was baptized (c. 1367). The interior, a single nave later enlarged by a narrow transept and a Gothic chancel, is supported by large, irregularly placed buttresses, built when the nave's vaulting seemed in danger of collapse. Rebuilding of the nave was planned during Bordeaux's prosperity under English rule in the fourteenth and fifteenth centuries. The project was dropped, however, owing to a subsequent recession. The *Porte Royale* (13th century) is embellished with later sculpture copied by Viollet-le-Duc from Notre Dame including ten apostles, a Last Judgment, and a Resurrection of the Dead. A gilded stat-

ue of the Virgin rests atop the cathedral's bell tower, which was built by the fifteenth-century archbishop Pey Berland.

An 1845 engraving of Bordeaux' interior

14 BOURGES *(see pages 72–77)*

15 CHALONS-SUR-MARNE

The Cathedral of St. Etienne at Châlons-sur-Marne is mainly a thirteenth-century edifice, although its west front, in the Classical style, dates from the seventeenth century. The choir, located between two Romanesque towers, is encircled by an ambulatory and three radiating chapels. In the Gothic nave, the glazed triforium is embellished with a multitude of tiny windows, reminiscent of those at Amiens. The cathedral's notable stained glass depicts, from the twelfth century, the story of Saint Stephen, the Passion, and the Church and Synagogue; from the thirteenth century, the Crucifixion, apostles, prophets, and past bishops of the diocese; and from the sixteenth, the legends of the Creation, the life of the Virgin, and the childhood of Christ.

16 CHARTRES *(see pages 56–63)*

17 COUTANCES *(see pages 126–29)*

18 EVREUX

A mixture of all architectural styles from Romanesque to Renaissance, the cathedral at Evreux further added to its disharmony by taking on two main towers of unequal height. Its incendiary history includes a fire kindled by Henry I of England in 1119 (which took the town as well as the cathedral), another stoked by Philip II in 1194 (which took the entire church with the exception of the main piers and arches of the nave), a third in 1356 during the reign of John II, and a fourth in 1940 (which destroyed the lead spire and the west façade's tower tops, one of which had supported a cupola and stone lantern). Evreux is especially known for its stained glass, which reflects the development of realism and perspective during the fourteenth century. Particularly notable are the windows of the choir, with the Virgin as a theme, and those of the Chapel of La Mère de Dieu, built under King Louis XI, which depict the French peers at the King's coronation, the tree of Jesse, and the Virgin amidst a reverent group that includes Louis XI himself.

19 LANGRES

Consecrated in 1196, the Cathedral of St. Mammès is typical of the twelfth-century Early Gothic style in its combination of pointed and circular arches. Its wide, symmetrical interior is far more impressive than the façade, which was redone rather clumsily in the eighteenth century. The beautifully sculpted capitals of the choir's monolithic pillars are particularly noteworthy, as are the excellent marble statues of the Virgin and Child and of a bishop at prayer (carved in 1341 by Evrard d'Orléans), the bas-reliefs of the Passion of Christ, and the screen (c. 1550) commissioned by Cardinal de Givny, who also gave to the cathedral the two tapestries in the transept that portray the life of the cathedral's patron, Saint Mammès.

20 LAON *(see pages 52–55)*

21 LE MANS *(see pages 122–25)*

340

22 LIMOGES

Although Limoges has been an episcopal see since the third century, its cathedral was not completed until about 1890. Construction began around 1273 on the site of an earlier Romanesque church and was continued in the sixteenth and nineteenth centuries. The lapses in construction may have resulted in part from the disasters that struck the town intermittently during those years—its capture by Edward, "the Black Prince," in 1370, famines, the religious wars, the plague in the early seventeenth century, and a major fire in 1790. Cruciform in plan, the cathedral has narrow, aisleless transepts and a massive west tower, whose base belongs to the earlier Romanesque church. The choir is Rayonnant Gothic and contains the tombs of three bishops. In the vestibule is a beautifully carved Renaissance rood screen, with reliefs representing the labors of Hercules, and on the north transept is the well-known Portal of St. Jean, whose magnificent Flamboyant carvings depict the stories of Saint Stephen and Saint Martin.

A nineteenth-century lithograph of Limoges

23 LYONS

The cathedral at Lyons, which combines Romanesque and Gothic styles, is considered one of the most interesting churches in France. The choir, the most remarkable part of the interior, was built during the period 1165–80 by Archbishop Guichard and contains excellent windows of thirteenth- and fourteenth-century stained glass, as does the nave. The Chapel of St. Louis (the Bourbon Chapel), a magnificent work of the fifteenth century, was commissioned by Cardinal de Bourbon and his brother Pierre, the son-in-law of Louis XI. Two crosses placed on either side of the altar during the Council of 1274 remain as a symbol of the short-lived union of the Greek and Latin churches. Above the three portals of the west front, begun sometime between 1308 and 1332, are a gallery and a beautiful rose window, finished in 1393 by the architect Jacques de Beaujeu and the glass painter Henry de Nivelle. Flanking the portals are two fifteenth-century towers. Between the doors are corbels decorated with both religious reliefs and scenes of amorous encounters, including one of Aristotle ridden by the courtesan Campaspe.

24 METZ

Foundations for the Cathedral of St. Etienne were laid in 1220, but a shortage of funds slowed progress, and work on the nave began again only in 1250 and was not completed until 1380. Incorporating an earlier church, Notre-Dame-la-Ronde, this yellow sandstone structure—with its two symmetrical towers, enormous pointed windows, slender attached columns, and numerous flying buttresses—is characteristic of the Rayonnant style of Late Gothic. The interior is not only one of the widest and most colorful in France, but, with the exception of the choir of Beauvais and the nave of Amiens, the highest French cathedral interior. Its architect, Pierre Perrat (responsible also for work done at Toul and Verdun), was buried in the nave in 1400. Occupying the entire north wall is a huge window containing stained glass dating from 1504 by Thibaud de Lixheim. The west front's rose window (*c.* 1384) is attributed to Hermann of Munster; a later, Renaissance-influenced window in the choir, to the Alsatian glazier, Valentin Bousch. The Bousch window portrays Antoine, duke of Lorraine, and his wife, Renée de Bourbon. The "Côté de la Place d'Armes" tower serves as a belfry. Its famous bell, cast in 1605, weighs over 11 tons.

Moulins as a lithographer saw it in 1839

25 MOULINS

Mainly of the Flamboyant style, the double-towered cathedral at Moulins was founded by the dukes of Bourbon and reconstructed by Agnès de Bourbon and her son, Jean II, in the fifteenth century. Its huge, rib-vaulted choir, which formerly served as the chapel of the ducal château, was finished in 1507, and its interior is higher than the interior of the nave. Built in Early Gothic style according to a plan by Viollet-le-Duc, the nineteenth-century nave was the last part of the edifice to be completed and combines the black lava and white stone typical of many churches of the Auvergne. Of particular interest are the choir's stained-glass windows (15th–16th centuries), its winding staircase, and, in the chapel to the right of the choir, a rather morbid sculpture of a worm-eaten corpse. In the sacristy there is a superb fifteenth-century triptych by the famous Master of Moulins. The Annunciation is depicted on its exterior, and the inside reveals the Virgin and Child being venerated by the triptych's donors, Pierre II de Bourbon (died 1503) and his wife, Anne of France (died 1522), the daughter of Louis XI.

26 NANTES

Of the cathedral at Nantes, begun at the request of Duke John V by Guillaume de Dammartin in 1434, only the nave dates from the Middle Ages. The lofty interior, with its columns rising in an unbroken movement from the ground to the ribs of the vault, produces a soaring

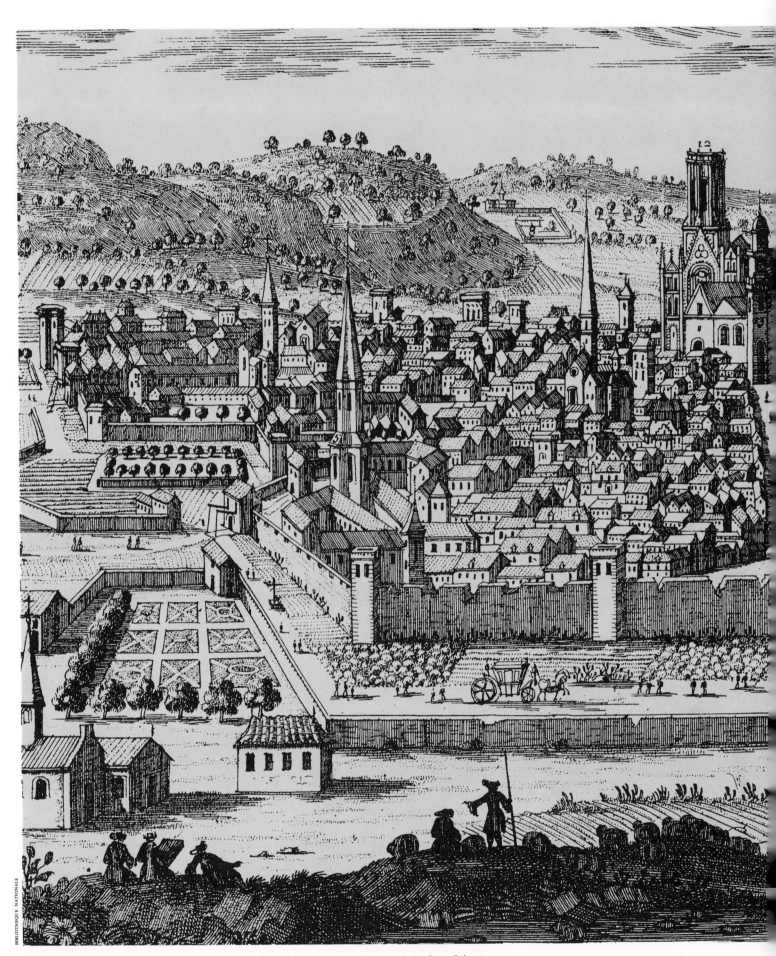

The Cathedral of Aix-en-Provence is shown in this detail from a seventeenth-century woodcut of the city.

effect. Nantes is particularly known for its fifteenth-century sculpture of early patriarchs and bishops and for the tomb monuments in its transepts. These include the tomb sculpture of François II, the last duke of Brittany, and his wife, Marguerite de Foix. Designed in black and white marble by Michel Colombe in 1502, it represents the royal couple reclining amidst statues of Justice, Prudence, Temperance, and Strength.

Nantes' façade; a nineteenth-century print

27 NOTRE DAME, PARIS
(see pages 90–103)

28 NOYON

The Cathedral of Notre Dame was begun around 1150 on the site of a ruined church. Its cruciform plan is unusual in having rounded transept arms. The west façade, with its three arched portals and two tall recessed towers, creates an impression of unimposing harmony. Internally, the feeling of space is enhanced by the nave's elevation of four stories—arcade, gallery, triforium, and clerestory. Arches are pointed in the galleries and rounded in the triforium, and two styles of coupled windows are set in the transept—one row early, and the other, later Gothic. Considered one of the best examples of the Transitional style of the twelfth century, Notre Dame, with its slender proportions and com-

pelling effect of verticality, influenced the design of many later cathedrals.

29 ORLEANS

Religious wars have taken their toll of the cathedral at Orléans, which was begun in 1287 by Bishop Gilles de Patay on the charred remains of an earlier Romanesque church. Around 1568, before the cathedral was completed, it was demolished by the Huguenots, whose siege left standing only the apse chapels and some exterior walls. When Henry IV began to rebuild in 1601, he followed the original Gothic plans; consequently, the cathedral achieves a remarkable uniformity of style. The façade, with its two spireless towers, five portals surmounted by three rose windows, and an open gallery, was rebuilt in 1759 by Louis XV's architect, Gabriel. Its bastard Flamboyant style implies that he had lost the Gothic mood. Inside, the choir stalls (1702–06) by Jules Degoullons are particularly beautiful. The stained-glass aisle windows by Jacques Galland depict episodes from the life of Joan of Arc, the city's patron saint.

30 PERPIGNAN

Founded in 1324 during the Majorcan reign and completed two hundred years later under French rule, this border-town cathedral retains the flavor of its Spanish origins. The flatness of its plain façade is broken only by a domed porch beneath a single, rectangular window. Within, the aisleless fifteenth-century nave is dark and lofty—a cool retreat from Mediterranean summers. A sense of mystery is captured in its vast proportions, and the Spanish mood is present in the exquisite decoration of its altars. The white marble reredos of Soler de Barcelona, depicting the life of Saint John, is an exceptionally fine work of the seventeenth century.

31 POITIERS

In 1162 Henry II of England, husband of Eleanor of Aquitaine, began construction of the cathedral at Poitiers. Although the west façade was finished in 1271, its asymmetrical towers were not completed until the fifteenth century.

The addition of the towers was perhaps not the very best architectural touch. Set outside the main structure, they greatly increase its width, but the overall effect has been described as too wide, too low, and too heavy. The large-proportioned interior appears longer than it really is because of the architectural device of narrowing the aisles and nave and lowering the arches toward the choir. The cathedral contains some excellent examples of stained glass from the eleventh, twelfth, and thirteenth centuries, and the fine thirteenth-century choir stalls are among the oldest in existence. Before the carved portals of the façade is a sunken courtyard, which formerly served as a court of justice.

32 QUIMPER

Although nearly three centuries (1239–1515) were spent in its construction, the cathedral at Quimper displays a particularly unified style. (Its two towers were not added until 1856, and then only with the help of 600,000 parishioners, whom the bishop solicited to donate one sou per year for five years.) One of the cathedral's most noticeable features is the misalignment of the nave (15th century) and choir (12th century). Some think this feature symbolizes Christ dying with hanging head, while others think it is the result of some obstruction.

An 1845 lithograph of Quimper Cathedral

In the pulpit, sculptured panels portray the life of Saint Corentin, Quimper's first bishop, who, legend says, subsisted all his life on the same self-replenishing fish. Between the spires is a statue of the sixth-century King Gradlon on horseback, which, until the eighteenth century, was honored by a yearly festival. Each July twenty-sixth a man would climb to the statue, tie a napkin around the king's neck, and offer him wine. After drinking the wine himself, the man would throw his glass to the street where any spectator catching it intact received 100 gold écus. During the struggles between the Huguenots and the Holy League in the sixteenth century, many townspeople sought refuge in the nave, and masses were performed amidst beds and other household possessions. Unfortunately, the plague broke out and 1,500 refugees died there.

33 REIMS *(see pages 32–39)*

34 RODEZ

Nothing certain is known of the history of Rodez Cathedral prior to a day in 1276 when the choir fell in. The presiding bishop, Raymond de Calmont, following the custom of the times, immediately began a reconstruction of the entire cathedral, but unfortunately he died before the new choir was completed. In place of an entirely new edifice, the old nave and new choir, of unequal heights, were simply joined together—a somewhat less than satisfactory merger—and work stopped. Funds for resuming construction were obtained by promises of vast spiritual favors to the generous and by threats of excommunication to the stingy. But construction continued slowly and was not yet completed when, in 1510, a fire broke out in the spire. According to a contemporary report, when the bishop lifted the bones of the church's patron saint toward the tower, "the strong wind ceased to blow and the flame, bowing suddenly, began to burn gently on its pile of stone as fire upon an altar. . . ," and the rest of the cathedral was spared. The rebuilt square-based tower, dedicated to the Virgin, is largely the work of François d'Estaing and is made up of three richly carved stages topped by four tur-

rets and, of course, a figure of Mary. In 1525 plans made by Cardinal d'Armagnac to complete the west towers were abandoned, and the surviving inscription—"Fall pyramids of Egypt, insensate masses, and let honor be given to the true marvels of the world"—seems a bit high-flown under the circumstances.

35 ROUEN *(see pages 84–89)*

36 ST. BERTRAND DE COMMINGES

Situated high on a peak of the Pyrenees like a great stone fortress, St. Bertrand de Comminges owes much of its beauty to the stateliness and dignity of its setting. Founded in 1082 by Saint Bertrand, the cathedral stands on the foundations of an older church, overlooking the ruins of a Gallo-Roman city of the first century B.C. The main body of the church, however, was constructed during the fourteenth century under the future Pope Clement V in the heavy southern Gothic style. The square, massive tower seems to rise up out of the rock itself, heightening the dramatic effect of the deep portal. Within, the aisleless Gothic nave arches to a height of more than 80 feet, and the long, narrow windows admit little warmth or light. The starkness is broken only in the choir, where the fine Renaissance wood carving of the rood loft, choir screen, and stalls adds a touch of richness and variety.

37 SEES

Built on the site of an earlier church burned by Henry II in 1174, the cathedral at Sées is a charming combination of Norman Gothic and French Rayonnant styles. The thirteenth-century Gothic nave provides an interesting contrast to the light, graceful lines of the choir. Constructed during the latter part of the same century, the choir is reminiscent of the choirs of the cathedrals of Amiens and Beauvais. The delicate tracery of the clerestory adds to the elegant, vertical proportions of the interior, and some of the original thirteenth-century stained glass still ornaments the windows of the clerestory and north

transept. The west front, which suffered heavy damage in the eighteenth century, has been extensively restored.

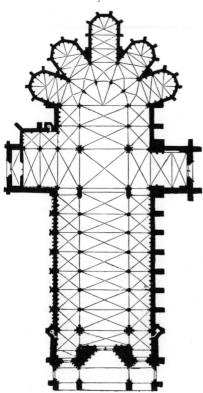

Sées; 1867 floor plan by Viollet-le-Duc

38 SENLIS

In 1153 Bishop Thibault received from King Louis VII letters of protection for collectors he was sending across the country to gather funds for construction of a new cathedral. Senlis' dedication in 1191 found the cathedral unfinished, and the moving oration delivered by the archbishop of Reims at this historic ceremony was in large part a plea for capital. Eventually, however, the building was finished. The center portal (c. 1175) of its three-portaled west front is adorned with magnificent statuary, and a particularly beautiful spire rises from the bell tower. Originally a Roman wall passed to the north of the choir, thereby constricting somewhat the ground lines of the radiating chapels that were added later. The lintel over the door of the porch represents the Death and Resurrection of the Virgin, and the tympanum shows the Coronation of the Virgin—inaugurating the use of the themes that caused the thirteenth century to be known as the "Century of the

Virgin." After a fire in 1504, the transept façades were marvelously reconstructed in the Flamboyant style.

39 SOISSONS

One of the smallest, most graceful of French cathedrals, Notre Dame (also called the Cathedral of St. Gervais and St. Protais) is an excellent example of the combination of twelfth- and thirteenth-century Early and High Gothic styles. Begun about 1176 and completed about 1250, it is in plan and structure very similar to Chartres, although on a more elegant and slender scale. Internally, the cathedral is divided into two distinct sections—the three-storied nave and choir in High Gothic and the Early Gothic four-storied south transept. Its west façade—three portals and a beautiful rose window—has a single tower (thirteenth century), a copy of that of Notre Dame of Paris. Although it suffered extensive damages in World War I, the cathedral was well restored and has been used as a model for the design of many small churches.

40 STRASBOURG *(see pages 104–9)*

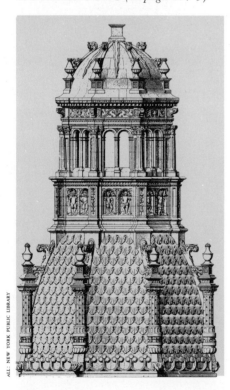

Tours' lantern; nineteenth-century print

41 TOURS

From its thirteenth-century choir to its Flamboyant west front, completed in 1547, Tours is a study in the evolution of French Gothic architecture. The transepts were finished in the fourteenth century; the soaring nave, begun early in the same century, was completed and vaulted in the fifteenth century. The façade, with its three lavishly embellished portals, reflects the unrestrained opulence of the Late Flamboyant period. Stained-glass windows from the various periods of construction give brilliance and color to the interior. Particularly noteworthy are the windows of the choir chapels, with scenes from the Old and New Testaments, and the clerestory windows, which depict the lives of the saints.

Troyes; engraving after J. M. W. Turner

42 TROYES

In 1228 Bishop Herve began to build the Cathedral of St. Pierre and St. Paul at Troyes, after selecting an unfortunately soggy site. This caused construction to progress slowly (over four centuries), with frequent interruptions to repair previously built sections. The present cathedral shows, therefore, a certain stylistic disunity, but its magnificent nave is one of the most elegant in existence. It is exceptionally light with particularly beautiful stained-glass windows, and its lines soar upward impressively. The cathedral has only a north tower; a central spire was blown down by a storm in 1366, rebuilt in the early fifteenth century, and destroyed again by a thunderbolt in 1700.

OPPOSITE: *The Cathedral of Lyons, seen from the east, is depicted in a nineteenth-century lithograph by Jacottet after a drawing by Chapu. The spireless towers of the cathedral date from the end of the fifteenth century.*

ENGLAND

1 BRISTOL

Founded in 1140 as a church for Augustinian Canons, Bristol Cathedral was built on the site of what is traditionally held to be the meeting place of Saint Augustine and the British Christians. Constructed in the manner of a hall church, Bristol (elevated to cathedral status by Henry VIII in 1542) has a number of striking architectural features. The absence of clerestory and triforium—the aisles rising as high as the nave and choir—creates a unique impression of spatial unity; and the openwork effect on the vaulting is among the earliest and finest examples of vault patterning. The cathedral's eastern section, rebuilt in the early fourteenth century, is considered by some authorities to be one of the finest works of the Early Decorated style.

2 CANTERBURY *(see pages 156–61)*

3 CARLISLE

When the foundation began noticeably to sink during the early building stages of Carlisle Cathedral (*c.* 1092–1123), the architects sensibly decided to wait several years before proceeding with the work. Then, finding the vaults had settled only several feet below the intended level, they carried on as though nothing untoward had taken place. The result is today's excellent example of the skewed Norman vault and asymmetric nave. In the early thirteenth century a fire destroyed a major portion of the church, including the choir, which was then rebuilt but unfortunately burned again in 1292. Apparently undaunted, the builders threw up a brand new church (Decorated style), which was finished in 1400—in ample time to be destroyed by the Scots under Leslie in 1645. Due to the loss of six of its eight Norman bays in that action, Carlisle is now one of the smallest churches in England. The east choir window has survived, however, and is considered one of England's most beautiful. Also notable is the excellent stone tracery, although it was left in an unfinished state now thought to be the result of delays caused by the Black Death.

4 CHESTER

Using the foundation of a convent dedicated to Saints Oswald and Werburgh, the earl of Chester, Hugh Lupus, a somewhat hefty individual familiarly known as *Le Gros*, erected a Benedictine abbey at Chester in 1093. Later his Norman structure was almost completely rebuilt in the Gothic style (13th–15th centuries) and at the Reformation (1541) became the Cathedral of Chester. Built of red sandstone, it has a very large central tower but a rather undistinguished west front. Its south transept is four times as large as its north one, a result of the clerical disputes that typified the times. The presence of monastery buildings to the north and the parish Church of St. Oswald to the south prevented the monks of St. Werburgh from extending their church, and so the St. Oswald parishioners were relocated and the present south transept built (14th–15th centuries). Later they returned, and until 1880 the south transept was separated by a partition from the cathedral and used as a parish church. The chapter house contains the cathedral's finest stained glass, depicting St. Werburgh's history, and the woodcarving on the choir stalls (15th century) is considered the best of its type in England.

5 CHICHESTER

Begun around 1085 and finished in 1108, the original Norman building caught fire six years later and was restored in the Transitional style. It managed to hold out a bit longer before burning again in 1186. It was again repaired in the thirteenth century. This time a good deal of fireproof Purbeck marble was used. The nave, narrow in proportion to its height, combines an Early English clerestory, Decorated aisle windows, and Norman arches and triforium. Unusual are the double aisles (also found in England at Manchester), created when the original series of chapels was converted to one. The northwest tower collapsed in 1634 and was not rebuilt until 1901. In 1861 the fifteenth-century steeple collapsed but was promptly reconstructed according to the original design. Still standing and 277 feet tall, it is the only cathedral spire in England visible from the sea. Other interesting features include the fifteenth-century detached bell tower, unique among English cathedrals, and the unusually wide intervals between the marble piers. The retrochoir, completed by Bishop Seffrid in 1199, is an excellent example of the transition from heavy Norman to the lighter Gothic style.

6 DURHAM *(see pages 168–71)*

7 ELY *(see pages 152–55)*

8 EXETER

Originally a conventual church, founded by Athelstan around 932 and replaced by a Norman structure (1112–1206), Exeter Cathedral was rebuilt and transformed in the Decorated Gothic style during the period from 1280 to 1370 by Bishop Walter Bronescombe and his successors. Dedicated to Saint Mary and Saint Peter, its huge Norman transeptal towers, an architectural rarity built by Bishop William de Warelwast (1107–1137), are, with the exception of those copied from them at Ottery St. Mary, the only ones in England. The preponderance of large buttresses outside bears little relationship to the small-scaled, perfectly symmetrical interior. Because the usual central tower is missing, the

Exeter; an 1818 engraving by H. S. Storer

interior of the cathedral is very light, and the emphasis is on texture and color, with the multiple ribs in the vaulting creating variety of light and shade. The many-shafted piers of Purbeck marble appear to have a somewhat rippling surface, and a feeling of compactness and warmth results from the combination of the cathedral's homogeneous style, low unbroken vaulting, and delicate carving. Exeter's ornate windows show the development of tracery from simple Geometric design to a later Flowing style.

Gloucester; an engraving of the cloister

9 GLOUCESTER

Gloucester, largely a Norman work constructed (1089–1100) under Abbot Serle, is an ornate edifice with a beautiful pinnacled tower. It achieved cathedral rank in 1540 under Henry VIII. In 1327 the body of Edward II (murdered at Berkeley Castle) was denied burial at Bristol and Malmesbury, but it was enshrined at Gloucester, where it became the object of an important pilgrimage. The vast revenue thus accrued enabled the monks to hire a court mason and rebuild in the new Perpendicular style then developing in London, making the cathedral the first successful example of Perpendicular architecture in England. The circular piers in the interior are massive and exceptionally high. The fourteenth-century choir, an excellent example of pure Perpendicular style, is unparalleled in England by virtue of the combination of its tracery, paneled walls, richly carved stalls, elaborate vaulting, and huge east window, the largest in the country. The cloisters (1350–1410), also unsurpassed in England, housed Cromwell's horses

in 1641 during the Puritan Revolution. In 1657, during the period of the Commonwealth, the cathedral was saved from destruction (already begun) only by a plea made to Cromwell by the town's mayor and citizens.

10 HEREFORD

According to legend, the ghost of Saint Ethelbert of East Anglia, murdered in 794 by Offa of Mercia, insisted upon burial at Hereford. One of Offa's successors accommodatingly built a stone church over Ethelbert's tomb in 825. A later Saxon church (burned down by the Welsh in 1056) preceded the present cathedral, dedicated to Saint Mary and Saint Ethelbert. Begun in 1079 and completed in 1535, it embodies an interesting mixture of architectural styles. The nave, of rich Norman design with its original eight massive piers and arches, contrasts sharply with the twentieth-century façade. Probably the most beautiful part of the building, the north transept has the tall, narrow windows, arches, and ornamentation of the early Decorated style and contains the shrine of Bishop Thomas Cantelupe (died 1282), a great attraction to pilgrims. In the Norman south transept is an old fireplace, an unusual feature in a cathedral. Interesting also are the choir's twelfth-century chair, said to have been used by King Stephen, the excellent Geometric tracery in the great window, and the famous *Mappa Mundi* (c. 1313) in its original frame, one of the oldest maps of the world. In 1786 the collapse of the west tower through the nave unfortunately gave James Wyatt the chance to reconstruct the nave in misconceived Gothic. The entire building was restored with greater success, however, by Sir G. G. Scott in the middle of the nineteenth century.

11 LICHFIELD

Called the "Lady of English Cathedrals," Lichfield is the only church in England with three stone spires ("Ladies of the Vale"). Mainly of the Early English and Decorated styles, it was constructed during the period 1200–1350 and dedicated to Saint Mary and to Saint Chad, the patron saint of Lichfield. The red sandstone used in the narrow-aisled interior gives it a feeling of warmth and richness. Formerly surrounded by a wall and ditch, the cathedral close was attacked in 1643 by Puritans, who demolished the central tower as well as many carvings, monuments, and windows. Although some restoration has taken place, the monuments are almost all modern, as are some one hundred statues lining the symmetrical west façade. The tall, airy Lady Chapel (c. 1230–36) ends in a polygonal apse, the only Gothic apse in an English cathedral. Seven of its nine huge windows contain the famous Herkenrode glass (c. 1530–40), purchased in 1802 from France. Interesting also are the choir (c. 1200), whose Minton tile floor depicts the early history of the diocese, and the presbytery (c. 1337–50), designed by the architect William Ramsey.

12 LINCOLN

Adapting the plan of Rouen, Bishop Remigius built a Norman church at Lincoln, which was consecrated in 1092. Damaged in a fire in 1141, it was restored by Bishop Alexander before collapsing in the earthquake of 1185. Restoration was then undertaken by Bishop Hugh of Avalon in the late twelfth century. Today Lincoln Cathedral contains the earliest pure Gothic architecture in existence as well as portions of the two previous Norman structures and samples of many building styles. The central wooden spire, thought to have been the tallest ever built in England, blew down in 1547; the two that had flanked it were removed in 1808. The choir, considered to be the oldest existing example of the Early English style, is also the earliest instance in which ribs were used solely for decorations. Two circular windows, known as the "Bishop's Eye" and the "Dean's Eye," peer from the transepts, and the lantern contains "Great Tom," a huge bell weighing five and a half tons. Perched on the turrets are statues of Saint Hugh and the "Swineherd of Stowe," who supposedly gave all his earnings to Hugh; below are numerous gargoyles, the best known being the "Devil Looking over Lincoln." Although its nave's vaulting is quite low ("the crazy vaults of Lincoln") and its bays are quite wide, Lincoln is still one of England's finest cathedrals.

H. S. Storer: Norwich seen from the east

13 NORWICH

Norwich Cathedral (or the Church of the Holy Trinity) has retained its Norman plan and structure almost as completely as has Durham. Begun in 1096 by Bishop Herbert de Losinga, it was dedicated in 1101 and completed by 1499 after a slight delay in 1272, when the townspeople revolted against the clergy and burned much of the cathedral's interior. A plain-looking building, it is unusual in having no monuments and a particularly long choir with an apse and radiating chapels—a French design very rarely found in English churches. Its fifteenth-century spire, the second tallest in England, is surpassed only by that of Salisbury. The Bishop's Throne is located behind the altar in the choir, a plan typical of Christian churches prior to about 1000, and a slab before the altar is dedicated to Bishop de Losinga, buried there in 1119. The painted retable in St. Luke's Chapel was probably donated in thanksgiving for the ending of the Peasant Revolt in 1381.

14 OXFORD

Originally the church of the priory of Saint Frideswide (8th century), Oxford Cathedral was rebuilt by Ethelred II in 1004 and restored in late Norman style by Robert of Cricklade (1141–80). To make room for his college, Christ Church, Wolsey pulled down half the nave in 1525, thereby making Oxford the smallest cathedral in England. Serving the dual role of cathedral and college chapel, Oxford is unusual in the arrangement of its massive piers, which are alternately round and octagonal, and its double arches, the lower of which rise from corbels connected to the piers. The east window, (c. 1330), a depiction of Becket's Martyrdom, today has one white pane, supposedly inserted after Saint Thomas of Canterbury's head was struck out by a Puritan trooper. Particularly beautiful are the choir's groined roof (c. 1490), the flowing tracery of the windows, the vault-bosses, and the octagonal spire, thought to be the oldest in England.

15 PETERBOROUGH

Like many other English cathedrals, Peterborough had a fiery early history. Founded as a Benedictine monastery in 656 by Penda, King of Mercia, it was destroyed by the Danes in 870, rebuilt in 971, and burned down in 1116. Begun again in 1117, its interior was destroyed by Puritans in 1643, but later restored. The ornate west front, composed of three enormous recessed arches, opens into a surprisingly light nave with beautiful vaulted aisles and a unique painted ceiling. Although they are massive in appearance, its piers were recently discovered to be only hollow shells filled with debris. In the transept, the restored wooden ceiling is the only original Norman ceiling still in existence. Beneath its south wall are foundations of the early Saxon church. The sanctuary, the

Peterborough in section by John Britton

oldest part of the building, contains interesting tombs and slabs: the "Monk's Stone," in memory of monks killed by the Danes in 870; effigies of twelfth- and thirteenth-century abbots, perhaps the best Benedictine memorials in England; the grave of Catherine of Aragon (d. 1536); and the original tomb of Mary Queen of Scots (d. 1587), whose body was removed to Westminster Abbey in 1612 by her son, James I.

16 RIPON

Though one of the smaller cathedrals in England, Ripon encompasses numerous architectural styles. Founded originally by Saint Cuthbert as a monastery for Celtic monks (c. 660), it was refounded as a Saxon church on a new site by Saint Wilfrid (c. 670). On that foundation, a church for secular canons, dedicated to Saints Peter and Wilfrid, was begun by Archbishop Roger of York (1154–81), later expanded (12th–15th centuries), and finally restored by G. G. Scott. Of Archbishop Roger's Romanesque structure, only the transepts and two Norman arches remain (the other two were changed to Perpendicular). The wide nave, unusual in its absence of a triforium, remained aisleless until the early sixteenth century. After two sides of the central tower collapsed in 1450 and were rebuilt in Perpendicular style, the tower became "unique in being divided vertically between two different styles of architecture." The west front, the only Early English façade with towers standing above the aisles, is relatively low owing to the collapse of the central spire in 1660 and the removal of the west tower spires in 1664. Of Saint Wilfrid's seventh-century church, only the Saxon crypt remains. According to legend, its narrow passage and opening, "St. Wilfrid's Needle," was used as a medieval test of chastity, for through it, it is said, only the pure were able to pass.

17 ROCHESTER

Though originally built in honor of Saint Andrew, Rochester Cathedral is now dedicated to Christ and the Virgin Mary. By the time of the Norman Conquest, little remained of the early Saxon church founded by Saint Augustine in 604. A new structure was begun in 1082 (consecrated in 1130) by Gundulf, the second Norman bishop and builder of part of the Tower of London. The present cathedral, built mainly between the twelfth and fourteenth centuries, resembles Canterbury with its double transepts, raised choir, and spacious crypt, one of the largest in England. The beautiful recessed doorway in the Norman west front is a compelling feature, as are the great Perpendicular window added in the fifteenth century and the ruins of Gundulf's tower. The elaborate triforium arches, which open onto both the aisles and the nave, and the choir's lack of aisle arcades are particularly noteworthy. For centuries pilgrims have been drawn to the tomb of Saint William of Perth, a thirteenth-century Scottish baker who was murdered nearby while on his own pilgrimage to Canterbury. Two of the oldest statues in England, of Henry II and Queen Margaret, frame the Norman west doorway.

Rochester's west front in 1816 by Storer

18 ST. ALBANS

The highest cathedral in England (320 feet above sea level), St. Albans is also one of the largest and plainest of all English churches, and although it is primarily a Norman edifice, it has the longest Gothic nave in the world. Founded by Offa of Mercia around 793 as a Benedictine monastery, it was largely rebuilt between 1077 and 1115 by Abbot Paul of Caen and was elevated to cathedral status in 1877. Mainly constructed of bricks from Verulamium, the most important town in southern England during Roman times, its plan forms a cross, with a central tower at the intersection. The nave, simple and solemn with its rather austere piers, contrasts with the central tower with its windows of various sizes and shapes. The west front, begun in 1195, was never completed; sharp practices on the part of the workmen, it seems, resulted in a shortage of funds. The painted ceiling of the choir survives from the time of Edward III (1327–77), and the chancel from the early reign of Henry VI (1422–61). The cathedral also contains the shrine of Saint Alban, the tomb of a brother of Henry V, Duke Humphrey of Gloucester (died 1447), and a brass tablet honoring Abbot de la Mare. Unfortunately, much of the cathedral was ineptly restored by Lord Grimthorpe in the late nineteenth century.

19 ST. PAUL'S, LONDON
(see pages 172–85)

20 SALISBURY *(see pages 144–51)*

21 SOUTHWARK (LONDON)

The cathedral at Southwark is considered by many to be the most beautiful Gothic building in London after Westminster Abbey. According to legend, the site was occupied in early times by the nunnery of St. Mary Overy (St. Mary of the Ferry), founded by a ferryman's daughter. Southwark itself, which has existed in one form or another at least since 852 A.D., was an Augustinian priory from 1106 to 1540 and achieved cathedral status in 1905. The cathedral has had an interesting history of births, marriages, and deaths. John Harvard, founder of the American college that bears his name, was baptized there in 1607 and is commemorated by Harvard Chapel. In 1423 the church was the scene of the wedding of James I of Scotland and Joan Beaufort, whose uncle, Cardinal Beaufort, rebuilt the south transept. The retrochoir, now called the Lady Chapel (an earlier Lady Chapel built by Peter des Roches in 1207 was torn down in 1830), was the site of the ecclesiastical courts of Bonner and Gardiner during the reign of "Bloody Mary" (1553-58) and the place where Bradford, Ferrar, Hooper, Rogers, Saunders, and Taylor were sentenced to death. The cathedral contains the tomb of the poet John Gower (1330-1408), a friend of Chaucer, and the unmarked graves of playwrights John Fletcher and Philip Massinger, and of Edmund Shakespeare (died 1607), the poet's younger brother.

22 SOUTHWELL

Paulinus, the first bishop of York (c. 630), is thought to have founded Southwell on the site occupied by the Church of St. Mary, although the first documented description of a church on the site dates from only about 730. The present building was begun during the first half of the reign of Henry I (1100-35), but it was not given cathedral standing until 1884. In the Decorated chapter house (unusual in having a roof not supported by a central pillar) are excellent naturalistic foliage carvings, which are considered the earliest of their type in England. A large Perpendicular window and aisle windows provide the nave with exceptional light, and in the choir the effect of height is increased by the clever manner in which the clerestory and triforium are combined. One of few early medieval cathedrals with three surviving towers, Southwell is also notable for the Roman mosaic paving that has been uncovered in the transept. The sculptured heads on the corbels—of the men in power when the choir was built—include Archbishop Walter de Gray and Henry III.

23 WELLS (see pages 162-67)

24 WINCHESTER (see pages 132-35)

25 WORCESTER

Of the eleventh-century Norman church built by Saint Wulfstan, only the crypt, west bays of the nave, chapter house interior, and some of the walls remain. Though all styles from Norman to Perpendicular are found here, Worcester Cathedral, whose plan forms a double cross, dates mainly from the fourteenth cen-

tury. The choir, which is embellished with narrow Purbeck marble shafts and delicate carving of the Early English style, merits particular attention, and the effigy on the monument of King John (buried in the cathedral at his own request in 1216) is thought to be the earliest existing portrait of an English ruler.

Worcester; a nineteenth-century engraving

Other interesting tombs include that of Prince Arthur, the older brother of Henry VIII, and one marked "Miserrimus," said to be the resting place of a minor canon who fell into disfavor when he refused to take the oath of supremacy upon the accession of William III. The interior's unbroken ribbed roof (387 feet long) is the only one of its kind in England, and the decagonal chapter house, whose vaulting is supported by a single central column, is said to have been the original example for all other circular chapter houses. The Norman crypt (1084-92), though similar to others in plan, differs in the grace and lightness of its piers. Worcester's fourteenth-century tower is one of the most impressive in England.

26 YORK

When Paulinus, the first archbishop of York, selected Easter Day, 627, for the baptism of King Edwin of Northumbria, a wooden church was hastily erected in a style that could be termed "Sudden Saxon." From then on York Minster had its ups and downs. A stone church, put up to replace the wooden one, burned down around 741; a third church, begun by Archbishop Albert (767-80), came down in the Norman Conquest; and a fourth (mainly twelfth- and thirteenth-century) was partially burned in 1829 by a madman and again in 1840, after which the mock stone roof, which had been destroyed, was replaced by another ceiling of wood painted to look like stone.

York boasts a number of features thought to be the finest of their kind in English cathedrals: the nave, the best in the Decorated style; the lantern, the largest; the chapter house, the most beautiful; and the windows, the best original stained glass. Of special interest are the Jesse Window (c. 1200), the oldest in the cathedral; the great east window, the second largest in England; and the Five Sisters Window with its original glazing, releaded in 1925 as a memorial to women killed in World War I. For the duration of World War II the priceless window glass was temporarily removed. An astronomical clock commemorates airmen based in northeast England during that war. Encircling the wide-aisled nave and the choir are painted stone shields of Edward II and the barons who held parliament at York in 1309-10.

J. Britton: 1819 study of windows at York

OPPOSITE: *Capital from Southwell Cathedral*

GERMANY

1 AACHEN *(see pages 212–17)*

2 AUGSBURG

The world's oldest representational stained glass may be found at Augsburg; it dates from the first half of the twelfth century (some say earlier) and depicts the prophets—rigid, forceful, and glowing with color. The ancient cathedral, begun as a Romanesque basilica around 995, had evolved by the fifteenth century into a fine Gothic structure famous for a long choir (possibly modeled after the choir at Prague) and four altars painted by Augsburg's great son, Hans Holbein the Elder. Other natives of Augsburg, such as the immensely wealthy and powerful Fugger family, added to the cathedral's treasures in the fifteenth and sixteenth centuries, founding chapels and erecting monumental tombs. Earlier, in the eleventh century, bronze panels were fitted to the wood of the building's southern door. They are striking for their uncluttered simplicity, described by one observer as "influenced by classical models, but unmistakably new."

3 BAMBERG

Weary of public life and chronically ill, Emperor Henry II of Germany set out for Bamberg, his favorite city, to build a cathedral. In so doing, he was living up to his appellation, "the Saint," which he had enhanced, supposedly, by living in the state of "*mariage blanc*" with his wife, Kunigunda of Luxembourg. Henry began his cathedral in 1007, but its heyday was not until 200 years later, when workmen from almost every part of Germany converged on Bamberg to transform the Romanesque *Dom* into the large Gothic Cathedral of St. Peter and St. George. Working side by side with these architects and masons were the sculptors who created a series of statues that are regarded by German critics as "of a quality comparable to that of Greece and Rome." The sculptors were men from the Upper Rhine, but they had undoubtedly studied in France, and some of them may have worked on the decorations of the cathedral at Reims. French influences notwith-

standing, their work has a distinctly Germanic bravura, especially evident in the bold equestrian figure known as "der Reiter." Three hundred years passed before other talented sculptors created a marble tomb in the cathedral for Henry and Kunigunda; both are shown chastely garbed on their separate beds.

4 BREMEN

The present Cathedral of Sankt Petri (as it is called in the northern dialect) was begun in 1043 by Adalbert, a statesman-bishop of northern Germany and Scandinavia. An imposing Romanesque structure, the cathedral boasts a thirteenth-century baptismal font, supported by warriors seated on crouching lions; an organ once played by Bach; and, in its cellar, seven mummies, including one of a fifteenth-century tiler who apparently fell from the roof while at work. A more impressive tomb, that of Adalbert himself, is located in the east crypt, the oldest part of the cathedral.

5 BRUNSWICK

The twelfth-century pillared Romanesque cathedral in Brunswick was built

by the Saxon duke, Henry the Lion, who is buried in the crypt. His tomb, depicting a life-size Henry and his duchess—their marble garments draped in classic folds —is one of the finest examples of German medieval sculpture. The most remarkable feature of Brunswick Cathedral is the fifteenth-century replacement of the north aisle with a double-aisled hall of unusual spiral columns and a complicated vaulting system.

6 COLOGNE *(see pages 198–203)*

7 CONSTANCE

Four stone pillars supporting the low-vaulted ceiling in the hall of the crypt in the cathedral at Constance recently have been identified as parts of an eighth-century Carolingian basilica. The cathedral proper was begun in the tenth century by Bishop Lambert; nearly 300 years later it fell victim to fire. A new structure was erected on the ruins, featuring two of the latest Gothic elements of the time: turrets and decorated window arches. By the early fourteenth century, a sturdy hybrid of Gothicized Romanesque was the pride of the ancient city. In 1356, however, an earthquake destroyed part of the building. New construction was then undertaken and continued until the nineteenth century with each era contributing its particular architectural features to both exterior and interior. One of the most interesting components of the cathedral is known as the "Schnegg" (dialect for "snail"), a spiral staircase, located in the transept and enclosed by an ornate Gothic stone tower.

8 EICHSTÄTT

Untouched by World War II, the exterior of the original eleventh-century cathedral at Eichstätt affords a good example of the Romanesque style once dominant in Germany. Inside, the style is Gothic, since much of the interior was rebuilt in the late fourteenth century; several Baroque elements are evident as well, especially in the west front façade (1714–18). Eichstätt's cathedral is the resting place of a family of eighth-century saints, the best known being Willibald, whose monument stands near the altar. Stained glass designed by Hans Holbein the Elder adorns the double-aisled cloister.

9 FRANKFURT

The Cathedral of St. Bartholomew in Frankfurt is one of the most history-laden buildings in Germany. Here, from the fourteenth century until 1792, all German kings and emperors were crowned—the result of a "Golden Bull" issued in 1356 by Charles IV. The thirteenth-century Gothic structure is notable for its choir frescoes (1427) depicting the life of the cathedral's patron saint and for a 309-foot spired tower with its 12-ton Imperial Bell, the "Gloriosa," and a famous view of the Taunus hills. In 1943, Allied bombing raids badly damaged the cathedral; reconstruction has only recently been completed.

10 FREIBURG (see pages 208–11)

11 FREISING

The 184-foot twin towers of the Romanesque cathedral, which was begun in 1160, dominate the small Bavarian town of Freising. Here, as in other Romanesque churches in Germany, Gothic ele-

ments were introduced into the interior during the fourteenth and fifteenth centuries. Three hundred years later, the interior was redecorated—probably in an attempt to unify the building's appearance. Two Bavarian artists, the Asam brothers, accomplished this with skillful stucco work and with frescoes on the dome and the chancel and chapel walls.

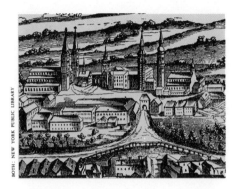

Freising; a nineteenth-century engraving

12 HILDESHEIM

It is not known whether the Saxon bishop Bernward, founder of Hildesheim's Ottonian cathedral, also planted the celebrated "thousand-year-old rosebush" that grows in its garden, but he did bestow an extraordinary treasure of medieval art works on the lofty edifice. Chief among these are the bronze doors (made for a smaller church in 1015 but promoted to the cathedral) portraying biblical scenes. Bernward commissioned a bronze commemorative column for the same church, and it, too, was later removed to the cathedral. Of a spiral design reminiscent of Trajan's column, it is decorated with scenes from the Passion in bas-relief. A font, resting on the shoulders of four allegorical figures variously known as the Four Cardinal Virtues and the Four Rivers of Paradise, is further testimony to Bernward's taste. The cathedral's interior was decorated in the Baroque style in the 1720's.

13 LIMBURG AN DER LAHN

In 909, Konrad Kurzbold, a Franconian count, founded the collegiate Church of St. George. The seven-towered building, which was completed by 1220, is among Limburg's chief historical achievements and is generally regarded as one of

the truest examples of the transition from Late German Romanesque to French Gothic. The French influence was brought about in the thirteenth century by Count Henry of Nassau, who had the interior redone in fond imitation of the cathedral at Laon—a Gothic masterpiece he greatly admired. The Gothic influence, however, remains largely in the interior of St. George's, whose nave and chancel resemble Laon, while the exterior is faithful to the fortress style of similar Romanesque cathedrals nestled along the banks of the Rhine.

14 MAGDEBURG

Begun in 1209 on the ruins of a Romanesque church, Magdeburg was among the first German cathedrals to incorporate French Gothic elements. A patron of the "new look," Archbishop Albrecht wanted his cathedral to contain the latest French innovations that he had admired at Senlis, Noyon, and Paris. Although the German architects were not always up to the demands of the new style, they did create a choir that is Early French Gothic in spirit. The nave and transept were finished by 1272 in a simplified German Gothic style, but they harmonize well with the French choir. The cathedral was miraculously spared in May, 1631, during the Sack of Magdeburg—one of the most violent episodes of the Thirty Years' War. Unfortunately, the building did not fare so well during the bombing of World War II.

A nineteenth-century view of Magdeburg

15 MAINZ *(see pages 192–97)*

16 NAUMBURG

As the thirteenth-century reconstruction of Naumburg's cathedral was nearing completion, Bishop Dietrich, overseer of the project, decided to create a fitting monument to the Thuringian aristocrats who had done so much to establish the city's episcopal see. The execution of his plan bestowed upon the cathedral its most famous single feature: the Founders' Choir, a gallery dominated by twelve life-size statues of the members of Naumburg's illustrious houses of Eckardin and Wettin, the latter being the ancestral family of Bishop Dietrich himself, as well as of the current Windsor family in England. The names of the sculptors engaged for this undertaking are lost, but there is no doubt that they were keen students of French sculpture and may have worked at Strasbourg or Chartres. Above all, they were master realists and captured what the noted medievalist Henri Pirenne calls "the first characteristics of what was one day to be known as the Prussian spirit"—a spirit epitomized by the popular figures of Margrave Ekkehart and his elegant wife Uta. The other members of the gallery watch with varying degrees of concern as the Lord's Passion is played out on a carved stone rood screen near by.

17 PASSAU

Overlooking three rivers—the Danube, the Inn, and the little Ilz—the domed Cathedral of St. Stephan stands on the highest point in Passau. It is a building of three eras: the Gothic, represented by the east end of the exterior, which was built between 1407 and 1530; the Baroque, by the west façade and the nave, built after a ruinous fire in 1622; and the nineteenth century, by the two west towers. Despite this diversity, the entire building has an architectural unity that is, strangely enough, Italianate. In fact, the entire town of Passau has an Italian quality that was imposed by Italian architects after the fire of 1662. In the design of the cathedral, they were responsible for the stucco work, the Rococo ornamentation, and the octagonal dome sur-

mounting the crossing of the nave. St. Stephan's houses the largest organ in the world: 17,000 pipes and over 200 stops.

Regensburg Cathedral (right) by Merian

18 REGENSBURG

At a meeting of the Council of Lyons in 1274, Leo of Tundorf, bishop of Regensburg, sought out Cardinal Archer, patron of the Church of St. Urbain in Troyes. The old Romanesque church at Regensburg had burned to the ground in 1272, and Leo wanted to build a new cathedral based on the cardinal's admirable elevation of the recently completed St. Urbain. The project was launched soon afterward, but St. Peter's required another 260 years to achieve any semblance of completion; in fact, its two towers were not finished until 1869. Now one of the glories of the Danube, the large Gothic cathedral houses some of the finest stained glass in Germany, as well as several richly carved tombs, including that of Karl von Dalberg, Napoleon's primate over the Confederation of the Rhine.

19 SCHLESWIG

Visitors to the thirteenth-century Gothic Cathedral of St. Peter in Schleswig invariably head for the chancel and the massive Bordesholm Altar—a carved masterpiece of 392 wood figures, which depicts several saints and the Fourteen Stations of the Cross in the strong, realistic style that is the hallmark of German

art. Hans Brüggemann finished the altar in 1521, and it was installed in a remote abbey at Bordesholm, where it spent nearly 150 years in obscurity. Not until the mid-seventeenth century did the duke of Schleswig move it to the cathedral, where it has been a focus of attention ever since.

20 SPEYER *(see pages 188–91)*

21 TRIER

The cathedral at Trier incorporates the remains of a Roman basilica. The exterior of the building is mostly Late Romanesque, having been erected in the eleventh and twelfth centuries, with vaulting and parts of the towers added later. The most unusual addition, the treasury, is an eighteenth-century Baroque structure capped by a bell-shaped dome constructed in three interlocking sections; it houses "the seamless robe of Christ," a relic shown to the public only once or twice a century. The cathedral at Trier is rarely considered by itself; alongside it is the Church of Our Lady, a Gothic building that served in the Middle Ages as a parish church, leaving the cathedral generally for aristocrats and clergy.

22 WORMS *(see pages 204–7)*

23 WURZBURG

The large Romanesque cathedral in Würzburg is named for the Irish saint Kilian. It was dedicated in 1034, and its exterior has remained largely Romanesque. Würzburg became one of the centers of German Baroque in the eighteenth century under the influence of the architect Balthasar Neumann, and the interior of St. Kilian's reflects this taste. From 1701 through 1726, Neumann and others added ornate chapels, stucco decorations, and Rococo statuary to the building, creating a somewhat startling contrast to the Romanesque exterior. Unfortunately, bombings during World War II damaged the cathedral rather badly, and much of Neumann's delicate work was lost.

OPPOSITE: *Limburg Cathedral as it was depicted by a nineteenth-century engraver*

SPAIN

1 ASTORGA

According to the original design, the Gothic cathedral at Astorga, begun in 1471, was to have two soaring towers, but only one (still incomplete) has been raised so far. On top of the cathedral stands a weathercock representing Pedro Mato, a well-known Maragato, or descendant of the Berber highlanders who settled in northwestern Spain. The cathedral's retable, depicting the lives of Christ and the Virgin and symbolizing the four cardinal virtues—wisdom, courage, temperance, and justice—is the work of Gaspar Becerra, a Spanish pupil of Michelangelo. The treasury contains some outstanding relics, including a segment of the True Cross and a silver casket from the tenth century.

2 AVILA

The term "church militant" might almost have been coined for the early Gothic Cathedral of Avila, whose huge battlemented apse forms a bastion in the city's medieval wall. The cathedral was begun in 1157—a time when Christians and Moors were still contending for power in Spain, and any Catholic church had to be built strongly enough to repel the sieges of the Infidel. Moreover, the boy monarchs of Castile, Asturias, and León traditionally took refuge in Avila from those kingdoms' predatory barons, who were not overly scrupulous about observing the sanctity of churches—at least, those churches that could be stormed with ease. As a consequence of all this, Bishop Sancho, who had assumed his seat in 1188 (and who was responsible for the safety of Alfonso IX during the king's minority), turned his church into a castellated fortress. Avila's interior is celebrated, even in a country where sombre churches are hardly exceptional, for its striking solemnity—a solemnity that must have accorded well with the temperament of the city's best-known native, the mystical Saint Teresa. The choir (c. 1190) was influenced by the choir at Vézelay, and the aisled nave is narrower than most, with a blind triforium and a large

358

clerestory. There is some excellent late fifteenth-century glass by Juan de Valdivielso in the main chapel, and a particularly handsome retable (1499–1508), the collaborative work of three Spanish painters, shows Saints Peter and Paul with evangelists and doctors and scenes from the life of Christ and the Passion.

3 BARCELONA

An almost palpable gloom pervades the interior of the Gothic Cathedral of Barcelona, obscuring its splendid proportions but investing it with an impressive aura of mysticism and gravity. The effect is further enhanced by the unusually high nave arcade, small triforium, and the use of oculi for the clerestory windows. Located in the picturesque medieval quarter of downtown Barcelona, the cathedral occupies ground that probably served as the site for a temple in pagan antiquity. A later, Christian, house of worship was partially destroyed by the Moors in the tenth century, was rebuilt in the eleventh, and then razed toward the end of the thirteenth to make way for the present structure. Although the major portions of the cathedral were completed by 1438, the elaborately decorated

west front (for which plans were drawn up early in the fifteenth century) was not finished until 1892. This extended lag notwithstanding, the facade harmonizes well with the rest of the building. Barcelona's choir windows are good examples of Late Gothic stained glass and, toward evening, suffuse the interior of the church with a rather eerie multicolored glow that has often been remarked upon by visitors to the cathedral. The many side chapels are filled with treasures (and with a good deal of fascinating trash), most of which, unfortunately, are nearly invisible. The cathedral's cloister (1382–1448), remarkable for its irregular arches and unconventional capitals, is one of the finest in Europe.

4 BURGOS (see pages 228–33)

5 CIUDAD RODRIGO

The city of Rodrigo was established by Count Rodrigo González Girón in 1150. Its beautiful Gothic cathedral was begun about fifteen years later and is modeled on the Cathedral of Zamora. Of its three doorways, the west portal is especially interesting for its wealth of varied carvings and its door jambs, which are miniatures of the Tower of Gallo in Salamanca. The choir stalls are the work of Rodrigo Alemán, an extremely gifted and witty carver, whose work is preserved in similar stalls in the nearby cathedrals of Plasencia and Zamora.

6 CORDOBA (*see pages 238–43*)

7 CUENCA

Founded by Alfonso VIII in the twelfth century, the Gothic cathedral at Cuenca stands in the Plaza Mayor, or Main Square. Much work has gone into restoring the original west front, after its poor reconstruction in the seventeenth century. Since the region around the city is rich in jasper, it is natural to find jasper columns in the sacristy and decorations of the same material on the high altar. The choir and side chapels all have beautifully worked grilles, and the east chapel is particularly notable for its splendid carved ceiling, which is considered to be one of the finest of its kind in Spain. The sacristy also contains some fine carving of another type—a Mater Dolorosa and a Madonna by Pedro de Mena, the seventeenth-century Spanish sculptor.

8 GERONA

In 1416 Guillermo Boffiy designed a tremendous vault for the aisleless nave of the Cathedral of Gerona. A committee of architects was assembled to ratify the design and attest to the safety of the undertaking. Apparently they approved, for today Gerona has the widest Gothic vault in existence (74 feet). Most of the cathedral's construction was accomplished between the early fourteenth and late sixteenth centuries. Earlier Romanesque constructions are the cloister and the Tower of Charlemagne (who built the first church to occupy the site in 786). A fourteenth-century stone bishop's throne, admirably simple in its design, is located in the choir, and the numerous chapels contain many noteworthy tombs.

9 GRANADA

In 1492 Ferdinand and Isabella claimed the Moorish kingdom of Granada for Spain and for Christianity—an event that was celebrated at St. Paul's in London with a special *Te Deum*. Thirty years later, work was begun on the Cathedral of Granada. Intended to be a monument to the Christian faith, it is more justly a memorial to the most Catholic monarchs of Spain. In the sumptuous main chapel, beside the arch leading to the high altar, are the kneeling statues of Ferdinand and Isabella. The huge royal chapel serves as a mausoleum for the couple. The sacristy contains mementos once belonging to the king and queen, the banner under which they conquered Granada, and a small but superb collection of paintings, including works by such masters as Memling, van der Weyden, and Botticelli. The cathedral, in Early Renaissance style, is the work of several Spanish architects, but French, Italian, and Flemish artists have contributed to its splendor.

Granada's royal tombs; an 1837 drawing

10 JAEN

Plans for the Renaissance cathedral at Jaén were drawn up in 1532 by André de Vandaelvira. Most of the church, however, was built by his successors. The two imposing towers that flank the west front, for example, did not go up until the second half of the seventeenth century, and the sacristy, although largely the work of Vandaelvira, did not assume its final form until 1801. The cathedral houses many relics, the most precious of which is one of the many Holy Cloths supposedly used by Veronica to wipe Christ's face on the road to Calvary.

11 LUGO

Lugo Cathedral (a suffragan to the see of Santiago de Compostela) is one of several churches that have borrowed stylistic elements from the cathedral at Santiago. Thus the interior, like Santiago's, has a long nave with nine bays and very low aisles. The three towers and west front were not built until the second half of the eighteenth century, although the church was founded in 1129. Above the north door is a carved stone figure of a serene Christ, beneath which, on the crowded pendant capital, the disciples gaze outward while partaking of the Last Supper.

12 ORENSE

Two saints watch over the Gothic cathedral of Orense. The patronage of Saint Martin began with the first cathedral, constructed in the sixth century. When the church was rebuilt for the third time during the first half of the thirteenth century, Saint Euphemia was given a share of the honors. As is the case with Lugo, the architects of Orense copied elements of the Cathedral of Santiago de Compostela. Indeed, the doorway leading to the nave is a near replica of Santiago's well-known Pórtico de la Gloria, with the same number of pillar figures and a central arch embellished with twenty-four saints playing string instruments.

13 ORIHUELA

Although built in the fourteenth century, the church did not become a cathedral until the middle of the sixteenth, when the ambulatory chapels were added to the edifice. In 1829 the city was hit by an earthquake that caused extensive damage to the cathedral. As is often the case, the restorers were overly ambitious, and their work has been repaired only recently to make the structure conform to its original design. The cathedral boasts two fine Gothic doorways; inside, the sixteenth-century vault with its twisted ribs is of interest, as are the grilles and the choir.

14 OVIEDO

The small, gracefully proportioned Gothic Cathedral of Oviedo is known for

The Cathedral of Barcelona is shown in longitudinal section in this illustration for a book published in 1837.

its 260-foot south tower, which provides a splendid view of the landscape surrounding the town. The cathedral proper was begun in the fourteenth century, but its most interesting feature, a chamber called the *Cámara Santa*, reached by a staircase off the transept, survives in part from the ninth-century church that occupied the site. Its rich collection of relics —thorns from Christ's crown, a sandal belonging to Saint Peter, a segment of the True Cross, one of the thirty pieces of silver—is contained in a coffer that cannot be opened without committing a sin against the church. The Holy Shroud is kept in this room and displayed on certain holy days. Another unusual feature of the church is the placement of the choir—in the main chapel. An interesting pillar, to the right of the choir, bears a figure of Christ thought to have been carved in the twelfth century; the capital is decorated with pilgrims' cockleshells.

15 PALENCIA

The ground above a cave reportedly used as a dwelling place by Saint Antoninus, a second-century martyr, was the original site of the church that antedated the Cathedral of Palencia. The cathedral itself was begun on the same spot in 1321, but it was not completed until the middle of the sixteenth century. As a result, its style is Gothic Transitional. During the sixteenth century many important works of art found their way to the cathedral, including two splendid altarpieces—one by a Dutch artist in the choir, the other by a Spaniard in the main chapel. The sacristy contains a painting of Saint Sebastian by El Greco and a diptych by Pedro Berruguete. The chapter rooms are enlivened by several fine sixteenth-century Brussels tapestries. One of the cathedral's more curious features is its clock, which is located high up in the south transept, where a knight and a lion strike the hours and quarter hours.

16 PALMA

Approached from the scenic bay of Palma, the "Gothic triumph," as the city's waterfront cathedral is called, stands out impressively against the rocky backdrop of the island of Majorca. The

Chancel window at Palma; a 1932 drawing

oldest part of the building is the *Capilla Real*, erected by Jaime I soon after he defeated the Moors in 1229 and added the Balearic Islands to the Kingdom of Aragon. But the cathedral itself, which incorporates this chapel, was actually founded by King Jaime II in 1306. Construction extended through the fifteenth century and did not actually cease until the late sixteenth century, but the builders followed the original plan and thereby ensured the aesthetic unity of the cathedral. The building is higher than any French cathedral except Beauvais. The inner space seems even greater because of the great width of both the nave and the aisles, the height of the columns, the lack of a triforium, and the rigorous suppression of decorative elements. There is no transept, and the impression is of a great waiting room for the complex choir.

17 PAMPLONA

Like many cathedrals of the Middle Ages, the Cathedral of Pamplona was dedicated to the Virgin. It was built during the eleventh century, but by the end of the fourteenth century it had fallen into such disrepair that it took over a hundred years to rebuild. The old Romanesque façade was finally replaced in 1783, and nothing remains of the original church. Indeed, change is still taking place in the interior. As recently as 1957 the choir stalls were removed to the main chapel, and their place was taken by the Burgundian-style tomb of King Charles III and his queen. The cathedral contains some fine sculpture; all the carvings over the doorways of the Gothic cloister celebrate a common theme: the cult of the Virgin. Particularly noteworthy are the death of Mary over the door leading to the cloister, and, inside the cloister, the fourteenth-century relief of the Adoration of the Magi.

18 PLASENCIA

The first cathedral of Plasencia was built during the fourteenth century. At the end of the fifteenth, however, another cathedral was begun on practically the same site. The section of the old church that survived the renewal became known as Santa María and contains a remarkable spiral staircase. Although the new cathedral, which is still unfinished, was begun as a Gothic structure, construction has continued for many years and with time has taken on more and more characteristics of the Renaissance style. Inside, the main chapel contains a magnificent, multicolored altarpiece done during the early part of the seventeenth century. Rodrigo Alemán is responsible for the elaborate choir stalls, with carvings that range from the sacred to the humorous.

19 SALAMANCA

Historically, Salamanca seems disinclined to put all its eggs into one basket. In 217 B.C. when the forces of Hannibal overran the city, the male defenders were easily disarmed, but the women supplied their

An engraving of Salamanca's interior

defeated menfolk with weapons they had concealed on their persons, thereby enabling them to turn the tables on the Carthaginians. In keeping with this early precedent, Salamanca today has not one, but two, cathedrals: the Vieja, a Romanesque and Early Gothic structure dating from the early twelfth century, with a Byzantine dome, and the Nueva, a sixteenth-century Gothic edifice whose plan resembles that of the cathedral at Segovia. The vault of the cathedral's Chapel of St. Bartholomew is interesting for its English influence and for its organ, dating from 1380, which may be the oldest in Europe. The new church is notable for its gallery, embellished with Flamboyant tracery; a thirteenth-century gilt-bronze Virgin; a Byzantine crucifix carried into battle by El Cid; and some sixteenth-century Flemish glass.

20 SANTIAGO DE COMPOSTELA
(see pages 250–55)

21 SANTO DOMINGO DE LA CALZADA

Founded by King Alfonso VIII, the Gothic Cathedral of Santo Domingo de la Calzada was to all intents and purposes completed in 1235, although a Baroque bell tower was added to the cathedral complex during the second half of the eighteenth century. A carved walnut altarpiece in the main chapel is interesting, as is the richly decorated screen of the Chapel of La Magdalena. The cathedral also houses a shrine designed by Felipe Vigarni, but visitors are most intrigued by a room off the south transept that serves as a coop for a rooster and a hen; the birds, killed every May twelfth, commemorate a miracle that occurred when a cock and hen prepared for dinner revived and assumed full plumage to prove a young man innocent of the charge of stealing; new birds are then brought in for another year's residence.

22 SARAGOSSA

Saragossa's eclectic cathedral began its existence as a mosque. Although the building was almost completely remodeled over the centuries, traces of its Moorish origins can be seen in a section of its exterior wall, decorated with a typical brick and tile mosaic, and in the square floor plan of the interior. Dedicated to the Saviour, the baldachin, resting on twisted columns in the middle of the *trascoro*, marks the spot where Christ is said to have spoken to a canon. All four walls are lined with chapels, including one dedicated to Saints Peter and Paul. Among the church's more noteworthy features are the magnificent grilles enclosing the choir and the alabaster altarpiece in the main chapel. The chapter house contains many fine paintings by Ribera, Zurbarán, and Goya.

23 SEVILLE (see pages 244–49)

24 SIGUENZA

Built and altered over the course of two centuries, the Romanesque Gothic Cathedral of Sigüenza is more French than Spanish in style. Specifically, the west front, with low, square towers, is derived from the cathedral at Poitiers. Within, there are many sumptuous chapels, the most notable of which is the main chapel with its elaborate grille and tomb of the first bishop of Sigüenza. The portal of the Chapel of the Annunciation is significant for its combination of Gothic, Renaissance, and Moorish elements. The chapel of the Arce family contains some fine tomb monuments, but perhaps the greatest treasure of all is El Greco's *Annunciation* in the chapter house.

25 TARRAGONA

Tarragona, the ancient Tarraco of the Romans, preserves much of its early heritage. The cathedral, begun in 1171, is a fine example of the Early Gothic style. The Moors had been forced out of the city less than a hundred years earlier, and fear of their return led the architects to fortify the apse. The main chapel contains a magnificent fifteenth-century altarpiece in florid Gothic style. The arched marble doorway leading to the cloister was executed by a local artist and decorated with Romanesque sculpture. The particularly handsome cloister consists of six bays, with three arches to each bay. Most of the capitals are decorated with the conventional foliated motif, but one stands out for the curious tale it tells—a cat, being borne to its funeral by a pack of rats, awakens from its pretended "death," presumably to do away with the pallbearers.

26 TOLEDO (see pages 264–69)

Tarragona; nineteenth-century lithograph

27 TORTOSA

The Cathedral of Tortosa was built on the site of a tenth-century mosque erected by Abd-al-Rahman III, one of the most powerful Moslem rulers in Spain. Its earlier history is preserved in the sacristy in the form of a Kufic inscription recording the erection of the mosque. Although the cathedral was founded in 1158, building was not begun until 1347; the elaborate Baroque façade dates from the first half of the eighteenth century. The most celebrated feature of the cathedral is its ambulatory with beautiful screens of pierced stone. The cathedral suffered much damage during the Spanish Civil War, and the choir was destroyed.

28 TUY

In 1170 Ferdinand II chose a new location for the ancient city of Túy, and ten years later the cathedral, a massive fortress-like structure, was begun. The nave—heavily influenced by French architecture of the period—dates from the first half of the thirteenth century, but most of the structure is more recent; the choir and west front, for example, were still being worked on in the fifteenth century, although the thirteenth-century style was retained. Túy is a river port with easy access to the Atlantic; as a result, the cathedral is dedicated to Saint Telmo (the English Saint Elmo), the patron of mariners.

29 ZAMORA (see pages 234–37)

ITALY

1 AMALFI

A flight of sixty steps leads to the roseate Cathedral of Amalfi, tucked in the Salernitano hills amid the shops and hostels of the town. Although the building itself is largely a nineteenth-century reconstruction based on thirteenth-century plans, the campanile dates from the twelfth century. The glazing and decorations of its turrets, however, are Baroque additions. The cathedral's elaborate interior is entirely Baroque, with gilded and molded panels on the ceiling, Rococo chandeliers of brass and crystal, and ornate plaster fronds and volutes over the altar. The relics of Saint Andrew, brought from the East in 1208, are kept in the thirteenth-century crypt.

2 ANCONA

A mixture of Romanesque and Byzantine styles marks the Cathedral of St. Ciriaco, begun in the eleventh century. The Byzantine influence is largely in the interior, which is shaped like a Greek cross, and in the pillars and capitals of the aisles. The exterior is basically Romanesque, with a thirteenth-century porch of rose-colored stone supported by the traditional carved lions. The cathedral's museum of sacred art contains many Christian artifacts brought from the East during Trajan's reign, when Ancona was a thriving seaport.

3 ASSISI

Two of the greatest saints in Christendom were baptized in the fonts of Assisi's cathedral: Saint Francis in 1182 and Saint Clare, his disciple, in 1193. Begun around 1140, the façade of the cathedral consists of a single gabled section, decorated with stone grillework and arches; a large rose window flanked by two smaller versions; and a pointed arch rising almost to the apex of the gable. The square campanile displays an old clock surmounted by a sun roof. The cathedral's interior, which was altered to conform with sixteenth-century notions of modernity, contains some excellent statuary.

4 BARI

The original Cathedral of Bari was destroyed by warfare in 1156. The subsequent structure was built in the Lombard Romanesque style, but retained certain exotic features, especially in the Saracen decorations around the windows and in the open-arched gallery with its slightly Moorish flavor. The façades of the cathedral are almost unadorned, its campanile is square with a peaked tower, and its cupola is octagonal—an unusual feature in the Lombard scheme. The interior retains the twelfth- and thirteenth-century mood, having been thoroughly purged of Baroque and later additions. A twelve-sided sacristy stands as evidence of the Baroque period.

5 BITONTO

The Romanesque Cathedral of San Valentino, probably the most beautiful and harmonious in Apulia, gives the impression that its nave and transepts were carved from a single block. The sturdy twelfth-century arches, the dignified decorations of the interior that draw all the elements together, and a wide, open southern gallery tend to enhance this impression. Dominating the central portal is a large rose window surrounded by stone lions, griffins, and other exotic fauna. A carved marble pulpit (1229) reflects certain Islamic styles in its tracery, as well as what might be called Adriatic pride in the bold eagle design of the Bible rest.

6 CATANIA

Owing to earthquakes and possibly to the eruptions of nearby Mount Etna, the eleventh- and twelfth-century cathedral has undergone various stylistic changes. Begun in the Norman style, it was revised in Baroque after the earthquake of 1693; in deference to the past the eighteenth-century architects incorporated the old columns onto the new façade. A Baroque cupola and campanile jut up above the gables, which are adorned with marble urns. The interior is similar in style but includes the ruin of an ancient Roman bath at the front of the structure. Several tombs are particularly interesting —especially those of the house of Aragon and the composer Vincenzo Bellini.

7 CEFALU *(see pages 286–89)*

8 COMO

The fourteenth-century Cathedral of Como, built entirely of marble, is one of the finest examples of Lombard Gothic building in Italy. There are, however, Renaissance elements throughout: Figures of Pliny the Elder and Pliny the Younger (both natives of the area) are ensconced in the niches on either side of the main door. The Renaissance is also at least partly responsible for the octagonal cupola crowning the cathedral; although constructed in the eighteenth century, it was inspired by fifteenth- and sixteenth-century designs. Original carvings and sculpture from the Renaissance may be found throughout the interior and on the façade of a structure that Symonds calls "perhaps the most perfect building for illustrating the fusion of Gothic and Renaissance styles."

9 CREMA

The thirteenth-century Cathedral of Crema, built in the Lombard Gothic style, stands in an arcaded square. The brick façade, because of its shallowness, seems to have been a happy afterthought. Dominated by three semicircular arches and a simple rose window, this flat façade balances the more ornate and integrated campanile in the rear. The overall thirteenth-century style of the building is interrupted slightly by the "classic" Baroque decorations of the lintels over the small side entrances to the nave of the cathedral.

10 CREMONA

The Lombard Romanesque style is well represented by the tower and gabled façade of Cremona's cathedral, built in the twelfth and thirteenth centuries. The campanile, the highest in Italy (498 spiraling steps), rises in ornate, octagonal elegance, offering a striking contrast to the shape of the cathedral itself. Statuary and rich detail stand out on the red-and-white-marble façade, begun in the twelfth century. These embellishments include a thirteenth-century rose window and an elaborate loggia, adorned by the sculpture of Balduccio and supported by columns resting on stone lions. The marble reliefs of the prophets that flank the main door are among the first French-inspired sculptures to appear in Italy. But it was the native school of sixteenth-century Cremona that enriched the interior of the building with paintings and frescoes. There is also a carved sarcophagus by the fourteenth-century tombmaker and sculptor, Bonino da Campione.

Ferrara; the cathedra and choir stalls

11 FERRARA

Three peaked gables of equal size and height dominate the façade of San Giorgio. Consecrated in 1135, the large building features Gothic elements in the arches on the upper façade and in the loggia over the central door. The sculptures of the main portal are attributed to Niccolò, a twelfth-century artist who may have studied for a time in Byzantium. His work consists of the usual lion-supports for the portal columns, but he has added tragic-looking men seated on the lions; they shoulder the actual burden. Unfortunately, the interior of San Giorgio was completely transformed in the eighteenth century—obliterating the work of the twelfth century and in no way improving upon the cathedral's general appearance.

12 FLORENCE *(see pages 304–7)*

Genoa; a nineteenth-century lithograph

13 GENOA

Because of its proximity to France, Genoa felt the influence of French Gothic architecture early in the fourteenth century when work on the restoration of the eleventh-century Cathedral of San Lorenzo was undertaken. Today a Renaissance dome tops the Gothic façade. The choir, on the other hand, is early Genoese Baroque (a kind of ornamented classicism). Taken together, however, the seemingly disparate elements of the cathedral make for a rather harmonious whole. Even the highly ornamented Chapel of John the Baptist,

365

containing relics of the saint, has its place in the overall design.

14 LUCCA *(see pages 326–29)*

15 MILAN *(see pages 314–17)*

Modena; a twentieth-century wood engraving

16 MODENA

By 1099, the old fourth-century church at Modena was in such a state of collapse that the rulers of the Commune commissioned the architect Lanfranco to build a new one. Seven years of work ensued before the remains of Saint Geminian, patron of the new cathedral, were laid to rest in the crypt. The style of the building is Lombard Romanesque. One huge gable rises in the center of the façade, dominated by a round window with peaked turrets standing on either side like horns. The campanile, which leans slightly, rises almost 300 feet from a square base to an octagonal lantern that was completed in 1319 by Arrigo da Campione. The interior of the cathedral, relatively unadorned, features a raised presbytery, common in Apulia.

17 MONREALE *(see pages 272–77)*

18 NAPLES

When the Angevins became rulers of southern Italy in 1266, they imported the French Gothic style for the Neopolitan Cathedral of San Gennaro (built between 1272 and 1323). Later, extensive rebuilding of the façades and interior, necessitated by earthquake damage, obliterated much of the structure's Franco-Italian Gothic character. The first major rebuilding occurred in 1407, the next in 1456, and the latest and most extensive between 1877 and 1905. The interior, however, retains some of the French elements —especially in the tomb of Charles I of Anjou. Otherwise, the Italian Renaissance style is dominant. Among other things, the cathedral is famous for its shrine of Saint Gennaro, containing the saint's skull and two phials of his blood (see illustration on page 368).

19 ORVIETO *(see pages 308–13)*

20 PARMA *(see pages 318–21)*

21 PIACENZA

The Lombard Romanesque Cathedral of Piacenza, begun in 1122 but not finished until the thirteenth century, incorporates sundry elements of both the Early and Late Romanesque styles; small open arches on the façade are Early Romanesque, for example, and the projecting porches with columns resting on carved stone lions are a later addition. The sculpture of the façade is attributed to Niccolò, a pupil of the ubiquitous Wiligelmo, the mid-twelfth-century artist whose work can be found up and down the Lombard plain. The harmonious outline of the cathedral proper is broken by the huge, square campanile (1333) with its conical tower and distinctive iron cage in which criminals were displayed to the crowds below.

22 PISA *(see pages 322–25)*

23 PISTOIA

In Pistoia, the *duomo* is famous for its solid silver altar of Saint James (13th–15th centuries), containing 628 figures in bas-relief. Even before taking its final form, the altar was recognized as a priceless treasure; in 1295 it was stolen, an act that so enraged Dante that he consigned the thief to his *Inferno*. The cathedral itself is mainly of the twelfth-century Pisan Romanesque style with rows of small arches on the façades and a polychrome wood-framed nave. Among the cathedral's art treasures are a Virgin and a superb terra cotta, in the central arcade, by della Robbia and a funerary monument by Verrocchio. Médici patronage was probably responsible for the cathedral's treasury of art, one of the acquisitions being the Gobelin tapestries, now hanging behind the altar of Saint James.

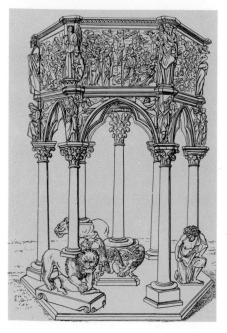

An 1815 engraving of the pulpit at Pistoia

24 PRATO

Originally, the thirteenth-century cathedral at Prato consisted of just a nave and a small choir. Beginning in 1317, a transept was added and the choir enlarged, both under the supervision of the artist and architect Giovanni Pisano, who united the separate parts of the building into an aesthetic whole and managed to create what has been called one of the most harmonious churches in Tuscany. The fifteenth century saw Gothic additions to the white-and-green façade. In the fifteenth century, great artists were encouraged to decorate the pulpits and chapels: Donatello made reliefs, della Robbia fashioned enameled terra cottas, and Fra Filippo Lippi painted frescoes. The dark interior of the church contains many comparable masterpieces and a handsome chapel dedicated to the

Holy Girdle of the Virgin—a relic reportedly handed to the apostle Thomas by the Virgin after her Assumption.

25 RAVELLO

Simplicity marks the exterior of the Cathedral of St. Pantaleone, founded in 1086. The patrician families of Amalfi preferred a rather somber aspect for their church and had it constructed along Norman lines, without arches or embellishments. The interior, however, is vivid and colorful. A marble pulpit stands on inlaid Moorish columns, and they in turn stand upon the backs of striding stone lions. Twelfth-century bronze doors (similar to those at Monreale) and bright mosaics tell the stories of Christ and Jonah, among others. There are also Baroque touches in the interior (on the capitals of the columns) and unusual sculpture derived from classical prototypes, such as the bust of a noblewoman over the pulpit stair.

26 ST. MARK'S, VENICE
(see pages 278–85)

27 ST. PETER'S, VATICAN CITY
(see pages 330–36)

28 SALERNO

Bare, symmetrical, typically Norman in its simplicity, the facade of the cathedral at Salerno is perfectly complemented by the ornate Romanesque atrium that leads to the building from the plaza. In the central portal are Byzantine bronze doors, decorated with niello relief (blackened silver inlay). The cathedral itself was begun by Robert Guiscard, a Norman adventurer who financed the project with his own funds. Pope Gregory VII, a friend of Guiscard who consecrated the building in 1085, was buried in the crypt one year later. The most famous sarcophagus in the cathedral, however, belongs to Saint Matthew the Evangelist, whose remains—or a reasonable facsimile thereof—were brought to Salerno in 954. His shrine lies at the entrance to the crypt beneath an impressive nave restored in the Baroque style.

29 SIENA *(see pages 290–95)*

30 SPOLETO

The influence of Lorenzo the Magnificent brought touches of Renaissance splendor—including a richly carved portico (1491) on the facade—to Spoleto's Romanesque Cathedral of the Assumption. Lorenzo's original impetus was the building of a tomb in the right transept of the church for Fra Filippo Lippi, the master painter who died in Spoleto in 1469. Filippino Lippi, the painter's son, was commissioned to design the tomb and to complete some of his father's frescoes in the apse and chapels. In the seventeenth century, the appearance of the cathedral was further enhanced by Bernini, who reconstructed the interior. The twelfth-century facade, which remained untouched after 1500, is notable for its mosaics and carvings and for two pulpits on the exterior of the portico, constructed for sermons alfresco.

31 SYRACUSE

The site of the Cathedral of Santa María delle Colonne in Syracuse may be one of the oldest places continuously devoted to religion in the world. In pre-Christian times, a Greek temple of Athena (whose Doric columns may still be seen in the south aisle of the present church) occupied the site. The Christians of the seventh century erected a basilica on the temple grounds. Later rebuilt in the Norman style, it survived until 1693 when an earthquake nearly wrecked the entire city. The subsequent facade (1728–54) is distinctly Baroque. Here, tapered columns are topped by ornate Corinthian capitals; lintels, niches, and gables are adorned with Rococo fronds and volutes; and the statuary is massive and Neoclassic. The interior of the cathedral was once similar, if not more elaborate, in style, but twentieth-century remodeling stripped away much of the Baroque, leaving the nave and transepts, according to one observer, "chilling and unrelentingly austere."

32 TRANI

This massive honey-colored building, begun in the eleventh century, stands alongside the seawall on the Adriatic.

The cathedral's nave was built above the 16-foot crypt of an early seventh-century church and is, for that reason, one of the loftiest in Italy. A colonnade of blind arches, a rose window, and a carved portal and its splendidly decorated bronze doors soften the austerity of an otherwise plain facade. The graceful campanile began to fall apart a few years ago and has undergone major repairs since 1952. Three years later, the interior was stripped of its post-Romanesque fixtures and returned to the plain, but effective, Apulian style.

33 TRENT

A German bishop-prince of the thirteenth century commissioned the architect Adamo di Arogno to create the Cathedral of San Vigilio in Trent. The work was immediately undertaken, but the building was not completed until the sixteenth century. Germanic influence is evident in the apse, with its upper gallery of round arches, its blind arches on the lower portion, and the recessed windows, guarded by griffins in between. The upper gallery of open arches continues around the entire church, dominating the façade and breaking off at the adjacent Pretorian Palace, which is joined to the apse by a wall. Several bishops of the Holy Roman Empire are buried in the transept, and the decrees of the sixteenth-century Council of Trent were posted in the Chapel of the Crucifix.

Troia's facade; a nineteenth-century print

34 TROIA

The eleventh-century cathedral at Troia at first resembled that of Pisa, with the usual profusion of small blind arches. Later revisions simplified the facade, bringing it closer to the bold Apulian and Norman styles. There is a large spoked rose window, surrounded by relief sculpture, and a series of blind arches (three on either side of the main bronze door) set against a wall of multi-colored bricks. The structure of the building is Pisan, with a half-rounded apse, no triforium, and a wooden roof.

35 TURIN

In 1497 the architect Meo del Caprina finished the facade of the extraordinary Cathedral of Turin, and at once it became the focus of life in Piedmont. Here the dukes of Savoy—who were eventually to give a united Italy her first kings—worshiped, were crowned, and were buried. Meo, a Florentine, worked in an early Renaissance style, mixing classic lintels with Romanesque arches and a square campanile with gracefully curving gables. When craftsmen of the seventeenth and eighteenth centuries imposed their Baroque restorations on the building, it seemed to be a natural evolution. The most thoroughly Baroque addition is the Chapel of the Holy Shroud, standing behind the presbytery. Rococo sunbursts rise from its altar, and its spired cupola, which dominates the building's profile, is somewhat similar to the architecture of St. Basil's in the Kremlin.

36 VENZONE

Giovanni Griglio designed the towered *duomo* at Venzone in 1308. The vaulting is Gothic; wooden beams crisscross the ceiling in the nave in distinct contrast to the large arch supports, which are formed of carved stone and jut out from the chancel. Several chapels have been added to the building since the fourteenth century, creating an amalgam of "planned and unplanned beauties" that as far as one observer is concerned "reflects the centuries of instinctive visual acuity . . . that make the writing of art history a hopeless task."

The patron saint of the city of Naples and of its cathedral is Saint Gennaro (Januarius), who was martyred at Pozzuoli during the persecution of Diocletian. When the saint's remains were transferred to Naples from the site of his martyrdom, his blood is supposed to have liquefied in the hands of Bishop (later Saint) Severus. Ever since then—and with documentation going back to 1389— the Miracle of Liquefaction (shown in the engraving at right) has taken place thrice yearly in Naples Cathedral. Concurrent with the triannual manifestations at Naples, a bloodstained stone at Pozzuoli is said to turn from a dull brown to a bright red.

Guthlac' edificat
sibi capellam.

Guthl'
lac'

Acknowledgments

BOTH: NEW YORK PUBLIC LIBRARY

The Editors gratefully acknowledge the valuable editorial assistance of Professor Whitney S. Stoddard of the Department of Art and Architecture of Williams College, Williamstown, Massachusetts, and of American Heritage staff members Edwin D. Bayrd, Jr., Karen Bowen, Margot Brill, Margaret Chou, Thomas Froncek, Michael Harwood, David Jacobs, Nancy Kelly, and Emma Landau.

Grateful acknowledgment is made for permission to quote from the following works: *Literary Sources of Art History*, edited by Elizabeth Gilmore Holt, Princeton University Press, 1947, Doubleday Anchor Books edition, vol. I, pages 49, 52, 53, 54, 57–8. *A Roman Journal*, edited and translated by Haakon Chevalier, The Orion Press, Grossman Publishers, pages 55–6, 58–9. *Mont-Saint-Michel & Chartres*, by Henry Adams, Houghton Mifflin Company, Doubleday Anchor Books edition, pages 4–5, 52, 57, 67, 75, 82, 96, 115, 117–8, 120–2, 123, 124–5, 141, 155, 304–5. *The Pilgrimage of Arnold von Harff*, translated and edited by Malcolm Letts, Hakluyt Society, pages 264–5.

Grateful acknowledgment is also made to the following individuals and institutions for their assistance in obtaining illustrative material:

Administration Communale de Tournai, Belgium
Bibliotheque Nationale, Paris
 Marcel Thomas, Department of Manuscripts
 Nicole Villa, Department of Prints
British Museum, London
 Department of Manuscripts

Jane Horton de Cabanyes, Madrid
Claire de Forbin, Paris
Mary Jenkins, London
Musée de la Ville de Strasbourg
  Victor Beyer
Museum of Fine Arts, Boston
  Elizabeth P. Riegel
New York Public Library
  Art and Architecture Division:
  Anthony Cardillo
  Donald Anderle
  David Combs
  Danica Jekich
  Jerry Romero
  Naomi Street
  Picture Collection:
  Lenore Cowan
  Letha Gregor
  Marion Wiethorn
  Arthur Williams
  Nils Briska
  Prints Division:
  Elizabeth Roth
  David Johnson
Osterreichische Nationalbibliothek, Vienna
  Hofrat Dr. Hans Pauer
Rosgartenmuseum, Constance
  Sigrid von Blanckenhagen
Bianca Spantigati, Rome
Maria Todorow, Florence

Special photographic assistance
  Jean Dieuzaide, Studio Yan, Toulouse
  R. B. Fleming & Co., Ltd., London
  Herschel Levit, New York
  Oronoz, Madrid
  Photographic Service, New York Public Library
  Jean Roubier, Paris
  Helga Schmidt-Glassner, Stuttgart
  Service Photographique, Bibliotheque Nationale, Paris
  Mrs. Le Monnier
Maps
  Cal Sacks

Index